Californians

A MAP OF
NORTH AMERICA
With the European Settlements &
whatever else is remarkable in the
WEST INDIES,
from the latest and
best Observations.

Works by James D. Houston

fiction:
BETWEEN BATTLES (1968)
GIG (1969)
A NATIVE SON OF THE GOLDEN WEST (1971)
CONTINENTAL DRIFT (1978)
GASOLINE (1980)
LOVE LIFE (1985)

non-fiction:
FAREWELL TO MANZANAR, with Jeanne Wakatsuki Houston (1973)
OPEN FIELD, with John R. Brodie (1974)
THREE SONGS FOR MY FATHER (1974)
CALIFORNIANS: Searching for the Golden State (1982)
ONE CAN THINK ABOUT LIFE AFTER THE FISH IS IN THE CANOE (1985)
THE MEN IN MY LIFE (1987)

editor:
WRITING FROM THE INSIDE (1973)
CALIFORNIA HEARTLAND: Writing from the Great Central Valley, with
  Gerald Haslam (1978)
WEST COAST FICTION: Modern Writing from California, Oregon
  and Washington (1979)

film writing:
FAREWELL TO MANZANAR, with Jeanne W. Houston & John Korty (1976)
LI'A: The Legacy of a Hawaiian Man (1988)
LISTEN TO THE FOREST (1991)

Californians

Searching for the Golden State

James D. Houston

James D. Houston
ASILOMAR
July 11, 1994

OTTER B BOOKS
SANTA CRUZ COUNTY
CALIFORNIA

Published by OTTER B BOOKS, November 1992

Published in the United States by Otter B Books, Santa Cruz, Ca.
Reprinted by arrangement with the author.
ISBN 0-9617681-6-9

Portions of this book have appeared in *San Francisco, Los Angeles, California
Living, Cal Today, The Santa Cruz Express, Quarry West #15, Blair and
Ketchum's Country Journal, Stanford Magazine,* and the anthology *Unknown
California,* edited by David Fine and Jonathan Eisen.

Endpaper illustration: *A map of North America, with the European Settlements
and whatever is remarkable in ye West Indies . . . ,* R.W. Seale, 1744. Courtesy Map
Division, New York Public Library, Astor, Lenox and Tilden Foundations.

Manufactured in the United States of America.

The map on the cover was provided by the Water Education
Foundation, a non-profit organization for developing and
implementing education programs on water issues.
Cover design by Lizardgraphics.

Start at the Beginning
Author's Foreword to the 10th Anniversary Edition

Ten years ago I went searching for the Golden state and wrote a book called *Californians*. You might say I started in the middle. Heading out from Santa Cruz I travelled north and south hoping to see again, or perhaps for the first time, the complex region I called home. If I were going to write this book today, I would start in a different place. I would start at the beginning, with some comments from the people who have lived the longest in this part of the world.

I would start with someone like Frank La Pena. He is stocky and brown-skinned, with a silver beard and silver hair receding from his smooth forehead. He lives in Sacramento now, where he heads the Native American Studies program at the state university campus. He grew up farther north, in a region bounded by the McCloud River, Redding and Mount Shasta, traditionally the home territory of his people, the Wintu. They have called it home for over ten thousand years.

Frank is a man so deeply rooted you can almost think the western earth speaks through him. He likes to talk about Mount Shasta, which dominates the landscape in Wintu country. For him this fourteen thousand foot volcanic peak is much more than a dramatic landmark and photographer's delight, much more than a challenge for climbers and skiers. It is a holy place he approaches with respect. For him the mountain can be a kind of mentor.

"If you sit still and listen to it," he says quietly, "it can teach you a lot."

He describes a sacred spring, one you reach via an old trail not marked or shown on any map. "I used to get water there to take as a gift to my uncle, who was an elder living on the Clear Creek Reservation. It was the best gift I could take him, because he knew where it came from, that it came from the mountain and was blessed. You have different kinds of springs up there, you see. Some are sulfur. Some are hot. This was a soda spring, with cleansing and purifying powers. You offer a prayer when you take the water. And all this would be carried in the jar I brought to my uncle."

Layered with generations of family memory, Shasta also serves as a chapel and a sanctuary. He talks about a pilgrimage he once made to the mountain when another uncle passed away. Frank went on foot and left behind a lock of his own hair, as he expressed his grief and prayed for safe passage. For the Wintu, who call themselves "the mountain/river people," Shasta is your final point of contact with this world, and your gateway to the next.

When I hear such stories, I envy Frank. I envy this kind of tie to a feature of the California landscape. He is linked to a majestic place by bonds both ancient and ancestral. No matter how much we may claim to care about the state or some part of it, few of us nowadays have been here long enough to have an ancestral sense for the region. Two generations are a lot. Seven is about the longest pedigree you hear anyone claim, if some forebearer happened to be with the Portolá or De Anza party. Half a generation is closer to the norm.

I can call myself a native, since I was born in San Francisco, of parents who immigrated west from Texas in the 1930's. Early in life I was following my father along trout streams in Mendocino County and tent-camping in the Yolla Bolly Mountains above Ukiah. So I have come to cherish the ridges and valleys of the long Coast Range, a realm I look upon as my natural habitat. Can you measure that against the earth-tied ancestry of a man whose people have inhabited the upper Sacramento Valley for many thousands of years and for countless generations? Of course, you can't. There is no comparison. But maybe there is a lesson to be learned. In this land of immigrants and runaway change, maybe we can learn something from the people who have lived here longer than anyone else. Now, more than ever, some reverence would help, to leaven the speed and the greed.

Like just about everywhere on Earth these days, California is a very different place than it was ten years ago. Nonetheless, certain features of the state remain the same. Some things change from hour to hour, while others turn on a slower cycle. Tom Bradley, who I interviewed in 1981, is still the mayor of Los Angeles. Though soon to retire, he has presided over the nation's second largest city for almost two decades. At Ridge Vineyards Paul Draper is still the winemaker. A Japanese investor owns the winery now, but this has not affected the careful aging of the zinfandel or forced any increase in the output, which remains steady at 40,000–50,000 quality-controlled cases per year.

The book's two main sections still apply—"Some Regions of the Earth," and "Some Regions of the Mind." I think this still provides a useful frame for talking about a state that has too often been perceived mainly as a region of the mind, a national haven for cults and lifestyle adventurers, the home of Hearst Castle, Disneyland, filmland, Silicon Valley. The regions of the Earth continue to be varied and diverse, from the oil reserves in the lower San Joaquin, to the rows of lettuce and broccoli that fill the long Salinas Valley, to the fault line that keeps reminding us where the true source of power resides. During this decade the San Andreas has shown signs of slippage and has shifted its weight numerous times between Shelter Cove and the Sea of Cortez. But its habits have not changed much, nor has its length or its subsurface structure.

The famous California Dream is still with us too, in some form or another, a bit harder to sight now that it has joined the condor and the grizzly on the list of endangered species. The idea of a land of promise with its endlessly magnetic appeal may be finally catching up with us. The numbers themselves are catching up with us, and looping around to catch us by the throat—the number of people, the number of cars.

It was back in the fall of 1962 that California's population surpassed New York's, to make this the nation's most populous state. An enormous counter had been positioned above the Oakland-San Francisco Bay Bridge. On November 24, when the counter registered 17,393,134 a general cry of celebration went up. In those days, bigger was still better, and Governor Edmund G. "Pat" Brown declared a four-day holiday.

As of 1962 the state's population had been growing at an average rate of about one thousand people per day for over twenty years, ever since the outbreak of World War Two. This continued until sometime in the mid-1980's, when the growth rate escalated, peaking at about two thousand people per day. As of early 1992 it was running around eighteen hundred per day. That was the net daily increase, state-wide, every day of the year. When *Californians* was first published, the population had risen to 24 million, and there was approximately one registered vehicle for each licensed driver. Ten years later we number 31 million, and vehicles now outnumber licensed drivers by several million. People have increased by 29 percent, while vehicles have increased by about 40 percent. In other words, the vehicle population has been growing faster than the human population.

Such numbers bring to mind the powerful winds that stirred up a dust storm over in the central valley near the town of Coalinga. The winds sent a wall of blowing sand across Interstate Five. It was Thanksgiving weekend, 1991. Four lanes were filled with vehicles speeding north and south, when visibility droppped to zero, creating the worst traffic accident in the state's history—over a hundred cars and trucks, including a dozen big rigs, with a death toll of seventeen, and 114 injuries. The wreckage spread for a mile on both sides of the highway.

As soon as I heard this I called my friend Gerry Haslam, a writer and valley historian who grew up near Bakersfield. He keeps track of what has happened over there. "My God, Gerry," I said, 'what a horrendous catastrophe! Have you ever heard of anything like it?"

Gerry said that as a matter of fact he had. He recalled another storm of sand and dust back in 1977, and it had also brought Interstate Five to a standstill, a bigger storm, which lasted longer, driven by higher winds. It didn't get as much media attention because fewer cars were involved. He reminded me that powerful winds across the broad expanse of the San Joaquin Valley was nothing new, nor was the rising of dust in the midst of a long dry spell such as we've had for the past six years, nor was a drought itself anything new. Most of California is semi-arid, with a history of dry spells.

In the central valley last November the habits of the Earth had not changed much. One big difference between 1977 and 1991 was the number of vehicles on the road, which had increased by some fifty percent the potential for trouble whenever the elements decide to do something we haven't anticipated.

In an eery way that sad pile-up echoes an event that happened almost 150 years ago, when the Sierras were providing this region with its essential mythology. When gold was discovered in 1848, and this remote western landscape actually delivered pockets and seams of the fabled ore so many adventurers had dreamed about, the world's imagination suddenly had a new touchstone. There was an Eldorado after all! And the Gold Rush was to become California's formative event—economically, politically, symbolically. But from that same era a twin legend has come down to us, a cautionary tale that has stood in the shadow of the Gold Rush, or perhaps has been bleached out by the blinding light of the boomtime so many have preferred to remember.

This second legend, or the under-legend, is the grim saga of the Donner Party, which had started too late from Missouri, fell prey to squabbling along the trail, entered the Sierra Nevada range well past the season when it was considered safe to cross, and thus found themselves trapped in the early winter of 1846. It is a story from a region where the weather can turn on you in an hour, where the landscape is no longer an ally or bountiful provider, and where nature is an adversary, or perhaps a mentor one can never afford to take for granted.

The story of the Donner Party contains a warning not unlike the warnings of John Muir, the great naturalist and patriarch conservationist who began to tramp the Sierra Nevadas some twenty years later. Be attentive to this land and its habits, he said; learn to enjoy it but never let down your guard.

One of the large California ironies is the way its very virtues sometimes seem fated to bring about the state's undoing. As the pressure on space and resources intensifies, one sees examples everywhere of how some cycle of nature is overlooked, or given low priority, in the rush to develop a parcel of real estate or maximize income or expand a city. Somewhere along the coast, a fragile slope, over-logged and over-built, is cut away by erosion, and six homes go sliding to the bottom. Somewhere in the central valley, over-irrigation coupled with poor drainage fills a hundred thousand acres of cropland with plant-killing salts and minerals.

The succession of such events, together with the ongoing debates over river use, air quality, offshore drilling and so on, has led us toward a revision of the original California legend, the one with the boomtown voice saying, "Take what you can while the taking is good." We are discovering, or re-discovering that this region is not a cornucopia of limitless reserves, but a well endowed place with very specific limits that have to be acknowledged and attended to. These limits, in turn, are fundamental features of the region—weather patterns, tidal patterns, wind and water flow, cycles in the soil and in the layers of earth below the soil.

As of the fall of 1992 there is a state-wide sense of crisis in the air. We find ourselves pushed up against the carrying capacities of a delicately balanced environmental network. The demand on every system seems to be at overload—roads, schools, housing, water. Thousands of voices are making recommendations for the future, and I listen to many of them. I listen to the engineer who knows how to anchor a building in the rift zone so it won't topple over. I listen to the grower and to the urban planner and to the police chief. I also listen to those people who have been here so long they have no record or memory of arriving. I listen to Frank La Pena, for whom each peak, each valley, each river has a life of its own and must be recognized and honored. Shasta is the Wintu's sacred place. But all places are sacred, he tells me. "It is really up to you. You can awaken that aspect of the place if you make your own connection with it."

I am thankful that these older forms of ecological wisdom are still available to us. They help me remember things my body and my nervous system tend to forget, spending, as I do, too much time in the world we have created for ourselves, the world of concrete and credit cards and carburetors and video cassettes. It is easy to forget that our strongest ties are not with the asphalt but with what lies just a foot or so beneath it. This is our oldest and most primal bond, and the Earth itself is always in command. We are here by grace, as lucky guests. We really have no choice but to revere its many cycles and its many wondrous forms.

Santa Cruz
September, 1992

Dedicated to my children,
Corinne, Joshua, Gabrielle,
and to all the travelers
who brought them to this crossroads—
from Hawaii, Honshu and Niigata,
from Cumberland Mountain,
County Antrim and Glasgow

CONTENTS

Contents

Californians

Anchors: A Prologue

People still fall in love with California. Not long ago a woman said to me, and these were her very words, "It's the closest place to heaven I have ever been. The weather, the landscape, the hot springs, the kind of people I have met—truly open, intelligent, seeking people, willing to take responsibility for themselves."

She was fifty-one years old, from London, England, and she was describing the two weeks she had just spent in Big Sur. Those two weeks had filled her eyes with amorous excitement.

"Everything is tried here first," she said, then added with a sly smile, "Of course, some things are tried that other people are quite glad to have experimented with outside their own borders."

"You sometimes feel safer watching it from a distance?" I asked.

She laughed. "Well, yes. You might say we wait to see if there are going to be any survivors to spread the news."

Her trip to the West Coast had been a pilgrimage, one she had been planning for years, and when she finally had to return to her native country it was with a lover's regret. She had found something on this coast that was instantly familiar and fulfilling, another kind of homeland.

I myself have never had the chance to fall in love that way. But after a lifetime in California I have not fallen out of love either. I think of this book as a kind of love story. Later on, if I say some things that seem to contradict this, please try to see them as the underside of love. I cannot honestly say I love all the people who reside in this part of the world

3

these days. But I love a lot of them. And I love the place itself, the multitude of places, even now, even after all that has happened in these last twenty years since California became America's most populous and popular location.

Many is the time I have found myself yearning for the good old days, back when I was younger and being a Californian, or merely being in California, was as simple as getting out of bed. When I was growing up, it was simpler than that. You didn't have to give it a thought. There were forty-eight states, and this happened to be one of them, prettier than some, better endowed perhaps, but less visible than others. Millions of people did not yet know where it was. After my folks moved out there from Texas in the early 1930s, relatives would sometimes wonder where they had gone.

"Gone to California," one would say.

"Izzat a fact," said another.

"My goodness," said someone else. "Why would anybody want to do that?"

"Lord only knows."

The name had a shine around it, flickers of romance. Hollywood was out there somewhere, and fast women, and citrus groves. Very little else was clear. I miss those days. There are so many Californians now —more people inhabit this state than lived in the entire country in 1850, when California was admitted to the Union[1]—such a gathering and so many strange and contradictory things occurring, it is indeed a region filled with paradox and riddles. This state leads the nation in pornography, divorce, suicide, home burglary, mind-meddling cults, and skateboard accidents. At the same time, perhaps for the same reasons, it leads the nation in micro-electronics, solar energy, accredited law schools, Nobel Prize-winners, women mayors, Olympic medalists, library use, salad lettuce, dates, figs, and nectarines.

In the fall of 1979, while facts such as these careened and collided all around me, I set out on a journey through the state. With delays and digressions of one kind and another, it lasted over two years. I was traveling partly by car, partly on foot, bicycling from time to time. My original aim was to wander at large, to look around, to satisfy my own curiosity about the kind of place California is becoming. It soon grew into something much larger than I had anticipated, and much more personal. I keep returning to a sentence from the preface to Henry Miller's *The Air Conditioned Nightmare*, the account of his trip across America in the 1940s, after living abroad for ten years. Explaining why he made the trip, he says, "I felt the need to effect a reconciliation with my native land."[2] That was precisely what I was starting to feel—the need to look again, and to look up other Californians, to find out more about the various people who live here now, work here, play here, die here, as well as those who, in certain cases, are transformed and resurrected here.

I see now that one could spend a lifetime in this pursuit and never reach an end, and that is due to the very nature of the place and the kinds of people who choose it. "Choice" is the key word.

Of Californians there are at least two broad categories: those who are born here, and those who are drawn or magnetized or sent here from somewhere else. I, by chance, am in the first category. That Englishwoman who spent two weeks at Big Sur is in the second. She is not a Californian by birth, or by naturalization, or by having spent a minimum number of months or years in residence, but by choice, and the nature of her own expectations, her personal dream.

Ever since the Gold Rush, this has been an identity that anyone can choose. The first crowd of men who started west in search of instant wealth were already calling themselves "Californians" when they were fifteen hundred miles away. It was a badge of honor, in those days, to be sharing this particular destination. "Here are some sixty men," one fellow wrote home to his mother in Youngstown, New York, "120 cows and oxen, all yoked and hitched to eighteen covered wagons, with a rope to the head of every yoke, and a Californian at the end of the rope with a large whip in his hand, plodding along at the rate of three miles per hour, pantaloons in boots."[3]

It was May of 1849. They were still two miles from Independence, Missouri, with half the Midwest and the Rockies yet to cross before they would glimpse the fabled landscape.

If Californians are an elusive breed, the place itself is equally elusive, and difficult to chart. From the outset I envisioned a book that could take the shape of a journey. Before long, I saw that it could not be a continuous journey, since there are now so many Californias, often layered one upon the other, that they cannot be explored in a linear way. I saw that it would have to be a sequence of trips and outings, into the river valleys, the mountain forests, the wine cellars, the film studios, the banks, and the border towns. A day here. A week there. Loops and switchbacks. A book of travels.

Traditionally in any such book the traveler is moving through a remote landscape—like New Guinea, or Central Asia—a realm that is new for the writer and usually, in some way, exotic for the reader. Early on, as I was returning from one of these trips, it occurred to me that

California, though it has been written about as much as anywhere on earth, still qualifies as that type of landscape. I was passing through San Francisco when it occurred to me that such a book could be an exploration through territory that is both totally familiar and totally unknown —familiar because most of my life has been spent in this region, unknown because the changes have been such, and the rate of change, that it is always exotic, remote, and strange, on some days entirely incomprehensible.

This double vision was sharpened, made especially poignant, by my angle of approach that day, from the mountainous north, and by the fact that I was approaching San Francisco. Like the state as a whole, this city is for me two things at once: the familiar place where I grew up, and *Terra Incognita* (as the old mapmakers used to say).

I had been visiting some friends who farm in Mendocino County. They live, by choice, in almost total isolation. I had started out that morning on unmarked logging roads, half an hour of dusty pine and redwood forest, then followed the coast to Navarro Head, where 128 turns south and east through a twenty-mile corridor of vaulting, shadowy, first-growth Sequoia. After that it was orchard country, and a broad meadow called Anderson Valley. In the last few miles the road dips and bends its way down through sparsely settled hills to intersect with Highway 101, the venerable route that hugs the continent's curve from the Canadian border to the Hollywood Freeway.

101 was busy, compared with the country I'd just passed through, but not a struggle, not outrageous. The towns are called Cloverdale, Asti, Geyserville, and Lytton, and they still have the rural feel. I pulled into a coffee shop in Cloverdale at 11 A.M. and found a couple of fellows from the county sheriff's office hunched over cups talking to some rancher in his cowboy hat and his neatly pressed rodeo shirt, also hunched over a cup of coffee. Outside the window, his pickup with the golden retriever asleep on top of the alfalfa bales was parked next to the county car, and I had the impression they all could stay parked at the coffee shop for quite some time.

That impression, that sense of the rural pace, stays with you through countryside and croplands for the next forty miles, carrying you along until you reach the outskirts of Santa Rosa, the most northerly city in the orbit of the San Francisco Bay Region. Nothing changes in the sky, nothing that a barometer might show. But something begins to thicken at the outer edges of the urban stew. You are plunging into another zone, like a space capsule at reentry.

If you zoom up for a satellite view, you can see how wide this orbit has grown. It fans out from San Francisco in all directions but westward

—toward Santa Rosa, fifty miles north, the Santa Clara Valley, fifty miles
south, and Vallejo, Concord, and the Livermore Valley to the east. San
Francisco might very neatly be described as the nub at the handle of
this fan.

Though all these towns were separate once, a town still hoping to
preserve an identity must fight for it day by day, hour by hour. The
nearby ridges of the Coast Range, which once created distances, have
all been tunneled or saddled by four-lane roads. The waterways have
all been bridged. Along this highway you feel anxiety thickening with
the traffic, in direct proportion to the condos and shake-roof subdivisions that begin to rise and spread on all sides as you reach Marin
County via 101, carried south into the accelerating flow.

In this mega-city of northern California, where communities merge,
sometimes disappear completely in amongst the tentacles and general
creep, San Francisco has long been a kind of anchor, a touchpoint, a nub
of fan and nexus. It was the original settlement, a mission site, with a
rickety Spanish fort to guard the entrance to this bay. From here the
miners fanned out north and east in search of gold. It is headquarters
nowadays for heavy chunks of corporate power, with many new and
glinting highrises downtown to house the main offices for Standard Oil,
Bank of America, Pacific Gas and Electric, the Southern Pacific Company, Crown-Zellerbach, Levi-Strauss. But in the end, what makes San
Francisco, what has saved it and preserved its definition, is the water
that surrounds it on three sides, so that in this region of otherwise
uncontainable runaway growth, the city remains a very specific place
on the map and in the mind.

As I came speeding through the tunnel cut into the hills at the top
of the last grade above Sausalito, and swung out onto the downside
slope, I had my first glimpse of the magical skyline.

It was just a glimpse, while the wide curve took most of my attention. Then the curve bottomed out, and I was pointed across the bay,
toward the north spire of the Golden Gate, and a straight-on view of a
city that seemed to be floating on water, with its fringe of parks, the
hilly thrust of white buildings, Coit Tower and the Transamerica pyramid, a choppy bay in the foreground, sharp blue sky beyond. In that
moment I could almost forget what happens in its desperate streets and
exploding neighborhoods. I wanted to celebrate whatever forces
created such a vista.

I wanted to stop and jump out of the car and wave my arms and yell,
"Hooray for skylines! Hooray! Huzzah! Congratulations! You did it
again!"

But as I approached from Marin, on a Friday afternoon, in the three southbound lanes of swooping traffic, there was no way to stop or slow down. I was carried out onto the legendary bridge, the very image of the West, opportunity's gateway, depicted on a million postcards, with the fabulous cityscape rising on my lefthand, the silvery Pacific opening on my right. In peripheral vision I could catch both sights while I raced along the perilous corridor between orange railings built forty-five years earlier when vehicles were smaller and fewer and not designed to cruise at these speeds. I was barreling across with inches between me and the trucks, the Greyhounds and sedans. One mistake, one lapse of concentration by any one driver, and we could all be swept into a domino tangle of torn metal and carnage. This was California living at its fullest and most nerve-wracking.

Six hours back, I had awakened in the absolute quiet of a Mendocino forest, with a silent fog creeping through apple trees and nine miles of logging road to the nearest town. Not that I myself would choose to live that far into the woods, but it sharpened the impact and double-edge of that crossing, and I was wondering, How long do we put up with all this? And, Why do we put up with it in the first place? And, Where, in the face of such hurtling motion for its own sake, does a person find any kind of footing at all?

Well, it is curious, watching what the imagination will grasp and cling to. When you live in a land of perpetual and high-speed transformation, you come to cherish anything that has survived—a building, a vista, a mountain's profile. That day it happened to be the bridge itself that stirred my personal sense of history and continuity. In my lifetime it had always been there, the golden gateway over the water, between the blustery headlands. As I sped across, each tower with its stack of arches made a gate. The lowest arch of the first tower framed the four silhouetted arches of the second, half a mile south, and the two towers were connected by downward-curving orange pipes, from which hung the many cables that hold up the roadway, making two long harps. It was an exhilarating approach, and another kind of anchor, the bridge, the look of the bridge, the very way it works. Entering that city which is my hometown and place of birth, I felt some rope connected to the bridge, reaching back through years, down through the layers and layers of change. . . .

One Sunday when I was eight, the entire city of San Francisco was reduced to the size of a billboard. This was the Sunday we received the news that Japanese aircraft had bombed Pearl Harbor and crippled America's Pacific Fleet. The billboard stood at the corner of 25th Avenue and Irving Street, half a block from the house my father had made his first payment on three years earlier. In what is now the classic scene of how Americans received the news that launched us into World War II, we all sat around the radio staring at the floor or at the speaker. When the somber announcement ended, my father switched off the radio. The mood in the room was so heavy I went outside, wandered up to the corner and huddled down behind the billboard I had come to rely on in times of stress and uncertainty.

It was a sandlot billboard with two surfaces to plaster ads across. They made a right angle just inside the concrete, one side facing 25th, the other facing Irving. I never knew what the ads said. My world was behind the signs, where all the struts, cross-pieces, and footings met and overlapped. Back there, when I was eight, you felt secure. The western wall broke the wind that usually poured down Irving from the ocean, twenty-five blocks away. If you fell from one of the cross-beams, or jumped, as we often did, like pirates abandoning ship or pilots leaving a flaming cockpit, the sand was there to break your fall. This whole district was built on sand, miles and miles of what had once been dunes were covered with houses. In those days there were still more miles waiting to be covered, dunes dotted with spiny beach grass of the same variety growing in this vacant corner lot. Wherever a parcel of houses ended and the dunes began, a little skirmish was going on. Half a sidewalk would be disappearing under wind-blown sand, sometimes half an avenue would be disappearing. People who lived in the final row of houses could look out across a mile or so of dunes and wonder how long before the next row would go in, so that *their* lawns and cars would no longer have to bear the brunt.

As a kid, I always wanted the sand to win. I loved the sand, hot or cold, dry or wet, day or night. In that district, the Sunset District of San Francisco, which was the world of my boyhood, sand was the alternative to civilization and its discontents, and so it is no wonder that on the day World War II broke out I wandered up to the corner sandlot to think.

None of my buddies were there, and I was glad. I wanted solitude. I was not in the mood that day for abandoning ship or leaping from the cockpit. Real planes could be appearing in the sky at any moment. This is what my parents were talking about. This is what I expected. Hawaii was twenty-four hundred miles west, with nothing between here and there but open water. My father had been to Hawaii. He had been stationed at Pearl Harbor for a couple of years during the 1920s, with a submarine crew.

"If they have a mind to keep on bombing," he said, "they'll have to fly clear over here 'fore they've got anything else to hit."

"You think they'll do it?" my mother asked.

"No tellin'," he said. "They might be able to git here. But I don't know how they'd ever git back. And if you cain't git back, there ain't much use in gittin' here."

A tall strip of lattice separated the two sides of the billboard, right at the corner, splintery boards painted green and nailed diagonally so you could squat back there, hidden from cars, and peer through the diamonds down Irving Street. I sat for a long time peering at the cloud bank above the distant ocean, expecting to see planes emerge, fighters, bombers. At times it seemed that the clouds *were* bombers, ingeniously disguised as broken clouds and moving toward the city like an inexorable fog.

Never before had the sky taken on such a threatening look. As the clouds drew nearer, my childish fears ebbed and flowed, and the air grew damp and cold. By the time they had covered the sun, my fearful solitude lost its savor. The day's news had emptied the streets. There was nothing else to do but go home. I came over the back fence, by way of another vacant lot, and from the yard I heard strange noises. I heard voices up on our roof.

It wasn't easy to get onto the roof. Counting the street-level garage, our house was actually three stories high. To reach the roof you had to carry a ladder up the back stairs to the second landing, and from there hoist yourself over the gutter. I saw the ladder leaning up there, climbed the stairs, climbed the ladder, got my chin to the gutter level, and found my mother and grandmother standing on the roof gazing west. This had never happened before. No one went up onto the roof but my father, from time to time, when a skylight needed putty. Seeing the women on the roof added to the strangeness of this day. Their panicky conversation confirmed the half-shaped worry I was carrying around. They too were looking for Japanese bombers and trying to decide what to do.

My grandmother was doing most of the deciding. Her idea was that we should head back to west Texas where it was safe. They had all come out from Texas the year before I was born, from a little Panhandle town right at the edge of the Dust Bowl. Shading her eyes, like a pioneer woman trying to see through mirages on a desert horizon, she kept saying things like, "Look! Look out there! Isn't that something flying to'rd the city? Look! Can you see it now?" Not only could she see and hear bombers over the Cliff House, she was certain San Francisco Bay was filling with enemy subs and that hidden infantry divisions would soon be marching out of Chinatown.

By the next afternoon a plan had taken shape. Three of us would leave first, me, my five-year-old sister, and Grandma. That way, at least the children would be saved. We would travel by train to Texas, where she still owned a farmhouse and a quarter-section of land. Grandma called the Southern Pacific terminal and reserved seats on the overnight train to Los Angeles, where we would meet up tomorrow with the southwest special heading east toward Phoenix and El Paso. She drew all her savings out of the Bank of America, which amounted to $300 or $400, money she had earned as a seamstress, doing alterations and hemstitching in her apartment here on the second floor. My mother packed our bags, cleaned us up and dressed us, so that by the time my father came home from work we were too baffled to cry, protest, or even speak.

The plan was perfect in all details but one: my father had not been consulted. The plan had taken shape after he had driven off to work that morning. When his old Plymouth pulled up to the curb, we were standing on the stairs waiting for him to drive us downtown to the terminal —me in my woolen suit, my sister in a pinafore Grandma had sewn and over the pinafore a red coat with simulated fur collar. My mother twisted at her sweater sleeve, caught between having to watch her children ride out of her life for who knew how many months or years, and her dread of the first air raid. Grandma stood over us, dressed in her city clothes, her long cloth coat, her round black pillbox hat garnished with cherries; but underneath these clothes she was the ranch-country matriarch, determined to protect her herd.

Dad climbed out of the car, still wearing his overalls. He was a painting contractor, worked jobs in all parts of the city—homes, apartment houses, office buildings. He smelled like paint. His bill cap was spotted with it, his shirt and his shoes. His hands were covered with a chalky film made of thinner and enamel residue. He had rolled up the sleeves on his blue shirt, so you could see a line across his wrists.

My mother broke into tears. "Dudley, please hurry. Load up as fast as you can!"

Grandma, looking mournful, waited until he had reached the stairs. "It's got to be, Dudley, it's just got to be."

He looked the situation over and finally said, "What has got to be?"

While they explained, he listened in stoic silence. He was not a talker. He took great pride in all forms of handiwork, but never put much stock in words. When they finished explaining, he stood there for a long time saying nothing. He squinted down at my sister and me and blinked and worked his jaws and fingered one of the brass buttons on his overalls, testing the callused tip of his forefinger.

The air was so charged, it was painful. I was looking around for anything else to concentrate on, and that was when I noticed his tattoo. It was a purple anchor. A rope curled around the anchor's stem, a purple eagle perched upon the crosspiece. At age eight my eyes were just about even with his forearm. What a relief to see his tattoo inches away. I gave it my full attention. I had looked at it many times, but on this day it occurred to me that the tattoo had not always been a feature of my father's arm. Someone had put it there. For the first time I wondered why, and when? His forearm was thick and brown, the hairs fine around the squinting eagle and the navy anchor. I thought I saw the eagle move. Was it breathing? Or was Dad barely squeezing his fist?

My mother had reached her limit. She cried, "Well, Dudley! My goodness! You going to stand here all day?"

He waited a while longer. I saw a trapped look come into his eyes, the voiceless alarm of a trapped animal. Then he blinked and the look went away. His jaws clenched one final time and his mouth opened. "Maybe I will," he said. "Maybe I'll stand here all day."

Grandma was a twenty-year widow who had raised her two children —my mother and my uncle—all by herself on that semi-fertile, semi-prairie quarter-section. It had put iron in her eyes. She fixed this iron glare on my father. "I *do* believe we ought to be gittin' along, Dudley."

The eagle stopped breathing. The anchor came to rest. He said, "I believe we ought to hold off a few days."

My mother was appalled: "HOLD OFF!"

Grandma was willing to bargain. "Now Dudley," she began, "if it's the money you're thinkin' about, you needn't . . ."

He passed between them, up the stairs, into the house.

For three weeks the bags stayed packed, while we waited on his approval of the plan. During those weeks the city braced itself for invasion by land or sea or air. The west sides of all the street lamps were painted chocolate brown. We draped our windows, taped up every place where light might leak, and sat through practice blackouts, staying off the streets, listening for bombers. They never came. The landing barges never landed. Grandma put her money back into the Bank of America. The sand continued to creep toward the last row of houses where the dunes began. My father never again mentioned the escape plan, nor did he ever acknowledge or even hint that such a plan had existed.

Twenty-five years later, I was again looking closely at his tattoo. We were at the University of California Medical Center on Parnassus Avenue, and a nurse was probing around on his arm with a transfusion needle.

"Your veins are very thin," she said.

He looked insulted, misjudged, but said nothing. She tried his left arm. "This one will do," she said. "The veins are stronger." And she slanted the needle through his white flesh.

He glanced at her with eyes full of suspicion, eyes that knew his right arm should be stronger, since that was the one he used most. With lips pursed she adjusted a valve on the thin, clear tube rising from his arm, watched the tube turn red. A scarlet bubble rose in the jar above his bed.

"This will take about four hours."

The trapped look came into his eyes. He wanted to ask her why so long. I knew he wouldn't ask. It was not his style. He rarely asked—for advice, for assistance, for answers. She noted something on her clipboard and padded out into the corridor, while I sat staring at the purple tattoo shielding his tender vein, watching that old eagle's slitted and arrogant eye.

After a while he said to me, "Why does it take so long?"

"Probably makes it easier for your system to adjust, assimilate the new blood."

A faint smile, while his body shifted restlessly under the sheet, impatient with the forced waiting. His jaws squeezed, the bunched muscles bulged, his lips began to part. He was framing another sentence, but he wouldn't speak it yet. His eyes roamed the room and gradually came to rest on the red bottle. It was always that way with him, the long slow pondering. I was never sure whether that reserve came from indecision or from caring too much, brooding too long over what was right and best.

"You'd think," he said at last, "that they could get somethin' like this done in less than four hours."

His eyes followed the infrequent climb of bubbles through the blood drawn from my arm earlier that day. My eyes were fixed again on his tattoo, wondering if this new blood had yet flowed under it. I searched for a richer hue in the eagle's wing, along the rope curling down behind the anchor's stem. He was grizzled by that time, coming through his third bout with intestinal cancer, a chronic ailment I connected to his lifetime habit of holding too much inside. His skin was pale and his blood thin, but the tattoo had not changed, the ink had not faded much at all. The eagle had not moved, the rope had not frayed, nor had the anchor rusted since I first took careful note of it in December 1941, or for that matter since his young right arm was decorated by the Filipino master on Hotel Street in downtown Honolulu one night back in 1926.

He saw me staring at his arm. I looked away, out the window, toward the vista to the north. The medical center stands high up the side of a steep wooded hill under the eucalyptus groves of Sutro Forest. From his room you could gaze out across several blocks of vintage flats and rooming houses pressed wall to wall in the San Francisco manner and cascading down the slope below. The houses end at Golden Gate Park. Beyond the park, beyond the Richmond District, beyond the city, rose the orange spires of the bridge, peeking over the forested hills around the Presidio.

That view was easier to watch, and it started me thinking about his life and mine. The spires had not been there when he first sailed into San Francisco Bay, on his way home from Hawaii, on his way home to Texas, when his tattoo was new. In those days there was a legendary waterway known around the world as the Golden Gate, but as yet no bridge had come rising out of the water to span it. He didn't stay long in Texas. A few years later he was back, with his bride. Something glittered for him here. I'm still not sure what it was, maybe all those things the bridge has come to symbolize, maybe something else entirely. I can only guess. We never talked about it. I do know this: the bridge and I are of the same generation. As it happens, construction began in the year I was born. I was three when police motorcycles escorted the first cars across. I grew up taking it for granted.

As I sat next to the bed of my father, I remembered the times I played along beaches in full view of the bridge, explored the Fort Point ruins in the shadow of its towers, bicycled out to stop in the middle, between spires, to watch the ruffling, endless Pacific, framed by the city on one side, the moss-ridged Coast Range on the other. On a sunny day the hills of white buildings still quiver with a brightness you only see in cities next to water. I wonder where I would have cycled had Grandma's plan carried through, and what other skylines might have beguiled me? And I wonder still at my father's particular form of delay. Was it uncertainty, or caution, or wisdom, or stubbornness, or fear that kept us in San Francisco till the war was past and the smoke had cleared?

Whatever anchored us, I know now that it shapes you to grow up in a city whose gate is golden. You leave, you return through its golden gate. Such a glitter can blind you to certain things. It can color all your expectations. Sooner or later you learn that from those railings people regularly plunge to their death, sometimes traveling thousands of miles to make the famous leap. But by the time you know that, the spires have already imprinted their gleaming image, and it takes more than suicides or heavy traffic to erase the eldorados flickering there.

I

SOME REGIONS OF THE EARTH

Once, fifty miles down the valley, my father bored a well. The drill came up first with topsoil and then with gravel and then with white sea sand full of shells and even pieces of whalebone. There were twenty feet of sand and then black earth again, and even a piece of redwood, that imperishable wood that does not rot. Before the inland sea the valley must have been a forest. And those things had happened right under our feet. And it seemed to me sometimes at night that I could feel both the sea and the redwood forest before it.

JOHN STEINBECK
from *East of Eden* (1952)

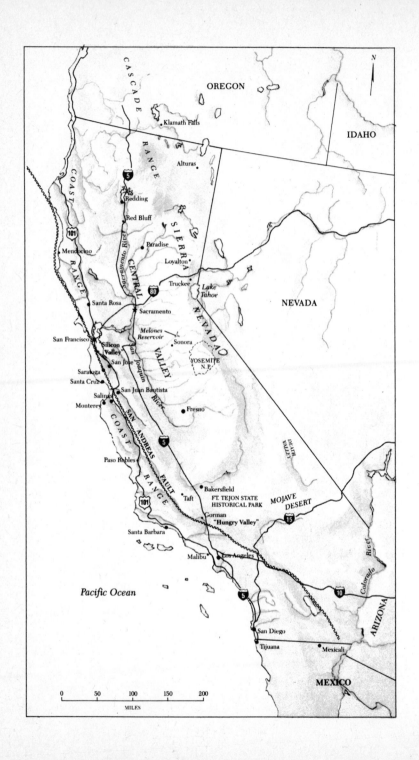

1

Maps

Traveling anywhere in California, starting out on any journey short or long, I make sure I have my maps. Even on the most familiar trips, through towns I grew up in, I take along the maps, because I never know which roads will be open, which closed, which landmarks will still be standing, which gone. New roads appear in the night, old ones may be rerouted. Lakes dry up. Rivers go underground. Buildings rise and fall.

Not long ago I had to break out the maps in San Jose, a town I thought I knew quite well. I went to high school there. I got lost in a district that had once been orchard land. For half a century the apple trees and pear trees had flourished. During the 1950s the trees were felled and burned, the land was scraped, and a vast housing tract was installed. Ten years went by, and half the houses were torn out to make space for an expressway. A few more years passed, the traffic load had multiplied, and a chunk of the expressway had to be torn out, along with a few more blocks from the tract, to make room for a freeway interchange, with frontage road fencing, a hooded pedestrian overpass, and exit ramps looping out among the highest aerials. That's when I got lost. It was after dark. I'd had a couple of beers. My guard was down. I was driving from memory, on the automatic pilot you ought to be able to use at least once in a while, after spending most of your life in the same part of the world. I learned once again that automatic pilot is a high risk in California, where everything changes as it moves.

Though I always take them, I know full well the maps can fool you too. They can be just as deceptive as the skyline. I am talking now about road maps from Shell and Texaco, and also those big and marvelous regional maps compiled by the National Geographic Society. The borders of this state, the outline you see there can be very deceptive. I know people who perceive California precisely as it is depicted on the *National Geographic* map of the United States—a straight line beneath Oregon, making its right angle with the north-south line that doglegs at Lake Tahoe, heading southeasterly toward the Colorado; another straight line slicing westward to the ocean, then the long belly of coastline curving northward against the Pacific. I have often seen this shape depicted on book jackets and in magazines, with no other part of the world attached, as if it were an island. I have also seen this shape breaking off from the rest of North America, as if preparing to become an island, or preparing to sink—an image usually associated with that cataclysm the Cal Tech geologists predict with such ominous regularity, the great quake that some people imagine will sever California as neatly as if cut away by a table saw. They imagine the entire state dropping out of the *National Geographic* and directly into the Pacific Ocean, leaving long straight lines of beachfront property near Klamath Falls and Reno.

This is not an uncommon view of California. It is the original view, and the one with the longest tradition. The first known mention of the name occurred in a sixteenth-century Spanish novel called *The Adventures of Esplandian* by Garcia Ordoñez de Montalvo, wherein he invents a fantastical island, "very close to the side of the Terrestrial Paradise, and it was peopled by black women, without any man among them, for they lived in the fashion of Amazons."[4] He called it California, in the same way modern writers of fantasy and science fiction conjure names for distant landscapes in imaginary or as yet uncharted galaxies. This was the name Hernando Cortez, who had evidently read the novel, gave to the tip of the Baja Peninsula when he sighted it in 1535, perhaps thinking he had reached a place as odd and improbable as the island Montalvo invented. His explorers, sailing halfway up what is still sometimes called the Sea of Cortez, assumed this long waterway continued on to the fabled Straits of Annian and the Northwest Passage. Thus the region called California was thought to be an island, and it appeared as such on maps of the world as late as the end of the eighteenth century.

Though explorers eventually disproved this theory, California was so far distant from the centers of power attempting to manage it—first Madrid and Mexico City, then Washington, D.C., and New York—that it continued to be thought of as a realm apart. The idea persists to this day. I have a little pamphlet issued by the Northrup-King Seed Company called *When and Where to Plant*. It charts the planting dates for all the popular garden vegetables, and next to the chart are five tiny maps of the United States, showing five main climate zones: COOL. MILD. WARM. SUBTROPIC. CALIFORNIA.

Now, anyone who has tried to grow vegetables on this side of the American continent knows there is as much variety in planting conditions as one can possibly imagine. Merely consider the difference between the desert gardens of the Imperial Valley, down there next to Mexico, and the fog-bound artichoke fields bordering Monterey Bay, six hundred miles north and west. Yet from the pamphlet writer's point of view, in Minneapolis, headquarters for Northrup-King, not only is California all of one piece, it is its own category, neither cool, nor mild, nor warm, nor subtropic but singularly itself.

In some ways, of course, this view is accurate. Certain events occur here precisely because it is a realm apart, with a reputation as the place where anything can be attempted. But bear in mind that this venerable island image, first provided by the earliest cartographers, must be viewed just as cautiously as the images conveyed by modern maps.

Early on, I thought I might begin my travels at the Oregon border, moving then from north to south. It didn't work. The Oregon border is an illusion. I drove up that way and looked around and I simply couldn't find it. Foliage and timber and landscape typical of southern Oregon actually begins in Mendocino, and in the mountains north of Redding, and in the lower Cascades around Mount Lassen. That straight line called the forty-second parallel is a political boundary through country that is in all other ways continuous, north and south of the line. And with the landscape come other continuities: rainfall, low population density, styles of living. It is logging and ranching country. On either side of this invisible line they vote in different primaries and lobby in different capitols, but the fact is, northern county residents have a lot more in common with the people of southern Oregon than with the people of Southern California. Their natural realm is closer to the one staked out by aboriginal tribes, the Klamath and the Modoc, who fished and hunted all through the Cascade region. Captain Jack, tragic hero of the Modoc Wars in the 1860s and 70s, was imprisoned for a while on the Oregon side, at the Klamath Lake reservation, before making his final stand out there in the lava beds, across the line near Tule Lake. Today the people of Tule Lake and Newell cross the line daily to shop in Klamath Falls. Californians from Alturas, the Modoc County seat, fifty miles below the line, will sometimes drive to Klamath

Falls to shop. It is handier than Susanville or Redding, and they pay no sales tax there.

Still searching for that point of entry, I climbed back into my car and drove eight hundred miles down Highway 5 to the other end of the state, where the maps show another straight line. It was easier to locate, but even harder to believe, much more political, yet in certain ways more imaginary than the line through the mountains. I know a number of people who don't believe it at all. I have heard Chicano historians say the border is largely myth, that the reality is the arid landscape it passes through, together with the continuum of language and culture that has linked northern Mexico and the American Southwest for centuries.

When you head out of Tijuana or Mexicali, there is not much in the terrain to suggest you have left one country and entered another. The desert, the mesquite, the dry arroyos, the fierce heat once you move a few miles inland, the intense greens of the irrigated fields—this enormous expanse, indeed all of Baja and Alta California, was originally a single political unit, a province of Mexico. After the first overland expedition in 1769, there began a back-and-forth flow of traffic through this land—soldiers, padres, Indians, settlers, traders, mules, horses and wagons—that has never ceased. It has continued and increased and has now escalated until there seems no way to control it, short of setting up heavy artillery and electric fencing from the Pacific to the tip of Texas. Mexico has one of the world's fastest-growing populations, and an impoverished economy. California has one of the world's richest economies. It works like a magnet.

Some Chicanos say more is involved than jobs and money. They say a sense of history, or destiny, has been built into the nervous system, that Mexicans have pushed northward the way Anglos pushed west, not so much by right as by instinct, by territorial impulse, and that the international border, in some recess of the national mind, is merely a recent and troublesome inconvenience. Immigration officials claim they apprehend about a thousand illegal border-crossers a day, while another two thousand or so make it through. They also observe that a good percentage of those coming in from Mexico, with or without approval, work awhile and return home. It is this constant motion, back and forth, from the towns and villages of Sonora, Jalisco and Sinaloa, into the towns and cities of Alta California, that makes the international border sometimes seem so artificial.

Though undocumented aliens blur the count, estimates for people of Mexican origin now living in California hover around 4.5 million, a bit under 20 percent of the total. Some have been here for five or six generations, others for five or six days. Theirs is a unique situation, fostered by borderland continuities. Most American ethnic groups, if they want to stay in touch with the homeland, have an ocean to cross. As the years go by, the connections get diluted. Not so in the Southwest. The second-largest Mexican city is Los Angeles. It is possible to travel by car, train, bus or on foot from Guadalajara, the third-largest Mexican city, into Los Angeles, never alter your dress or your diet, stay with relatives, see the same movies, read the same magazines, hear the same songs on the radio, and watch Mexican television shows. You can do this for years and never have to speak more than a few words of English.

Such things are possible much farther north than Los Angeles. Santa Cruz County, where I live, is not thought of as a border county or as part of the Southwest. Though the Spanish Mission heritage is often noted, a Mexican population does not figure in the county's imagery. Advertisements from the Chamber of Commerce feature the Boardwalk, the Roller Coaster, the annual Miss California Contest, the wide beaches warmed by a southern exposure and protected by a benevolent arm of the Coast Range. Recently I attended the Santa Cruz County Fair. It was a regular, old-time fair with a livestock auction, a lumberjack contest, carnival rides, hot dogs, corn on the cob, prizes for the largest cabbages, Golden Delicious apples and hubbard squash, and the added attraction of a Mexican-American Day, scheduled on September 16, anniversary of the proclamation of Mexico's independence from Spain, which was originally delivered by Padre Miguel Hidalgo in the town of Dolores in 1816. Since September 16 happened to fall on a Sunday, this event was also the county fair's finale.

A talent show had been flown in from the state of Michoacán—a mariachi band in charro outfits, an M.C., a comedian, a romantic baritone wearing maroon jacket with darker maroon striping his lapels. Everything was in Spanish. The jokes were Mexican jokes. The songs were Mexican favorites. The crowd of some three thousand listeners was entirely of Mexican origin. They came from Watsonville, Hollister, Salinas, San Juan Bautista, and Santa Cruz. Some were born in those towns, others were recently arrived and looking for field work. There were many Indian faces, the skin bronze, the hair straight and black, the eyes often almond-shaped, giving that oriental cast. Many of the women were tiny, under five feet, even when wearing spike heels. As I stood in this crowd of three thousand brown faces, at the county fairgrounds on Mexican Independence Day, listening to the handsome baritone lean in close to the mike to announce, "Con mucho gusto y mucho cariño, me voy a cantar QUE LINDO ES MICHOACÁN . . ." ("With great pleasure and much affection, I am going to sing HOW LOVELY IS MICHOACÁN . . ."), it was easy to imagine that the border had dissolved or that geography had reversed itself, and we were not five hundred miles north but a thousand miles south, in Uruapan or Patzcuaro.

The western boundary of California is the most visible, the most famous, the most often written about. Because of its place in history, the Pacific coastline has come to represent much more than the border of the westernmost states, much more than the line where the land ends and the ocean begins. Standing at the edge of the continent, it has loomed as some final destination, a terminal zone for that great surge outward from Europe toward the New World that began in the fifteenth century. Many writers have voiced this sense of destiny—Walt Whitman, Robinson Jeffers, John Steinbeck, Joan Didion. Beat poet Lew Welch, in *The Song Mount Tamalpais Sings,* described this coast as "the final cliffs of all Man's wanderings."[5]

It is a heady notion, especially when you are in the presence of those awesome cliffs along the Point Reyes peninsula or the granite bluffs that defy the ocean at Big Sur, or the softer bluffs of sandstone that turn orange with the late sun at Santa Cruz. I walk along some part of this coastline almost every day, and it is easy to brood upon the great events that somehow find conclusion here. Such splendid cliffs seem capable of bearing tremendous freight. And indeed they do, if you or your family arrived from an easterly direction, as my father did. One of his ancestors had left Ireland in the 1700s, heading west, much the way another ancestor, a few decades earlier, had left Scotland, heading west in a boatload of Presbyterians who had been encouraged by the Church of England to practice their unwelcome rituals elsewhere.

This view of the coastline, however, this map of the region's destiny, does not tell us all we need to know. Hundreds of thousands have approached it from the other direction, bearing other histories. They came first to build the railroad, when that was the most vital work to be done. They dug the mountain tunnels and laid the track. But they had no voice in the making of the legends, so there emerged the most marvelous and beguiling of all the images of transcontinental conquest, the great engines that finally linked the East Coast and the West, with very little said about the infusion of energy from Asia. Because Anglo voices have dominated the literature and the myth-making, this notion of coastline as terminus has prevailed. Yet for Californians of Asian ancestry—Chinese, Japanese, Filipino, Indian, Korean, Vietnamese—

the coastline has played quite a different role. Historically, it has not been the conclusion of something, it has been the point of arrival.

Like the coastline, the border to the east of California is palpable and inevitable. You can touch it, climb it, see it coming toward you, see it looming. The peaks and bulges of the Sierra Nevada rise beyond the central valley, the long and ragged bulwark of some ancient kingdom. By the time you have crossed those mountains you know you are leaving one region of the West and entering another. The license plates begin to change, and so does the terrain. Yet here again we must be wary, for the border to the east is the most elusive. To the east there is another continuity, not of landscape or style of life or ethnic origin, but what you might call a continuum of the mind. What the map shows, the political and geographical boundaries, does not take into account the centuries of hopes and ambitions that have flowed toward California with the flow of history toward the Pacific.

You hear a lot of talk about the California Dream, or about its failure, that the dream is still alive, or is vanishing, or has become a nightmare. I have a friend, a native son of the Golden West, who recently moved to central Oregon, saying he does not want his children growing up amidst the pollution, the congestion, and the crime rate of the San Francisco Bay Area. He was not bitter about this. He had found a pleasant spot for himself outside a small town in the Willamette Valley. But he felt betrayed. One of life's promises had been unfairly broken. "Since I was a kid," he said, "the population of this state has tripled. All the things we used to do, you can't do them anymore without standing in line. I can't even take my kids to a state park to camp out overnight without making reservations through Ticketron."

The week my friend left his home state for good, I met a fellow who had just moved his family and belongings from Boston right into the center of that same congestion, and he was filled with the enthusiasm of a man for whom life had new importance. Why? He was already making a small fortune in real estate, and there were no more brutal winters to assault him.

A while back, at a party in Los Angeles, I was talking to an architect's wife about roots, about whether it was possible to feel rooted in California, to have a sense of origins and a sense of place. She laughed and shook her head and said what she liked most about living on this coast was the total lack of roots.

"I don't have any family here," she said, "no relatives, no community of people I grew up with. I love it. When we moved, I left all that back in the Midwest, and it has been absolutely liberating. Out here I can be exactly who I want to be, on my own terms. That's what this so-called permissive society is all about. It permits me to be myself and be free of all those hometown limits, most of which were inbred and totally unexamined, and repressive. I don't think of California as a place, you see. It is a certain kind of opportunity."

She was clear-eyed and confident, she seemed of sturdy character and capable of handling as much space as the world could give her. California is full of people like this, who thrive on the available emotional and psychological space. But while she talked, I was thinking of others I have known, who have grown up in this same permissive society and been obliterated by it, people who have collapsed into the available space like exploding dolls. In all parts of the world people are defeated by circumstances, by social injustice, by disease and natural disaster. In California it is also possible to be defeated by one of the key features of its much publicized dream: available space.

The fact is, this notorious dream is born and dies and decomposes and is reborn in a million new shapes every day. It is important to remember that the shapes it takes remain connected to all those places where the dreams and hopes and ambitions originated. This is what blurs the boundaries to the east. East is the direction most Californians have come from. Junípero Serra's vision of glory for God, Spain and the Catholic Church took the shape of a string of Missions, which still survive, built and maintained by the enslaved coastal tribes, who did not survive. His vision was hatched in Madrid and on the island of Mallorca where he was born. The vision of another religion for a later age, which took the shape of The People's Temple in San Francisco, was hatched in Indiana, where the Reverend James Jones grew up and was ordained as a minister in the Disciples of Christ. Visions of a fortune in gold and silver, which lured the father of William Randolph Hearst, were sharpened by the narrow prospects facing him in his home state of Missouri during those days when the news from Sutter's Fort was igniting young men all across the land. The zinfandel grape, which has found its ideal support system in the soil and sunlight of California's coastal valleys, was one obscure varietal among the hundred thousand cuttings shipped in by the Hungarian Agoston Harazthy, part of the dream he carried west from Europe in 1862. My own father's dream of a new and better life was hatched in east Texas around the family blacksmith shop, in the dusty fields of the 1920s. He piled what he owned into a rickety sedan and started driving toward El Paso, the Grand Canyon and points west, looking for work, looking for beaches, looking for a change.

People call this state the nation's testing ground, or its early warning system. The phrase "a window on the future" is used, sometimes "cutting edge," with its most adventurous and sinister connotations intertwined. Such words are used because this has become a realm where things are tried, attempted, acted out. One way to think of it is as a region of the Euro-American landscape that has been selected—through certain accidents of history, location, climate and other natural endowments—selected as a place where many of our collective yearnings and possibilities and expectations and hallucinations, for better or for worse, find their full expression. Here jet aircraft are designed and tested, and advanced models of farm machinery, and renegade views of property tax. Diets are tested, and telescopes, and sexuality, and new ways of risking your life.

Yogis teach that this physical world we call reality is actually an invention, a product of the mind. If any place on the planet fits that description, it is the state of California. On the Shell station and *National Geographic* maps, it is clearly a region of the earth. Yet by another set of charts it is an elaborate, Byzantine, unwieldy work of our communal imagination, perhaps a vast novel, begun in the mind of Montalvo back in 1510 and still being written.

How Various Large and Small Pieces of California Move Around from One Place to Another

Gary Griggs is a geologist here in Santa Cruz County. In his view, any account of where people live, and why and how, should properly begin with the earth itself, with the rocks and the riverbeds and the soils beneath our feet. Why? These things were here first. They have seniority.

It may seem obvious to point this out. But in California it is not obvious.

A while back, Gary drove me up the coast a few miles to look at a pile of sand by the side of a very famous road. As he saw it, this humble pile of grimy sand was a perfect metaphor for something about the way life is lived out west. It was half an hour north of town, up Highway 1, not far from where the sign says NEXT GAS TWENTY-THREE MILES. Row crops, brussels sprouts and artichokes, spread back on one side of us. Toward the ocean, it was sand dunes sprinkled with sparse tufts of grass. The dune grass used to be thicker, but the four-wheel drivers and the Honda three-wheelers with the big balloon tires had been coming in there chasing each other up and down the dunes and across the tide flats near the surf line and in and out of the sandy hillocks, and this played hell with the dunes.

"It takes a long time for this stuff to root," Gary said. "Once it's rooted, the sand and the grass and the wind have a nice system going. The sand stays put, and the dunes hold their shape for years and years. But now you have these huge patches of open dune where the grass has been torn away or mutilated, and you have this onshore wind which picks up the loose sand and pushes it out toward the highway. When it gets too far out into the road, it is a traffic hazard. Since this is supposed to be one of the state's great scenic drives, the road crews have to come in with their sand movers and dump trucks, load it up and carry it down the road a ways and dump it. So, in addition to the ecological fact that the dunes are being systematically destroyed, there is a direct correlation between the damage done by one set of vehicles and what it costs the state to bring in another set of vehicles, at probably a hundred-and-eighty-five dollars an hour, to clean up the mess."

"They ought to be keeping those four-wheelers out of there," I said.

"They try," said Gary. "It's county beach. The county has passed an ordinance. But they don't really have the personnel to enforce it. And the four-wheel drivers don't always see the connection between the fun they are having on the beach and the sand drifting toward the traffic a hundred yards away. 'Put up some barriers,' they say. 'Turn off the wind. Who's responsible for the goddam wind anyway?' they say."

The earth has seniority, yet we who live here overlook this all the time. Who can blame us, living where the land and the dream have this inverted relationship that goes back so many years. The earth has seniority, and yet the dream came first.

Like America itself, California was dreamed about long before anyone knew it was really here. Montalvo's novel was published in Madrid twenty-five years before Cortez named the lower peninsula, thirty-two years before the Cabrillo expedition first sailed up this coast. "Their island," Montalvo wrote, "was the strongest in all the world, with its steep cliffs and rocky shores. Their arms were all of gold, and so was the harness of the wild beasts which they tamed and rode. For, in the whole island, there was no metal but gold."[6]

It was a concoction that actually influenced the hopes of the earliest adventurers. And this sequence—the dream running well in advance of the reality—has shaped the life of the state from the outset. Nowadays the dream shifts and turns and trembles, while the earth itself refuses to stand still. These two coexist, in a zany and tumultuous kind of marriage, a tug-of-war. They are never going to separate. They are going to tough it out to the bitter end. You can see the evidence everywhere, along the beaches, in the mountains, in the deserts and in the delta marshes, and in certain subdivisions built across a fault line, in the broken pads of concrete there, where sports cars were meant to park.

My nearest vantage point happens to be my own front porch. For almost twenty years I have lived in the same house, watching Monterey

Bay, observing the change of seasons register in the colors and rufflings of the bay, in the surge of tides and the angle of the waves approaching shore. In the summer, waves roll up from the south, stirred to life by storms below the equator, moving straight across the bay to meet these beaches head-on. Sometime during the fall the approach angle shifts, as the storm centers shift to the north Pacific. By November or December the waves are rolling down from Alaska. They swing around the headland west of here, which protects our inshore waters from the colder, harsher currents of the open sea, and they approach the beach with a northeasterly turn, usually with great force. This delights the surfers and alarms the yachtsmen and the fishing fleet, since these fall and winter swells not only send breaking waves into the harbor mouth, they can haul sand in too.

The sand fills the channel between the jetties, and then the great, gloomy, non-pastoral, non-resort town dredge is put to work sucking sand and sludge from the channel so the sloops and launches can continue to glide in and out. A twelve-inch pipe is strung along the beach for a few hundred yards, to carry the sludge back into the tide, and you can hear the gravel and scraps of clam shell rattling along inside the pipe and smell the stink of buried boat oil and refuse that spreads across the beach in a murky fan. A good onshore wind will send the fumes back into the neighborhoods. On those days you hold your nose and watch the sunset backlighting the spectacular winter surf that humps outside Seal Rock, at the headland of this historic bay, and you are fully in touch with both the glory and the undoing of the California Dream.

In the dream, pleasure holds a high priority. And this harbor exists primarily for pleasure craft—yachts, ketches, Boston whalers, catamarans. People from all over northern California berth them here or haul them in on trailers to be launched down the concrete ramp into the inviting waters of the sunny and irresistible bay. The sailing is so good, so exhilarating, and the mooring so benign, there have never been enough berths to go around. It is like Yale or Princeton in the old days: you put your newborn child on the waiting list. Then, when the fall and winter swells arrive you watch with dread as the pleasure principle collides with the stubborn will of the coastal sands.

Carried by wave-generated currents, the sand moves down the coast from northwest to southeast. Thousands of tons are swept up and swirled along by wave action. Whole beaches are transported from one district to another. The Army Corps of Engineers designed these jetties to fend off heavy swells, but they underestimated the flow of sand. The westward jetty has trapped acres and acres of it, creating a vast beach that did not exist before 1965. This now forces sand around the jetty and into the harbor mouth until sometimes nothing wider or deeper than a kayak can move in and out. During a minus tide in December, even the kayak is stuck.

Griggs the geologist, who has studied this coastline for most of his life, says the habits of the sand are not likely to change. The sand, he says, has been carrying on this way for thousands of years. To solve the problem, the harbor must be redesigned. But the county doesn't have that kind of money at the moment, and the Corps is reluctant to accept any blame. So every winter there is panic and consternation, followed by a gloomy reaching into the public pocketbook, while the dredge is called in to pump out the sand and the accumulated sludge, which in turn befouls the beach and fills the neighborhoods with noxious fumes and a day-long, night-long industrial rumbling like the sound of a tug-boat pulling us all toward deeper water.

The dredging only lasts a few weeks, of course. Then the bulldozers roll in and push over the mounds of debris that have piled up around the mouth of the overflow pipe. A couple of high tides later the beach is restored, and all of us who use these sands, tides, offshore waters and stirring vistas are content—the boaters and fishermen, the surfers and surf casters in their hip boots waiting for perch, the joggers, skimboarders and scampering dogs, the Frisbee masters with dogs trained for startling mid-air catches, the scuba divers and volleyball players and young meditators in the lotus, the ponchoed smoker who wants a hassle-free toke while the tawny sun goes down, and the retirement couple right behind him in their straw hats, who hike the sand most evenings.

According to Griggs, this annual skirmish between the harbor users and the restless sand is another typical California event. Whenever I talk to him, I am reminded again how delicately balanced is this seemingly solid surface we walk and drive around on. I am reminded of the many fluid tendencies our human plans keep running counter to. In this ongoing contest, Gary is a kind of attorney for the earth and its habits, filing briefs on its behalf. He often finds himself explaining or defending these habits to people who see the earth as an adversary or who don't seem to see it at all.

He also happens to be a born-in-Pasadena Californian, and an unrepentant native son. For most of his life he has lived within hiking or biking distance of a coastal beach. His father taught school in San Fernando Valley, and Gary remembers many summer trips into redwood country and the northern mountains. There is no denying that this influenced his chosen line of work. He is endlessly fascinated with the land and landscape of his home region, the way it behaves. Right now he lives on a wooded slope, at the top of a four-mile uphill road, with a view of the Pacific, in a house he designed and built himself. The house is made of fir and redwood. His office at the University of California's Santa Cruz campus, where I was meeting him for another lesson in the geology of recreation, is made of concrete: floors, ceilings, and the walls which are covered with slope maps, satellite photos, tiers of books.

His field is called Earth Sciences. He made full professor not long ago, at 35. This is like making brigadier general when you're 35, or senior vice-president at Humble Oil, where he was once offered a job. He looks and dresses younger. In his office he wears jeans, a buff-colored leather shirt, and hiking boots. He would make an excellent frontier scout, lean and hardy and intently pleased to be doing what he does. He is away from campus much of the time, looking at where people hope to locate buildings or moor their boats or maneuver their off-road vehicles. This work has taken him to New Zealand, to Greece, and to all parts of California. The day I called on him was a typical day. He had invited me to join him on a little trip to a place called Hungry Valley, below Bakersfield, where he had been measuring the impact of dirt-bikes and four-by-fours, the ways they reshape the surface of the world.

The State Department of Parks and Recreation had hired him for this project. Before we left the office, he showed me some of the material he had gathered, beginning with a photo of a hilly region taken from five miles up. It resembled a cross-section of human flesh, with the capillaries and nerves exposed. The capillary lines were dirt-bike trails in the high desert. He showed me close-ups of gullies etched into one of those same hillsides. One was four feet wide, eight feet deep. Gary stood inside the gulley with a measuring rod. It was an impressive sight, the way serious damage is always impressive, and awesome—a crumpled front-end, a wind-torn tree across the road. The damage, he told me, was even more impressive than it looked: tons of soil torn loose by that kind of gullying was displacing valuable water storage space in Pyramid Lake, part of Los Angeles County's intricate reservoir system.

"Off-road vehicles have been in there for six or seven years now," Gary said. "And we are talking about thousands of vehicles. Part of the valley is National Forest, part of it is private property. As usual, the state gets involved after the damage is done. Now they are thinking about buying up some parcels and turning a big area into an ORV park. You can't keep them out, so you look for ways to legalize the activity and contain it."

When he describes these dilemmas Gary has a way of laughing, not *at* anyone in particular, but *with* the way the world goes. He has compassion for the state officials who inherit these headaches. He understands the will of the riders who want to scale those hills. But his deeper sympathies lie with the will of the rainfall to flow where it has to flow, with the will of the sand to migrate through these coastal waters like schools of whales.

We were out of town right after lunch, cutting cross-country toward the San Joaquin, where we would pick up the highspeed north–south trunk route. Heading past Watsonville, we followed the Pajaro River east along Highway 124. On its way to Monterey Bay, the river has carved a trough through this fold in the Coast Range. The trough is called Chittenden Pass, and it happens to be a place where the river crosses the San Andreas Fault. I would not say that Gary is obsessed with the San Andreas, but the substructure of this state is on his mind most of the time. As we were leaving his office, with its layers of maps, charts, graphs and high-altitude photos, I had asked him if he could describe in twenty-five words or less a line of work that included a blocked harbor mouth, the price of real estate, earthquake prediction and four-wheel drive.

His eyes opened wide, as if he had never thought of it quite that way before. Then he laughed his way-the-world-goes laugh.

"I guess you could say that I spend a lot of time thinking about how various large and small pieces of California move around from one place to another."

Of all this state's innumerable moving parts, the rift zone is the one that interests him most. He never wearies of discussing it, speculating, pondering. When he pulled to a sudden stop, halfway through Chittenden Pass, we were two pilgrims paying homage to the visible signs of certain planetary forces greater than our puny human selves.

The fault line marks the zone where two pieces of the earth's crust meet and grind together, the Pacific Plate and the North American Plate. Thanks to deep cuts through this pass made by highway crews in the 1930s, we could stand on the road that follows the river and see the meeting ground of these two vast slabs, spread before us like an open-faced sandwich. On the western side there was a chunky wall of granite, overgrown with brush and, higher up, with eucalyptus. To the east, a brighter wall of buff-colored shale, stratified at about a forty-five-degree angle, pointed up and west, as if the granite side were steadily nosing in under the shale. Above this layering there was a low dip in the ridge, the kind of dip that makes the trace line visible from airplanes.

In 1906 the concrete pillars holding up the railroad bridge at Chittenden cracked and almost toppled. The tracks were thrown so far out of alignment that a train moving through just after the main tremor hit was rolled on its side like a toy. It is said that in the old train depot at Chittenden a thousand-pound safe was overturned. Nowadays there is a granite quarry working full-time, right across the river. We stood and contemplated the million years of silent grinding made visible there, and listened to the distant clank of conveyor belts at the quarry, the heavy trucks hauling out gravel, and the various creaking and clanking machines of men chipping away, chipping away, at the surface of the earth.

We had stopped there once before, back in 1973, when Gary first introduced me to the mysteries of the fault line. We had followed it that day for about fifty miles, examining the surface effects on the land and in the towns. We saw sag ponds, little avalanches, displaced creek beds. Outside San Juan Bautista we had stopped at a fence that happens to straddle the fault, where students of his had driven markers to measure the creep. As we passed it again, Gary glanced at the same markers, and told me the fence line had moved a bit less than an inch this year.

In Hollister, we took five minutes to swing a few blocks off the highway. Gary turned down a side street notable for an asphalt warp he likes to check from time to time. On both sides of the street stand immaculately kept Victorian cottages and farm-town homes. Sighting down the center of this street, we could observe the tar line, which is offset about eight inches. Hollister sits right in the rift zone, as does the Almaden winery a few miles south, on La Cienega Road. The winery is being gradually torn in two. For students of ground flow, the winery is a historic site—it is where the fault line's pattern of steady creep was first identified, back in 1956. A government plaque stands by the side of the road, outside the tasting room:

> This site possesses exceptional value in illustrating the natural history of the United States. (U.S. Dept. of Interior, National Park Service, 1965.)

That is exactly the role it played for me, driving down there with Gary in 1973. Until that day I had not given much thought to the look or the behavior of this fault line. Dimly I had imagined a long gash or trench that stretched like a zipper from somewhere in the north to somewhere in the south. I had lived most of my life within a few miles of this region's most influential natural feature, and knew it not at all. I began talking to other Californians about this and discovered that most of us were in the same boat. For a couple of months after a major quake, such as the bad one in San Fernando in 1971, or the 5.5 near Livermore in January 1980, you will hear a swell of conversation, a run of gallows humor. Meetings will be called and legislation passed. But interest soon wanes. If a tremor measures less than 4.4 on the Richter, few people care to read past the headline. They seldom give it a passing thought.

A passing dream, however? That was another matter. I ran into a number of people who confessed to vivid and recurring dreams such as this one:

> The ground opens up. We are running in a panic, screaming and yelling, and then this tidal wave is moving toward shore. I am riding the wave, kind of body-surfing, when it turns to ice. It freezes before it breaks, and I am hanging there, frozen too, inside the wave.[7]

Lurking underground the fault line lives its hidden life, while on the surface the busy rush prevails, with a disregard that sometimes seems calculated, some kind of testing, or challenging, like the bullfighter who turns his back on the bull.

As we dropped through Pacheco Pass, with the broad valley before us, Gary said, "Back there in Hollister, not far from the winery, there is an ORV park called Hollister Hills, which happens to be bisected by the fault line. Where the bikers ride, you can see two kinds of damage, depending on which side you look at: sedimentary rock on one side, granite on the other. For some strange reason, the San Andreas also skirts the northern edge of the Hungry Valley site. Isn't that bizarre? I mean, when you think about all the things in this state that occur right on top of the San Andreas—high schools, dams and reservoirs, housing projects, parking lots, Pacific Gas and Electric substations, a winery, one of the original Spanish missions, and now these off-road vehicle playgrounds."

"Don't forget the late James Dean," I told him.

"What does he have to do with it?"

"Star of *East of Eden*, set right over the ridge there, in Salinas. Star of *Rebel Without a Cause*, sad saga of southern Cal teenagers cast adrift in the fifties. It is a little-known fact that in 1955, when Dean's Porsche piled into a station wagon at a hundred and ten miles per hour, killing him instantly, he was crossing the San Andreas Fault."

"I don't believe it."

"He was driving west on Highway Forty-six out of Wasco, on his way to Paso Robles. He crashed at Cholame. That is a historical fact, and you know yourself that Cholame is right there in the rift zone."

Gary grinned. He wanted to believe it. He muttered, "I'll be damned," then, after a moment, "but what does it mean?"

"Cars," I said. "Vehicles. Traffic and geology. It is the whole story of California."

"That's right! Traffic and geology," exclaimed Griggs the geologist, stomping his accelerator, pushing his van to seventy miles per hour as we swung through the intersection and out among the semis and diesel rigs barreling south on Interstate 5.

Like so many of the world's fertile regions, the central valley was once under water, a flat-bottomed sea, contained on one side by the Sierra Nevada, on the other by the Coast Range, and at its southern rim by the Tehachapi Mountains which, a couple of hours later, were looming in front of us, mountains with a character all their own, bringing to mind the sharp-edged tropical peaks at the center of Tahiti and Kauai. Geologists call this the Transverse Range, for the way it cuts across the grain of the state. According to the theory of Continental Drift, the Pacific Plate, of which the coastal edge is an exposed lip, pushes north and west against the North American Plate. In eons past, as this movement confronted the southern end of the deeply rooted Sierra Nevada, the mountains of the Transverse Range occurred. Some say this bend in the landscape and in the fault line blocks the steady creep. Thus, they say, accumulating stress makes it the most likely region for the next "big event."

The San Fernando quake was centered in these mountains, as well as the legendary Tejon quake of 1857, the first to draw wide attention to this feature of California life, since it was the first to hit after major settlement began. That quake, an estimated eight on the Richter, was centered at Fort Tejon, a small outpost built by the army to control a narrow pass which is still the main pass connecting the central valley with the L.A. basin. The pass itself happens to be a feature of the rift zone, and once again we crossed the San Andreas, at four thousand feet, surrounded by the produce trucks and highballing Peterbilts that grind through there all day and night, back and forth between the world's richest agricultural valley and the world's most improbable collection of appetites.

We left the Interstate at Gorman, a cluster of filling stations just over the brow of the pass and just inside the L.A. County line. A mile out of Gorman we turned onto Hungry Valley Road, where a sign said ENTERING LOS PADRES NATIONAL FOREST. Past the sign there was a dusty clearing, rimmed with trees, a camping site that had become the staging area for what lay beyond. Vans and campers were scattered around, with dirt-bike trailers attached. There were high-wheeled pickups with dirt-bikes braced upright behind quadruple spotlights. Young kids in helmets and masks whipped Hondas and Yamahas around the clearing, warming up. The sound was like a heavy-duty chainsaw, that same high sputtering whine. Half-a-dozen were revving up near the campsite, careening through the blinding dust, making the sound of half-a-dozen chainsaws.

In the middle of the clearing, like a totem for the circling riders, stood a Forest Service bulletin board, where signs and pamphlets were stapled. One was large enough to read from the road:

Save Our Vegetation. Stay On The Roadway.

Beyond the bulletin board, beyond the line of trees, we could see the first hillside, perhaps sixty feet high, totally denuded, striped with wheel tracks, lined with ruts and parallel gullies, as if the fingers of some enormous hands had been dragged through what used to be the topsoil of this slope.

One of the kids who had been kicking up dust swung out onto the road, made a wide turn, gathering speed, and roared up the far side of the hill, his thin arms tense, his body rising over the handlebars. From his build I figured him to be about thirteen. We watched him make the climb and level out at the top, with a couple of triumphant revs from the whining engine. He was motoring across the ridge against a gorgeous blue sky.

I said, "It looks like fun."

"It is. That's the whole trouble. It is a hell of a lot of fun."

Past the campsite the road followed a low rise and the valley opened before us, high desert country, the flat zones rugged enough to challenge the riders, the slopes and ridges rising on both sides, some denuded, others sprinkled with scrub juniper, low oaks here and there, all striped with trails, gouges, ruts, deltas where several tracks intersected at the top of a climb.

Kids on bikes roared toward us down the road, more vans, more campers, more pickups. Across the valley we could see them parked— a van next to a clump of juniper where a fellow squatted adjusting his wheel. Halfway up a slope, two camper rigs awaited the return of their owners, who had taken off across country. A VW bug with an exposed engine rumbled up a barren incline, swerving with the effort, in the loosened dirt, to join two other VWs up on top. A young girl came toward us popping a wheelie, lifting off the ground in exuberant greeting. Behind her a father and son were riding together along the narrow asphalt road, the father's bike a size larger. The son looked to be about eleven. They wore matching Yamaha T-shirts.

It was late afternoon. As the sun dropped, the light spread, catching sharp edges, throwing the convoluted dips and arroyos into shadow, brightening the juniper's dusty green. We parked below a high straight ridge that blocked the sun. Its top emanated a buttery glow, an aura, and a young rider whined along up there, raising a plume. From that altitude his view must have been even more spectacular than ours on the valley floor. I envied him. He had climbed high to make his own connection with this glorious landscape. He whirled and motored back the other way, and I thought of other pastimes that put you *into* nature. I thought of surfing, and skiing. You want to take the rising wave, or the snowy slope, make your mark upon it and, for that brief run, possess it. The difference is, after you have drawn your line across the wave's sheer wall, it breaks. It turns to water and the line is gone. The snow melts, and the skier's tracks melt with it. The tracks of the dirt-bike do not go away. Just below that lone biker, there was a bare hillside streaked with tracks, a steep slope that had been climbed so many times no one climbed it any longer. There were too many ruts, sunk too deeply into the soil, gullies too dangerous for the churning wheels.

We locked the van and hiked a hundred yards to the foot of this slope, then climbed to the lower end of the deepest gully and followed it until we were in up to our waists. It was about three feet across, three-and-a-half feet down, a ragged channel cut into the slope and littered with large cobbles, tumbleweeds.

"When you're a biker," Gary said, "the steepest hill is the biggest thrill. It is also where you can do the worst damage to the soil."

He leaned against the embankment, picking at the sand and gravel and talking about the fragile systems that hold the thin layer of topsoil together in these semi-arid regions. When the vehicles arrive, the vegetation goes first, and with it the root networks that help control the natural erosion rate. Over time the wheels and the weight compact the soil, which makes it less receptive to water, thus more difficult for vegetation to recover, if any topsoil remains to grab onto. Here on the western edge of the desert, it seldom rains. But for a day or two it can fall in torrents. Then, instead of flowing evenly down a slope, the water will pick out a wheel track and turn it into a channel, deepen it into a rut, and the gullying begins. Soil and sediment pour down onto the flat basin below the gulley we were standing in. Gary noted how the runoff had deltaed out. It would have been grazing land, he said. Now it was covered with coarse-grain sand and gravel. Nothing would be growing there again for many years. Multiply that by dozens of hillsides and thousands of wheel tracks, and eventually the drainage system of an entire area is thrown out of balance.

"The sediment heads toward Piru Creek, just south of here," said Gary. "And since Piru Creek empties into Pyramid Lake, a lot of sediment ripped loose by ORV activity in Hungry Valley ends up displacing water in what is supposed to be a reservoir for the city and county where most of these bikers come from. Isn't that a twist?"

The previous winter, he had been there during a storm and had the chance to measure sediment displacement in three parts of the drainage basin: one where there had been *no* ORV use, the second where there had been *limited* use, the third in an area of *heavy* use. The differences were appalling. Sediment yield from this desert in its natural state was about fourteen tons per square mile per day. In the area of limited vehicle use it was fifty-one tons, while in the area of high use it was seven hundred and twenty-one tons per square mile per day— topsoil, sand, and gravel torn loose and swept along in the hundreds of gullies twisting down barren slopes, across the vales and deltas.[8]

According to studies made in 1968, before Piru Creek was dammed, and before the ORVs arrived, normal erosion would fill six percent of the proposed lake in fifty years. Gary's figures suggested that wheel damage in Hungry Valley could double this rate. The evidence was all under water, of course, and he was only guessing. The effects on L.A.'s water system interested him as yet another result of the ongoing battle between human and earthly habits. But the precise numbers were outside the range of his assignment, which was to consider the feasibility of turning some thirty square miles of this region into a permanent park for off-road vehicles. He was here to measure rainfall, soil composition and erosion rate, and to think about ways to arrest or slow down the flow of so many thousands of tons of the state of California from one place to another.

As we hiked back to the van, he talked about reseeding the soil. He talked about hydro-mulching and erecting sediment traps to contain the runoff. I asked him about the deep gullies. "What can you do, on a hill that steep?"

"Not a whole hell of a lot," he said. "You can't use equipment. The slope is too critical. It's hand work, and that gets expensive—laying jute netting, in-filling with rocks. They figure anywhere from two to six thousand dollars an acre to start, to restore land like this. Then, it is only effective if you can keep the riders out. So you can close this area for a while and work on the hillsides and let them ride over on the next ridge, or the next one. But eventually this area gets opened again, and the whole process starts over."

"So what's the solution?"

"You are looking at the solution. The theory is, you sort of give them

Hungry Valley, which they have already taken, plus a little more surrounding space for expanding into, because what has usually happened,
you close off one area entirely, they go out and find another area. They
move on to some other spot that has the rolling hills and the bumps and
the climbs, and they start working that place over. They use a hillside
like this one until it isn't good for anything, not even ORVs, then they
move on. So you sacrifice Hungry Valley, and you hope to save a few
other places from this type of invasion."

Gary wasn't laughing his zen laugh now. He was trying not to let his
feelings boil over.

"That heats your blood, doesn't it," I said.

"To be perfectly honest," he said, "sometimes it's hard to maintain
the professional distance. A lot of this land is supposed to be National
Forest, for Christ's sake! It's supposed to be dedicated to preservation,
not destruction. Back there on that bulletin board one of the pamphlets
says, 'Off-road Vehicles Are Welcome in Los Padres National Forest,'
followed by a list of rules. They are supposed to stay on the marked
roads. Some of them do. A lot of them don't. The state has never had
the personnel to enforce the rules. And they might *never* have the
personnel, because that requires heavy backing in Sacramento and
Washington, D.C., and the American Motorcycle Association has a
lobby that makes as much noise as the bikes do."

Back in the van we followed the road a few more miles, and I was
prepared to see a regiment of Hell's Angels come over the rise with
afterburners blazing. Grizzled gangs would not have surprised me,
wielding chains and buck knives to terrorize the rangers and hold sway
over their desert domain. They did not appear. What we saw were more
kids wearing Yamaha jerseys, more loners, more young guys in cowboy
hats roaring along in the pickups, more folks from the cities looking for
a way to let off steam. Families. Husband-and-wife teams. Fathers and
sons, the father a carpenter, or an auto parts salesman. They live in
Altadena or in Fresno. They get up early on Saturday morning and pack
a lunch, fill the thermos, grab some beer, hop into the truck or the van
and head for open country. They want to be cowboys for a day or two.
Who can blame them? We all want to be cowboys for a day or two. In
the movies you usually see one or two cowboys at a time, galloping
through the canyon. Butch Cassidy and the Sundance Kid. But what
would that canyon be like if a thousand cowboys all decided to gallop
through at once? Or a hundred thousand? On a fall weekend you might
have a hundred thousand cowboys, or more, out there tearing up the

dirt in places like Hungry Valley. There are nearly as many motorcycles registered in the state of California (about a million) as there are human beings in the states of Wyoming and Montana combined. This is what makes it interesting, and also ominous and alarming. More dirt-bikes, more four-by-fours, more leisure time, more money to spend on it, more sunny days, more people, more undersupervised public land to ride around on, and generally more support for pursuits that draw people toward this region in the first place: outdoor living, self-expression, personal fulfillment.

That young dirt-biker at the top of the ridge, backlit against the faultless desert sky, was the perfect photo for an article on what people will do in their searches for fulfillment, especially here, where vehicles are more sacred than the soil, sometimes more sacred than life itself. And that waist-deep gully we stood in was the perfect photo for an article about what the earth will do when it is ignored or underestimated. It is a pairing Gary sees everywhere he goes, in one form or another. It is both commonplace and shocking. An attorney for the earth, he marvels at the forces conspiring against it.

In the case of off-road vehicles he sees a clear example of ego gratification taking top priority over whatever is being done to the land. With a great deal of property development, it is ego gratification mingling with profit. People continually put money into properties poorly located, he says. They build on the fault line, in a tide zone, or on some slope where the erosion is going to cut them to pieces and send their deck sliding into the ravine. But the investment is so great, the property becomes so valuable, they won't abandon the location, so they pour money into it, trying to counteract the sands or the tides or the gullying or the slippage.

Such costs add up to a kind of interest, or holding fee, exacted by the earth for overlaying this precarious geology with one of the world's heaviest concentrations of capital and investment. The town of Santa Cruz now wrestles with the problem of how to contain the San Lorenzo River, because a century ago someone decided to locate the commercial district in the middle of a flood plain. To counteract a river's will to flood and silt's will to gather, the city may spend millions. It is now costing the public half-a-million every winter to pump the restless sand out of the harbor mouth. It cost the state over sixteen million dollars to buy up the private parcels in and around Hungry Valley, in order to contain that particular form of damage. The purchase was completed soon after Gary submitted his final report to Parks and Recreation. During the first full year under Parks and Rec (1981), another $200,000 went into soil protection and erosion control. And bills such as these are nothing, Gary says, compared with the bill that will come due if the San Andreas ever releases the stress some experts say has been accumulating under our feet since 1906.

We had wound our way back to Gorman. We stopped for a six pack of Rainier ale, then eased out onto the Interstate, heading north toward Bakersfield, where we would listen to some country music and spend the night. Tomorrow we'd be back for a day of photos and measurings.

After the first sip I said, "I don't think the Santa Cruz city leaders would appreciate being put in the same bag with the bikers."

"It's just one point of view," he said. "When I am being totally objective, these are the two forces pushing back and forth all over the state. The people have this will to build where they are going to build, or ride where they are going to ride. The sand and the silt and the surface of the earth has this will to go where it is going to go. Can you stop either one of them? I tell people what I see happening, and then usually I stand there and watch the process work itself out. Just look at this!" he exclaimed. "This highway! Six lanes wide, all these cars racing from Bakersfield down to L.A., all these trucks hauling stuff through Tejon Pass, right here where the Interstate crosses the rift zone!"

At that very moment his van was thrown sideways, the road beneath us seemed to swerve. I gripped the seat, while the windows rattled. I blinked away the ale's first rush, staring out at a sky that was suddenly darker. I saw that the shadow was cast by a high wall of moving metal. The windows vibrated again in the wake of air, as a passing diesel rig doing eighty registered 4.7 on the Richter Scale for rolling stock.

With a nervous laugh Gary straightened out the wheel. A mile later, we were coasting down the Grapevine grade, and the valley's lights were twinkling in the distance.

In Pursuit of Excellence, in Pursuit of Excellent Reds

Bob Moesle is a Californian who lives in the Loire Valley. A while back he came home for a visit and appeared at my door with two bottles of wine. He had just bought a case of the 1976 Paso Robles Zinfandel from Ridge Vineyards. He was shouting that this was one of the finest red wines he had ever tasted, and he insisted that we drink one bottle immediately.

I have no pretensions to being a reliable judge of wine. My only basis for opinion is the embarrassing amount I have personally consumed in the past twenty-five years and the many rambling conversations this has led me into. But I trust Bob's judgment. We went to high school together, and now he lives in France, in the middle of a famous wine region; his wife is French, and between them they have sampled a good many French and Italian wines.

I agreed to help Bob evaluate this bottle of zinfandel. When we finished it, he was so full of convivial feelings he insisted that I keep the second one, with the understanding that I would lay it away. We would drink it together when he returned the following year. I agreed to this, and we talked wildly about what the wine would be like after another year of aging.

The next day I betrayed Bob's trust and opened the second bottle. I told myself I wanted to share the experience with my wife, which was at least half the truth. The other half was, I couldn't wait: the wine was too good. When Bob found out what had happened, he said mine was a peasant's attitude. A peasant, he said, has trouble getting a wine cellar started because he drinks everything as soon as it comes into the house. So be it. I am a peasant with a taste for the big dry reds, and this is what sent me off on my next pilgrimage, to Ridge Vineyards, where they are known for their cabernets and zinfandels, particularly the zinfandel, a wine I happen to savor in almost any form. There are two reasons for this: (1) it usually lives up to those adjectives you read on labels—*robust, sturdy, complex, full-bodied, earthy, bold;* (2) regional identity. Loyalty would not be too strong a word. In a region often belittled for its shortage of authenticity, zinfandel is hailed as California's most authentic grape. The chardonnay, the cabernet, the pinot noir, the merlot, they have thrived here for decades, but they have also thrived in France. For reasons that are still not universally agreed upon, the zinfandel has flourished here as nowhere else.

These days you hear a lot about the full flowering of the post-Prohibition renaissance and the coming of age of California wine. I had been hoping to meet one of these renaissance wine-makers, of which there are dozens scattered up and down the coast, from as far north as Mendocino to as far south as Temecula, near San Diego, each working at some cutting edge of the viticultural advance: premium reds, premium whites, or the adventurous packaging of bulk reds or whites, or the frontiers of dessert wine, or the volume production of quality champagnes. Paul Draper, the wine-maker at Ridge, held a special fascination: He had worked wonders with the zinfandel, a grape that had long been considered a mainstay of good jug wine and what you might call the affordable daily tipple, but had not—until Ridge and a few other new-age adventurers came along to test its virtues—been thought capable of producing bottles you would presume to stand in the company of wines from a fine château. Something extremely Californian was going on here, it seemed to me, and I wanted to get to the bottom of it. At first, I thought it was simply a matter of grapes.

There are two lines of approach: from the east through spreading subdivisions, and from the south through rising foothills. In pursuit of wine, in pursuit of excellent vistas, I choose the southern route and, following Highway 9 out of Saratoga, suddenly enter heavy forest just beyond the town, then take a right and start climbing. My destination perches on top of one of the ridges I am glimpsing through the trees, Monte Bello Ridge, or "Beautiful Mountain," named by the Italian doctor from San Francisco who established a winery there almost a hundred years ago.

This landscape is the ideal route for approaching a winery, so rich in vineyard lore it is actually a back-roads synopsis of a chapter in this

state's agricultural history. Around a couple of hairpin turns I come
upon an iron gate and a wide sign with the world-famous name, PAUL
MASSON. *By Appointment Only,* say the words below, meaning access
up this driveway to the original family estate. This morning the gate is
locked. As I continue winding along Pierce Road, looking for my next
checkpoint, I am thinking about Masson and the old San Francisco
doctor named Osea Perrone, and that first flamboyant crowd who came
west from Europe in the late nineteenth century, who saw the Mediterranean possibilities and set up their vineyards, their châteaux and their
baronial estates along ridges such as these and in the valleys below, from
Santa Clara north to Napa—Le Franc, Masson, Perrone, Krug, Harazthy, de Latour. The Masson name is owned by Seagram's now. The
big modern plant—number twelve on the list of the nation's one hundred largest wineries—stands on the valley floor next to the wide boulevard that connects Saratoga with San Jose. But on days when this hillside gate is open, you can curve another half-mile up to the top and look
around and get some feel for how things used to be. One afternoon last
summer I was up there to hear Stephane Grappelli, the great French
jazz fiddler, in the annual concert series called "Vintage Sounds" which
is staged under trees and patio umbrellas in front of the original winery.
A date, 1852, is cut into its stone façade, commemorating the year the
first growers connected with the Masson family planted their earliest
vines in this region. The old stones are neatly fitted and give the look
of a castle entrance. There is a fleur-de-lis under the date, and a venerable pair of wooden doors hang on metal hinges. Thick ivy climbs the
wall of this warehouse/castle made of stone.

At intermission we adjourned to the upper plaza where the bottle
shop is located and where the chilled French Columbard flowed gener-
ously, as much as you could drink before the bell clanged to announce
the second set. It was a rare privilege, to be standing in the lee of sloping
vineyards, to sip in the Sunday sun and look out upon the broad valley
a thousand feet below. Though the valley now is gagging with traffic and
every day a few more fruit trees fall before the bulldozers, the free
Colombard helps you overlook all that, for an afternoon. Up there you
can't hear the traffic, and you can't help but admire those wine-loving
explorers who arrived early and—whatever else they may have done or
failed to do—had the taste and vision to pick out such majestic spots for
planting their vines and living their lives.

At Mount Eden Road I take a left, well into the foothills now. The
trees part, and the landscape opens up. Along here sections of the
narrow road are lined with orchards. Many houses have been built
along this road in recent years, comfortable houses on expensive land,

but across the slopes that rise toward still higher ground you can see stretches of orchard that remind you how this whole region must have looked in the 1930s when wine-maker Martin Ray bought his acreage and began to plant the rows of chardonnay and pinot noir. Half a mile down Mount Eden Road, I pass his mailbox. He has been dead several years, but his name is still there in small letters, another famous name and label in the wine lore of this little range of mountains that Masson called *la chaine d'or*, the ridge of gold.

Martin Ray was an archetypal figure in the next phase of California wine-making, which is to say he came along right after Prohibition. That was the cutoff point, the traumatic event. Though it ended half a century ago, Prohibition comes up continually when wine-makers talk about the business and the history and the quality of wines in California —the way filmmakers talk about the advent of television, the way Southerners still talk about the Civil War. Businesses failed. Vineyards were uprooted. Families sold their holdings. Where there had been hundreds of wineries before 1920, when the law went into effect, afterward a handful remained. A tradition that would have been continuous for well over a hundred years went into suspended animation, and the adventure of wine-making out west, especially the pursuit of fine wine, in effect started over with Repeal in 1933. Ray bottled his first vintage in 1935. Before he retired, he had bottled forty more vintages, the latter half from grapes grown, pressed and aged up the hill here, on this mountain called Eden. Like so many of the new breed of wine-makers who, one might say, are following trails he helped to blaze, he aspired to make great wine. And, by all accounts, he did. His wines were often compared with the finest whites and reds from France. It is said that he also produced some terrible stuff from time to time. He was a man of extremes, willing to experiment and take risks. This is why he stands as one of the forerunners and early contenders. As I am soon to learn from Paul Draper, the grapes—such as the abundant and long-under-rated zinfandel—the fertile soil, and the fabled microclimates—these tell half the story. If there has been a wine-making renaissance, it has depended equally on that other climate, that other kind of soil, hovering to an altitude of six or seven feet above the visible contours of the land, nurturing the whole multitude of California's crops.

The road drops down to a streambed and follows Stevens Creek through sparsely settled forest. Though not quite on automatic pilot, I assume I'll have no trouble finding my next turn. It will be well marked. I am heading for a winery after all, in certain circles thought to be a star, a jewel, a prize of a winery. In the now legendary blind tasting in Paris, in 1976, the tasting that validated the Golden Age and officially admitted California into the international big leagues, a Ridge cabernet was among the six reds that measured up against the best French reds of recent years. Ridge is, moreover, a winery with a tasting room, and every tasting room has a sign next to the road that says, "Tasting Room, One Mile, Visitors Welcome." Up in Napa Valley, where they number tasters in the hundreds of thousands each year, I have seen parking lots large enough for Gray Line tour buses to turn around without backing up, outside tasting rooms that include mini-theaters where wine films are shown on triple-frame screens with four-track stereo.

I am so programmed for some kind of sign pointing uphill toward the tasting room that I miss the turnoff at Monte Bello Road. There is no sign. You really do have to know where you're going. As I back up and begin the spiraling ascent, I see that it also helps if you are highly motivated. You climb from riverbed to twenty-three hundred feet in four miles, on a road that requires full concentration, with scant leisure for studying mailbox numbers. Again I figure some sign will mark the way to the tasting room. And again I figure wrong. Where the climb finally levels out, with half of San Francisco Bay in panorama behind and below, and the Diablo Range across the bay dark and distant under high rain clouds, I see a box with a number I recall. But nothing more. Could that be it? A number? No sign? No name? No invitation? I turn into the muddy drive and come upon a fork. I try the left. It leads me twenty yards to an old fence and broken-down gate which, if open, would admit me to an empty field. Wheels spinning, I back up, take the other fork up and over a rise, arriving in a wet yard where dogs begin to bark. I see a Doberman, a farmhouse, a few scattered cars, an old barn set into a hill that slopes down below the house. No people.

It's starting to rain, a cold rain almost like hail. What the hell is going on? We are a week into spring. It's not supposed to hail in the wine country in the spring. A small porch leads along one side of the barn, with a roof to stand under and doors to what might once have been offices. As I climb the rickety steps, in search of shelter, I see the first indication that I may actually have come to the right place, a small hand-carved sign tacked to the wooden planking of the barn: Ridge, California.

I open a door and find half-a-dozen people eating lunch at a long wooden table. When I ask for Paul Draper, they all laugh, as if finding him is a hopeless task. A woman talking on a wall phone holds the receiver away from her ear. "Are you from the Advanced Tasting Program?"

"I'm a writer. Maybe you could say I'm from the advanced fiction program."

She says, "Did you say 'fiction' or 'friction'?"

"It's all about the same," I say.

A friendly bearded fellow sitting next to the door says, "Here, sit down, have a glass of wine. We'll get Paul on the phone as soon as she's finished."

He wears jeans, flannel shirt, bill cap. They all wear jeans, the men and the women, boots, warm jackets, sitting around on wooden benches. It's all rustic, inside and out, what I would call West Coast Rustic, Well Informed. No mountain people here. No banjos on the back porch or inconvenient family idiots wandering in the yard. There are old vehicles under the trees and the barn siding could use some attention, and dogs outside are barking in the mud. But the backers come from the Stanford Research Institute, and the people on the crew seem pleased to be involved in an operation that is both high-class and low-key. The mood in the room is expansive, generous, full of high spirits, loud talk. They are drinking wine with lunch, as they do every day, and talking about the wine, as they do all the time. Two bottles stand open on the table, a Souverain 1974 Burgundy and a Ridge 1977 Paso Robles Zinfandel. Someone is troubled by the Souverain. "It was a bad deal, trading for this. When you see Burgundy on the label, no telling what they put in there."

They drink it nonetheless, along with their sandwiches, their burritos, the bearded fellow's goulash which he confesses is a mixture of his leftovers from the past three nights. He drives tractor here. He pours me a taste of the Paso Robles, and I mention my ecstatic memory of the '76. He agrees it was a very big, very cinnamony, and unforgettable wine, which will probably be surpassed by the '78 Paso Robles they have just bottled.

Outside it is hailing heavily. Icy gravel pelts the window. The dogs come sprinting toward the porch for cover.

I say, "Unusual for vineyard country, isn't it?"

He laughs. "Some people think this shouldn't be vineyard country."

The tractor man is looking out at the rows of dormant vines across the nearest slope. "Doesn't seem to hurt 'em, though. Look at those babies. They've been there thirty, forty years. We got one vine must be a hundred. It's this big around," he says, making a two-foot circle with his arms. "I know just where it is 'cause I got to plow around that sucker."

The far door opens and Draper walks in. You can tell he is the man in charge. Questions hit him from three directions, the kind people ask

when they don't know how long it will be before they have him standing still again, urgent but not anxious questions, asked by people who
have each put away half a bottle of good wine with lunch. He seems to
enjoy being scheduled to the limit, being almost too busy to deal with
all this, yet not *quite* that busy. In two days he is leaving for New
Orleans, for a week of tasting, lecturing, wine consulting. In three
months he leaves for a trip to Burgundy and Bordeaux.

He is in his early forties, wears Levi's, a red wool shirt, wide-lens
glasses. With each answer his smile opens up between a black mustache
and chin beard salted with flecks of white.

The woman just now hanging up the phone has a question about a
price change on some wine they're ready to ship, and another about
some restaurant owner's request for sample bottles. Then he has made
his way across the room, and we are out the door I entered by, standing
on the porch exchanging greetings and hunching against the weather,
which has turned to a cold, windy drizzle. The hail cloud has moved on.
The sky is lighter. He observes that this is not unusual. It has snowed
up here every winter since he joined Ridge in 1969, worst in 1974 when
seven or eight inches stayed on the ground for a week. This doesn't
harm the vines, he says. As it turns out, Paul is in favor of a little
hardship. A certain amount of stress, he says, is good for the grapes. He
talks a lot about stress. We are walking through the semifrozen yard
outside his warehouse and storage shed, squashing mushy hailstones
underfoot, and he is telling me stress on the vines is a key factor in
delivering the kind of grapes he looks for.

"All other things being equal," he says, "the older the vines, the
higher the quality of grapes. All this means is that the greater the stress
on the plant, and the lower the yield per acre, the chances are—with
red wine—the smaller the berries will be, and therefore the more
intense the fruit."

"That has a European sound to it," I say, as we climb into his car.
I am thinking of Bob Moesle's French wife, Suzanne, who looks at the
size of the carrots and cabbages at Safeway and shakes her head with
regret. "They are so *big*," she will say, "and yet, where is the taste?"
As the Gallic lips pooch and the shoulders rise.

"I am giving you vast generalizations," Paul says. "But any French
wine-maker, any European would say, 'Of course, that's what you learn
from childhood on.' But in California it is not always quite that clear.
We don't have that tradition, and many people have grown grapes to
sell, not to make wine themselves. Therefore, the more tonnage the
better. The bigger, the lusher the berries, the more juice and the more
you are going to earn. If you can get six or eight tons to the acre, why

8192

should you be satisfied with two tons or two-and-a-half, which is the kind of yield we find in the vineyards we do business with. From a grower's point of view, the higher yield is good. But it doesn't necessarily mean a better wine."

It's a way of talking about grapes. It can also be a way of talking about character and the living of one's life, connections that float right at the edges of Paul's conversation. In the late 1950s he left Stanford with a degree in philosophy. There is still something philosophical, you might even say scholarly, in the set of his glasses, the cut of his beard, the amount of detail he is able to command. But it is philosophy applied, not theoretical. If small is good, it is good because it means a lower ratio of juice to skin, which means proportionately more color and tannin and phenolic components, thus more intensity in the final product, which is the dry red wine that sends such elegant fumes rising toward the portals of philosophy. Later, when he begins to talk about the pursuit of excellence, he is talking about nothing more, nothing less than something you can pour into your glass and drink and then remember.

"I had grown up in the country on a farm," he said once, in a book called *The Great Winemakers of California,* "and it was an intriguing idea to be able to take something from the earth, to carry it a step further through artisan ability, and make of it as sophisticated and complex a thing as fine wine, and to have that also be something that would give pleasure."[9]

The main winery is a mile farther up Monte Bello and two hundred feet higher. When we park in front, at the bottom of another muddy track, it is hailing again. The ground is white with hail. We rush inside, through a heavy wooden door that shuts with a thunk. For the first few years after Ridge Vineyards was founded, in 1959, the lower sheds housed everything. This building, the former Monte Bello Winery, had long been idle, empty and neglected. It was gradually refurbished and restored. Nowadays the lower sheds house the bottled wine, the sales counter, the Spartan tasting room. Up here is where the wine is made, fermented, aged. You can smell it aging. The pungence of wine-soaked wood hangs in the air like mist.

Paul's desk is just inside the door, overshadowed by vats and stacks of bunged casks, underneath ceiling beams that go back to the 1880s. In the midst of the casks and cases we pull chairs up to the desk, littered with wine magazines and loose pages of calculations. Across the wall hangs a display of antique tools, and above the tools stand three long shelves of empty bottles, maybe sixty in all, from France, Italy, Germany, Chile, Spain, California.

On a narrow shelf in front of where he sits there are two rows of the most memorable empties, among them Château Mouton Rothschild 1962, Château La Pointe 1945, Château Latour 1946. Paul finds his measure of quality in bottles such as these, from regions of France where he himself spent time during four years in Europe. Here at Ridge the original dream was to make wine from cabernet sauvignon, the world's most highly valued red-wine grape, and traditionally the main ingredient in the great clarets from Bordeaux. The estate wine here, their pride and joy, is a cabernet made from grapes grown on this mountainside. They would like to produce more, and plan to. The problem has been to find grapes with that low-yield, high-stress character. When they first started looking around, they soon learned that the few older cabernet vineyards were tied up, contracted for.

"It was just impossible," Paul says, "to go out and find a twenty-year-old, let alone a fifty- or an eighty-year-old cabernet vineyard producing the kind of fruit we wanted. Whereas, we discovered that all over the state were these old zinfandel vineyards. Survivors of Prohibition."

"Survivors," I said. "Terrific." The vines themselves, their old stocks thick with history, just like the redwoods standing in the coastal fog, clocking events, the turn of eras. "But why? What were they doing there? Why the zinfandel?"

He settles back and begins to tell a story about Italians. You can't talk for long about California wine without telling an Italian story. In Paul's view, they are the ones who developed an early taste for the zinfandel.

"It's still not clear why it was planted so widely and why it took off. But from very early on it was clear that the quality of wines it produced, prior to Prohibition, was exceptionally high. The Italian growers saw that. In those days there were thousands of vineyards, each with its own winery. And the Italians had figured out that zinfandel would deliver a better-tasting wine. It was not an Italian grape, at least not to the knowledge of the people here then. And it wasn't an idea brought over from France. Cabernet, which was a much more exotic grape as far as Italians were concerned, and not familiar, works best with trellising, whereas zinfandel does not need trellising or wire support. But mainly I think it was just that the zinfandel made this rich and interesting wine for those early growers. Even as big as it could be—not just in alcohol and size, but in tannin, and therefore in its roughness—it could be drunk younger and could give a lot of pleasure when it was young. You could have an interesting glass of wine even when it was a year or two old, whereas cabernet made the same way would be unbearably tannic and closed-in and uninteresting. These people enjoyed their food and their wine, and zinfandel was just what they wanted. So they planted it all over the state."

In Paul's personal cellar he has bottles labeled zinfandel, with dates as old as 1893 and 1901, which he takes as evidence that by the end of the century some vintners were already treating it as a better varietal: another flicker from the far side of Prohibition, which brought the industry to a halt. The small growers, in Paul's opinion, were the ones who had made the finest zinfandels in those early days. Many of them had to sell their ranches, or turn to other crops. Small wineries shut down, or, like the winery on this mountaintop, staggered on for a while and then shut down. Most of them disappeared forever, but by the 1960s there were still some vineyards to be found, old zinfandel vines that had survived into modern times.

"The grapes were being sold to go into the big blends of some of the huge wineries. Nobody was telling these growers how good they were. Nobody was paying any more than they were paying some grower who had planted his vineyard eight years before and was getting three times the yield. No recognition was being given that these were two very different kinds of grapes—the one a young fully producing vineyard in the valley, the other an old and struggling vineyard in the hills. We could go in there and talk to these people and buy their grapes and show them the results, and they themselves became involved in the fact that in their vineyard something was being produced of better quality, instead of just dumping it into the big blend. In our case we were also identifying the vineyard on the label, so the grower could begin to take pride in what he was doing. That has played a real part in our ability to work with the growers, many of them descendants of people who planted the vines, thus many of them Italians. It was the father or the grandfather who planted the grapes."

Paul likes this connection. It makes him sit up and lean forward, energized. He likes the continuities, the vines that have survived, the families who have held on to some land, these old barrels stacked around us that have continued on from vintage to vintage, the winery itself, renewed yet elderly, patriarchal, almost a hundred, which out West is next to ancient. It connects him to Europe, lets him live in California but be almost physically connected to those European ways he admires.

The doctor who built this place was wealthy and popular, and legend has it that each time a visiting opera star arrived in San Francisco from Italy, there would be a weekend spent here at Monte Bello, with much zinfandel to be consumed and spontaneous arias ringing through the dining room and out across the vats and barrels. Many features from those times still survive—the beams, the massive doors, the stonework and planking and invisible insulation.

As we descend a steep, ladder-like stairway to the lower level, Paul says, "They packed dirt between the upstairs flooring and the ceiling below. Six inches of dry soil, and it's still in there, keeps the temperature where we want it."

We push through another door and come out upon a landing where barrels are stacked in rows. Below us, down another set of steep stairs, more barrels belly into their racks, hundreds of them quietly aging away in the stone-lined cellar. It calls to mind a tale that scared me deliciously when I was twelve: Edgar Allan Poe's *The Cask of Amontillado*. If the old insulation were leaking just a bit, to send some water dripping down these walls and across the floor, this could be a fine setting for Poe's tale. It has a medieval setting, and for a moment, in this cave light, Paul takes on a medieval look. He has picked up a strange-looking piece of equipment, a curved metal tube. If his beard were longer and his shirt not quite so woodsy, he might pass for an alchemist. Yes, he is a philosopher and a wine-maker and a scholarly kind of alchemist who has a taste for both hard facts and mysteries, for lab terminology and what some might call superstitions. He calls them old wives' tales.

He tells me about his view of fermentation, how he prefers to let the juice ferment on its natural schedule, on its own yeast. Though all California wineries now use a commercial starter yeast, he prefers to save that as a last resort.

"We are wine-makers," he says, "not wine chemists. Our main job is to keep the wine on its path."

He tells me about filtration, another process he goes out of his way to avoid, if at all possible. It has to do with the body, the complexity, the nuance of taste. He prefers to let the sediment settle in the barrel on its own time, and this means racking the barrels every three or four months, pumping the wine out, scouring the insides, pumping the wine back in. It takes a lot of careful hand labor. Right now a fellow is moving around down there below us, in the shadows between the rows, racking the 1978 Montebello Cabernet.

Everything they do here takes a lot of hand labor, Paul says. It's one of the reasons they stay small, thirty-five thousand cases a year, about eighty-four thousand gallons (compared with Paul Masson's thirty-three million gallons of storage in 1979, and E. and J. Gallo's two-hundred-

and-fifty million gallons)—some delicate balance between the quality they aim for and the methods they choose.

Paul shows me the tube he has been carrying, a racking tube of his own design, made of stainless steel. Smooth bends give it the look of a short handrail. This is used to draw the wine from stacked barrels where access is hindered by those above. It is joined to a length of glass tubing so the cellar-man can note when sediment begins to show. Paul thought he had invented this device, until he came across a catalogue printed in France in the 1860s, called *Articles du Cave*—"Cellar Equipment." There he found the identical item, made of bronze.

His eyes flash, remembering this discovery, this reaching back for the old continuities. Though fully in touch with the mood of contemporary California where he makes and markets his wines, Paul regularly looks to France for support, not so much the France of modern times, where he began to train his palate and learn these skills, but to the France of fifty or a hundred years ago, when devices like this racking tube were common.

"Most wineries today have no use for such a thing," he says with a grin. "Filtration processes take care of the sediment."

He grins again as he begins to talk about the barrels, which are filled to the bunghole with aging wine and old wives' tales. They should be small, for one thing––fifty to sixty gallons is the traditional size—and made of oak. The wood flavors the taste, the size affects the rate of oxidation and the quality of aging, since in small barrels more wine is exposed to the inside surfaces and thus to the slow penetration of air through the oak.

"I have an assistant here who recently graduated from the oenology program at U.C. Davis. He was with me before going to Davis, so he was already familiar with the way we do things. About six months after he returned we were beginning to rack this same wine you see down below, which is of supreme importance to us here. One evening I asked him what he was planning for the next day, and he said, 'We're planning to rack the cabernet, the 'seventy-seven. In fact we've already started the first couple of barrels.' 'I know I approved that,' I said, 'but with this storm that moved in last night, the barometer has surely dropped severely.' He was looking at me and I saw a grin spread across his face. I said, 'Normally I prefer not to rack during a storm.' It was a horrendous storm, you see. And he said, 'Are you serious? I checked the wine yesterday, and it was brilliant.' I said, 'Yes, I know. I saw it. But why don't you go down and draw me a sample now, from the barrels you're just starting to rack.' In three minutes he was back and he said, 'My God, it's not clear. What's going on?' I said, 'Well, the old wives' tales say you don't rack during a storm. The reason, I think, is that when you have not rough-filtered and you have not fined, when it has not been processed, and everything is in there, and it has been settling three or four months before this rack—there is a sediment at the bottom, and with the change in pressure it seems to me you get some currents started that put the sediment back into suspension. Maybe that isn't it. But it's the only thing I can think of. I'm not sure, but I do know the sediment is in suspension again.' He said, 'I'll put those three barrels back, and we'll wait till the weather clears.' I said, 'Yes, you do that,' and he was just amazed. But that is a tale I would hesitate repeating to too many people in California. This concern would not even apply much here, because almost everyone would have clarified the wine earlier. There wouldn't be any sediment down there to get stirred up by a pressure change. So in that case it *does* become an old wives' tale, from some remote and older era."

We are descending again, toward the bottom level. Paul is halfway down the ladder when he stops, looks up and says, as an afterthought, "One thing they used to do was rack by the phases of the moon. They would rack at a high-pressure time, but also during certain phases of the moon."

"Have you ever tried that here?"

"No, that's further than I'm willing to go. But I'm willing to believe there is some effect."

A loud ring fills the cellar. Paul turns toward a phone extension on one of the support posts. "I'd better get this."

It's another wine-maker, seeking his opinion on the price per ton of a certain grape. While they confer I introduce myself to the cellar-man, down here by himself and quiet as the walls, methodically squiring a hose nozzle that pumps wine back into the clean casks. He is Mexican, dressed like a ranch hand, in jeans and a straw cowboy hat. He speaks little English, so we talk in Spanish. His home state is Michoacán.

"Do you know the town of Paracho?" I ask.

"Oh yes, I know that town. Have you been there?"

"I bought some guitars in Paracho."

He laughs. "Did they charge you much money?"

"No. Not so much. Tell me, have you worked here very long?"

"About six years, five or six years."

"And was this your work in Mexico?"

"No, there is no work like this in my district." He lifts one flattened hand above his head and laughs again. "I think the mountains are too high."

Paul returns, dipping his head now, tapping at the barrels, listening for one that's full. He carries a "wine thief," a glass tube shaped like a long-barreled pistol, which will fill through a small hole in the bottom until you thumb shut the small hole at the top. Finally he hears a full thunk and opens the bung.

As he does this I am struck by the mix of things, the improbable mosaic—a cellar-man from Michoacán, in this cave of a winery designed by an Italian, where methods worked out long ago in Bordeaux and Burgundy are practiced by a modern master of the dry reds who grew up on a farm in Illinois—all converging to flavor this wine that Paul now draws from the freshly racked barrel and pours into a glass he brought along. He regards it, sniffs up a noseful of the aroma, takes a sip and then begins to talk about it.

"This has just gone through one of the traumas of its life. It has been racked out, pumped into a tank, mixed with a hundred other barrels and then the next day flowed back down. So it is not quite as calm, not quite as subtle as it could be. With the settling in the barrel it develops what we call barrel bouquet. Once it's bottled and has been laid down a couple of years, that develops again in the bottle. It's still in this, there's a nice nose, a nice smell to it. This is 'seventy-eight, a very rich year, one of the excellent years. Here, taste it."

I do what you are supposed to do. I swirl. I sniff. I sip, I hold it on the tongue, savor, swallow, and it is . . . well, what can you say about a superb wine that does not sound like something off the label? It is without question a wine I'll be telling Bob Moesle about. It has, I will tell him, that high-quality buzz up through the nose as you inhale, that satin thrill across the tongue going down, and an instant later the little rush to remind you that a great deal more than alcohol is happening. The subtler intoxicants are all at work, the fumes, nuances, hints of spice, and, on this particular afternoon, the old stones, the stacks of barrels each filled each with its sixty gallons of this marvelous stuff, aging away in the wine-pungent cellar Osea Perrone sank into the top of his ridge. In here you can get drunk on the atmosphere, just breathing the air. One sip of the wine and you're soaring.

When we step out into the parking lot, the sky has opened. We squint against the brilliant light pouring down between the thick, white and no longer threatening clouds. The wind has dropped. It's a good time to take the air, which is clean and crisp after the hail and the rain. We hike up the next rise, along a road that cuts through long rows of cabernet vines, neatly trellised, fifteen acres of them up here at twenty-six hundred feet, where altitude and weather conspire to provide that stress Paul values. They are eight years old and bearing well now, he says, urging me to lean in close and note the first tiny pink nubs of spring budding.

His house is in the distance, a small frame building set back against a knoll a hundred yards away. We don't go over there. His wife is giving someone a piano lesson. "She is addicted to the keyboard as I am to the barrels."

They don't own the land, he says, they couldn't afford it. They hold it on a long-term lease. Together they designed the house, then had it built, facing west, with a view toward the Pacific, which is visible through a V in the landscape, a silvered, gleaming wedge fifteen miles away.

It is an overwhelming location, to have in front of you this mountain range folding out of the Pacific, and behind you a view of one of the most congested urban areas in the United States. From the rise beyond their house, or from the road we followed to reach the upper winery, you can see the sprawl—the lower end of San Francisco Bay, surrounded by the mesh of suburbs, subdivisions, housing tracts, boulevards, expressways and parking lots, the semiconductor towns of San Jose and Sunnyvale and Mountain View where the great hangars at Moffett Field Naval Air Station are reduced to the size of canopies ejected from troubled fighter-bombers and left there, unrecovered, in the tidelands. It spreads before you like a map or, from this altitude, a satellite photo such as the one I saw in the tasting room before we left the lower buildings. As you step out the door of that rustic shed and walk across the barnyard to a point where you can contemplate this view, there on the doorpost is what you are about to see, from a somewhat higher elevation: the Sierra Nevada rises dimly at the far horizon, beyond the central valley, with the clean lines of the Diablo Range above the encircled and embattled Bay. Standing on this ridge is like being in some kind of satellite that must sooner or later return to that kind of earth. And yet, when you turn around and look the other way, here are six or seven more ridges that appear to be empty, ridge upon ridge of the Coast Range forest. We are in fact at the edge of wilderness. Paul is talking about the animals they see up here, wild pigs, coyote, deer, hawks, white-tailed kites, and eagles.

"Once I saw these eagles with spots in the middle of the wings. I went and looked it up, and sure enough they were immature golden eagles. The mature birds are enormous, you know. The wing span is just a few inches smaller than the bald eagle's."

As we discuss such wonders, another kind of excitement enters his voice. In the winery it was the controlled eagerness to share details of a craft he commands. Outdoors in this high vineyard, talking about the house he and his wife designed and the animals they see when they go out jogging in the early morning, his voice makes another sound. He becomes exuberant, amazed by the spectacle, by the memory of a mountain lion who once leaped across the road in front of his jeep. Weaving his hands he describes how the big cat looked from behind, as it loped away, the front and rear legs swinging in and out of alignment.

He is reminded of what brought him to this particular spot on the planet, from the family farm forty miles outside Chicago. He came West the first time for education. His first choices had been Princeton and Stanford. "Someone said to me, Go to California. It's a different culture, a different world out there, it will give you another perspective on things." He is glad he took the advice. He liked living in these mountains above the campus, he liked the looseness and the independence of things. Wineries had nothing to do with it then. His affection for wines began to blossom during the years in Europe, in Italy and France, though he did not start making wine until his travels took him to Chile in the mid-1960s. When he came back to take this job at Ridge, after twelve years abroad, it was because his travels had taught him that here was an extraordinary situation. As usual, his reference point is somewhere in the south of France.

"In Bordeaux, if you buy a small château, it has been classified since 1855 as a fifth growth, or a bourgeois or an artisan cru, and the chances, no matter how good your wine, of getting your class changed—since there is very little class mobility—the chances are poor you will ever move up a notch. Maybe. In twenty years of trying. Whereas here we can aspire to be number one, right from the beginning. Every small winery here aspires to make and be recognized for making the finest wine in California, if not in the world. Because we don't have a tradition to buck, in terms of who is top dog, we all feel we have an equal shot at being the best. For me that is the great challenge and the greatest source of excitement and satisfaction. The Frenchman, his wine is classified by a system that has barely changed since 1855. Here, no matter where you start from, you have that chance to aspire to be the best, and then, if you do well, to be *recognized* in that position."

For the man in pursuit of excellence, in pursuit of excellent reds, what more could you ask: the soil, the climate, the grape growing history, the broadening market, and this elusive but essential feature, available space.

Paul had things to do, as usual. But when you're on that ridge, you don't want to rush back down. We stood there a while longer and talked about California, as Californians will do when something insistent in the landscape starts you thinking about why you came here, or, if you were born here, why you stay. That day it was the almost irreconcilable contrast on either side of Monte Bello, the Beautiful Mountain—on one hand, the freeways, the sea of aerials, Lockheed's Space and Missile Division; on the other hand, the mountain lions, the wild pigs and eagles—and surrounding us on the very brow, those fifteen acres of trellised rows suddenly gold-tinged as another window opened in the high cloud cover floating south.

In Search of Oildorado

California's best-known exports nowadays are not things. They are images, composed of such unnatural resources as life-style frontiers and the shapes of leisure—not the bottled wine itself but the chilled chardonnay in the hot tub; the kid on the trail bike, on the rim of the bluff, at sunset. The images depict all varieties of the West Coast adventure in Life with a capital L, the Living and Exploring and Spending and Expanding and Exploding. They are exported on film, on record and tape, via the covers and inside pages of the *National Enquirer, Road and Track, TV Guide, People, Self,* and *Us.* Meanwhile, more traditional resources, such as timber, cotton, cattle, hogs and poultry, crude oil and natural gas, come to the public attention when some feature of the environment has been violated or is about to be swamped. But for the most part, though they fuel and finance the rest of it, these tend to exist in the shadow of The Great Post-Industrial Experiment, which dazzles us with such a blinding light.

To see this other part of California, the resource-full part, it helps to get away from the coast from time to time, and head inland, which is why I found myself on the road to Bakersfield again, over there in Kern County. About 7 percent of the cotton grown in the United States comes out of Kern County. According to Bill Rintoul, it is also the nation's fourth largest oil-producing region.

"If Kern seceded from the rest of California," says Bill, "which of course it is not planning to do, at least not right away, but if it were separated off, this county all by itself would be running fourth in oil, after Texas, Alaska and Louisiana. For that matter, it is the eighteenth largest oil producer in the world."

Bill is a Kern County patriot. I do not mean he would defend his county's honor with guns and knives. But he likes the place, he has spent most of his life there, and takes its flaws along with its virtues. He actually prefers the unrelieved flatness of the landscape. We were talking once about the heavy groves and wooded canyons characteristic of the northern coast, and he said, "You know, it's funny, but there is something about that kind of country that just doesn't feel right. Those trees all around you. And the rain it takes for that kind of growth, the way it drips down through the trees. The way the mountains rise up. Half the time you can't see the sun. I suppose it's just what a person gets used to. You get used to a certain idea of what the world is supposed to look like. I'd just rather see the sun and know where I'm going."

Bill makes his living as a petroleum journalist. He writes columns for the Bakersfield *Californian* and the Tulsa *Daily World*. When I called and told him I might be heading his way, there was a pause. He is not a fast talker. He thinks things over. After a moment he said, "Well, if you time it for next weekend, you could be here for some of Oildorado. I am going to be the Grand Marshal in the parade this year. Maybe you could ride along with me in the limousine."

I had heard of Oildorado, but didn't know much about it. The fact is, on the day I called him, everything I knew about oil in California could fit easily into the spare can I carry around in the back of my Mercedes, which has a diesel engine, by the way, an old 1960 190D. It will give me thirty-five miles to the gallon on a trip like this, where the roads are straight and flat.

Naively I asked, "Does the parade run through the oil fields?"

"No, it runs right through downtown Taft. On second thought, maybe you'd be better off watching from the sidewalk. That way you'll be sure to see all the floats and the Oildorado Queen and the Maids of Petroleum. If you want to see the fields themselves, my suggestion is to drive down Highway Thirty-Three. There is no other road quite like it in the eleven western states."

In literature, Kern's finest moment comes in that scene midway through *The Grapes of Wrath*, when the Joad family stops at Tehachapi Pass to take a first long and thirsty look at this land they have struggled so hard to reach. Ruthie and Winfield, the youngest, are awestruck by the sight, "embarrassed before the great valley," is the way Steinbeck described it:

CALIFORNIANS

The distance was thinned with haze, and the land grew softer and softer in the distance. A windmill flashed in the sun, and its turning blades were like a little heliograph, far away. Ruthie and Winfield looked at it, and Ruthie whispered, "It's California."[10]

The vista Steinbeck chose, in 1939, to flesh out the dream these immigrants carried with them from Dust-Bowl Oklahoma is a long way from the world most Californians inhabit now. The largest cities, the densest networks of subdivisions, mobile home parks and retirement towns are found along a coastal strip, some forty miles wide, between Sonoma County and San Diego. By and large, this is where The Big Experiment is going on. It is also a zone of intense tourism. People living in or near the coastal communities often find themselves caught in that mind-boggle between how a place once looked and felt and how its packaging looks once it has become merchandise on the international travel circuit.

In Kern County you do not have to put up with much of this. In the 1979 *Atlas of California,* on the page where "Major Tourist Attractions" are marked with circles and dots of various colors, Kern is blank. Gray Line buses do not linger in Bakersfield or Oildale or Taft. Movie stars and sports celebrities seldom buy homes there, though they might well invest in the land. People don't visit, as a rule, unless they have business there, or relatives, or have come searching for Oildorado.

Heading east out of Paso Robles, I cross the county line halfway through a lonesome dip in the Coast Range called Antelope Valley. The hills along here are so dry and brown they shine in the sunlight as if ready to burst into flame. Just as the county sign flashes past, I hear Conway Twitty on the radio, station KUZZ out of Bakersfield coming in clear now. His voice rich with stoic remorse, Conway tells some lost sweetheart she is standing on a bridge that just won't burn. It seems perfect. This land could torment you for years without ever quite killing you. And the road signs for what lies up ahead don't seem to promise much relief: Bitterwater Valley, Devils Den, Lost Hills.

The first blur of color is startling, almost uncanny, when this narrow passage opens out into cotton fields, hundreds, perhaps thousands of acres, with bolls white and ready for picking. A couple of miles go by, and one side of the road turns from cotton into a long orchard of dusty almond trees. As the last slopes level out, where Antelope Valley joins the broad San Joaquin, the first grapevines appear, their leaves half green, half rusty brown after harvest. To the south the rows look about a mile long, stretching across to the base of the Temblor Range. To the north there is no telling how far the rows extend, no limits visible up that way. Vines merge toward the horizon.

A few more miles go by, and the vines give way to another stand of almond trees, older and thicker, bearing well, and then a peach orchard, and now, across this highway, facing the orchards you can see what all this land looked like once, and would look like now without the aqueduct. The contrast is spectacular. In this landscape almost nothing grows naturally. No shrubs, no trees, no houses. No people. Out this way there aren't even any beer cans. Without the aqueduct that intersects this highway a few miles up ahead, there would be nothing here but tumbleweed and sagebrush and the diesel rigs powering past on their way to Interstate 5.

Water is one of three resources that have shaped Kern County. Oil and country music are the other two. The water is imported from rivers farther north. The music is what you might call a hybrid product, transplanted southwestern and Okie energy finding new roots here, giving Bakersfield its nickname, Nashville West. The oil, however, is indigenous. While the guitars and the fiddles and the gospel quartets float through the airways a few feet above the ground, and while the piped-in water taps the riches in the first foot of earth, thousands and thousands of wells suck up the riches farther down, planted there fifty or sixty million years ago when uncountable generations of plankton sifted downward through the fathoms of this one-time inland sea and left tiny skeletons behind to be transformed into crude.

When we talked on the phone Bill told me Kern County is now producing more oil than some of the OPEC nations. He said this with such genuine pride in his home region, I felt obliged to ask him which OPEC nations he was referring to.

Again there was a pause, as if he had forgotten. He had not forgotten. Bill is a living encyclopedia of petroleum lore, but he will hesitate like this, as if the facts are elusive and hard to pin down. "Oh, I think Qatar is one," he said. "Gabon is another. Ecuador is in there somewhere."

On the radio Willie Nelson is singing, "Whiskey River, don't run dry." Out here on Highway 46 the crops have disappeared for a while. Sand and sagebrush stretch away on both sides of the road. It's odd to be comparing this alkaline wasteland with Ecuador.

Standing all alone in the sand and the wind, where Highway 46 meets 33, there is a cafe with a couple of gas pumps called Blackwells Corner. I swing right, as Bill instructed me to do, heading south. Within a few miles I am surrounded by walking beams, steam generators, derricks and fields of grimy pipe. No crops at all grow along this side of the San Joaquin. The soil is parched. Animals are scarce. The only movement in this moon-like realm comes from the pumps, their metal beams nodding with the motion and profile that has stirred several dozen writers to compare them to praying mantises. I now see why. This type of field pump resembles nothing in the world as much as a mantis on a string. What you see from the road are hundreds of praying heads, painted orange or yellow or black and connected by cable to something underground that seems to pull each one by the nose, so that they are all, on their various cycles, silently, ceaselessly bowing.

I will soon learn from Bill that if there was a Guinness book of financial records, this oil field would be in it. Late in 1979 Shell bought it for what was said at the time to be the largest sum ever to change hands in a corporate transaction. The field, called Kernridge, which now produces fifty thousand barrels each day, was sold for three billion, six hundred and fifty-three million, two hundred and seventy-two thousand dollars. Shell's geologists estimate three hundred and sixty-four billion cubic feet of natural gas are waiting underground here, along with five to six hundred million barrels of oil, most of which had long been considered too expensive to get at or too viscous to pump. Soaring prices changed that view.

South of this field, and near the village of McKittrick, I enter a much larger and more valuable oil field, a legendary field that has created five towns and numerous fortunes. It is called the Midway-Sunset. It is over twenty miles long. As Bill is soon to tell me, it is among the twelve largest fields in the United States. It was the fourth in the history of the country to deliver a billion barrels—as of 1967—and they are still a long way from the bottom.

I have some trouble with figures like a billion barrels, or three hundred sixty-four billion cubic feet. I have some trouble with the scale of this whole business. It is almost too much to grasp. These fields and Bill's almanac memory are filled with numbers that simply bring the imagination to a standstill. Standard Oil of California grossed $42 billion in fiscal 1980. Kern County produces nearly four million barrels of oil per week. The United States still imports about five million barrels per day. A typical reason, or symptom: there are 5.1 million automobiles in Los Angeles. These cars alone burn fifteen million gallons of gasoline every day. There are forty-two gallons in a barrel. By 1967 this field I'm driving through produced a billion barrels. In other words, forty-two billion gallons, a hundred and sixty-eight billion quarts. But where are they now? And how big a cavity does that leave below? Is it bigger or smaller than Carlsbad Caverns? And how much bigger can it get before the roof caves in?

I am beginning to wonder if it helps to drive out through these oil fields. Even here, right in the middle of it, along Highway 33, which displays the most elaborate collection of field equipment west of Oklahoma, there is not much to see, not much to hold to, nothing nearly as immediate as that vast field of cotton with its bolls like a field of white eyes along the roadside watching you pass.

I think it was easier in the old days, when they had gushers that would blow the tops off the derricks, puddle the earth with lakes of oil and fill the air for miles around here with an oily haze that would stain the laundry and cloud the sun. The most dramatic of these, Lakeview Number One, blew in on March 14, 1910, with such force and volume it could not be brought under control, and it was never brought under control. People still talk about the soaring column of oil and sand and rock. Unable to cap or channel it, they used timbers and sandbags to construct great dikes and holding sumps. Of the nine million barrels said to have come pouring forth during the year and a half it gushed and geysered, some four million were trapped and processed. The rest just ran free and seeped back into the earth from whence it came. This went on for five hundred and forty-four days without restraint. Then one day it stopped as suddenly as it had begun. The bottom fell in, due to some shift of underground pressure, and that was the end of the Lakeview Gusher, but the beginning of flush times in the Midway-Sunset, as well as the true launching of Taft, the largest town among these west-side fields. (The sign at the edge of town listing weekly luncheon times for Kiwanis, Lions, Optimists and Rotary, claims a population of 18,500, but a plumbing contractor Bill introduced me to confessed that the true population is closer to twelve thousand. "People will throw these numbers around," he said. "They will try to rope in Fellows and Tupman and some of the outlying areas, but as long as I've been here, which is forty-four years, the population of the town itself hasn't changed that much one way or the other.")

Taft happened to incorporate in the same year Lakeview Number One burst forth, and it looks back upon that event as a grand and almost supernatural announcement of the town's arrival. Emblazoned across the 1980 souvenir T-shirts being sold in Taft, where Oildorado originated, is the phrase SEVENTY YEARS OF BLACK GOLD.

Seventy years. Even in the foreshortened history of California this place is very, very young. My house in Santa Cruz is older than any two-by-four in Taft. In this part of the world the coastal mission towns, like Santa Cruz, go back as far as towns go. The central valley had to wait until after statehood. And Taft's side of the valley had to wait even longer. As late as 1900 there was still nothing here but sagebrush. In 1902

Southern Pacific ran a spur line out this far, to service the new wells. The end of that spur line gathered a dusty collection of shacks and tents and converted boxcars. The town is still built close to the ground, in a hollow between hills studded with producing wells. The view in all directions is of dry, oil-bearing hillsides, their bare slopes defined by a few wooden derricks that survive from the early days—the same kind of definition trees provide.

Hills like these are uncommon in the San Joaquin, which by nature is as flat as a football field and about the same shape. Geologists call them anticlines. Where they rise from the plain, oil from sand and shale layers farther down has been gathered upward, within easy reach of the surface. Just out of sight, a few miles east, there lies another low range called Elk Hills, an unassuming cluster of tawny ridges that offer almost nothing to the passing eye, yet Elk Hills happens to be California's number-one producing field. Since 1912 it has belonged to the federal government, as a naval petroleum reserve. For a while in the 1920s, it was famous for its role in the most notorious oil scandal of all time, though never quite as famous as Wyoming's Teapot Dome field—another naval reserve—which gave the scandal its name.

In 1921 Albert Fall, then Secretary of the Interior, brought the control of these fields into his department and promptly leased them out to high-rolling cronies. Elk Hills went to Edward Doheny, the original California oil baron and L.A. entrepreneur, in exchange for "a personal loan" of $100,000. After the dealings were exposed, Fall became the first cabinet officer in American history to be convicted of a felony and sent to prison. Doheny was acquitted. Elk Hills spent the next fifty years rather quietly, as a low-production reserve administered by the navy. It was not until the Arab oil embargo of 1973, and the new pressure to develop domestic fuel supplies, that the idea of reopening Elk Hills for commercial use was seriously considered. Bill Rintoul says a hundred and sixty thousand barrels a day come out of there now, and two hundred million cubic feet of gas.

At a small shop called Oildorado Headquarters, on the main street in downtown Taft, I pick up a couple of the black and gold T-shirts, an official program, and the special issue of the Taft *Daily Midway Driller*. In a back room, beyond the cash register, bright lights are shining. Life-size costume boards have been set up, with notches at the top for neck and chin. The costumes are old-time and turn-of-the-century Western. People are waiting in line to have their pictures taken standing behind these boards, as souvenirs of this festival which is already three days along. It started Wednesday with the queen contest and the official opening of the Westside Oil Museum. Things will begin to peak tomorrow with the big parade and hopefully climax with the World Championship Welding and Backhoe Races at Franklin Field.

Outside this shop, where I am meeting Rintoul, numerous sheriffs are passing by, numerous vests and cowboy hats, bonnets and gingham dresses. Bill is easy to spot. He is not in costume. A man of simple tastes, he never overplays his hand. As Grand Marshal of tomorrow's parade he could get away with almost anything, but he shows up in checkered slacks and a short-sleeved sport shirt. No string tie. No turquoise. He has a brand-new cowboy hat, which he has left in the car. He pretends to be worried that the parade committee might get the wrong idea.

"If they see that hat they might start talking about horses. Then I might have to tell them to forget the whole thing." He grins a weathery grin, as if he is turning into a heavy wind to look at me. "I think the Grand Marshal deserves a limousine, don't you?"

Whatever they give him to ride, Bill is going to do well as Oildorado Marshal. His heart is in exactly the right place. He is an oil fields aficionado, a man fascinated with every feature of the way this business works. He grew up here in Taft, joined the army during World War II, came back for a few years in the fields before going off to Stanford for a degree in journalism. Secretly I suspect he writes his daily columns and his feature pieces for *Pacific Oil World, Well Servicing,* and *The Drilling Contractor* so he can continue to roam among these anticlines at will. He loves all of it, the mathematics, the geology, the look of a drilling rig, the lore of the roughneck, the gusher legends, the way a late sun tints steam plumes rising from the generators. He jumped at the chance to meander once again through his own home territory, to take me on a little tour, which now begins, in the Veterans Hall, where the Oildorado Civic Luncheon is being served, and where the Grand Marshal's attendance is expected.

We walk in moments before the invocation. Bill moves directly to the head table, while I find a spot, a vacant folding chair, at one of the long tables lined up in rows across the hall. Maybe two hundred people are here, merchants and their wives, the civic leaders of Taft, dressed as cowhands, schoolmarms, desperadoes. The brightest outfits are black and gold, worn by a dozen young girls dressed as saloon dancers, 1890s style, with high fringed skirts and high-heeled shoes. These are the girls who ran for queen, sponsored by such groups as the Taft Rotary, the Desk and Derrick Club, the Moose Lodge. The winner, sponsored by Veterans of World War I, Barracks 305, is a slim and pretty senior from

Taft High. She wears a glossy beauty-contest banner that says OIL-DORADO QUEEN. The others each wear a banner saying MAID OF PETRO-LEUM. Later, two hours from now, after speeches by Oildorado presidents, mayors, and council members past and present, after all the testimonials to the community of Taft and the Oildorado tradition, these fourteen girls will dance a cancan routine to taped music, a high-stepping, side-kicking, skirt-lifting dance that will end with their back-sides first to the speakers' table and then to the crowd. They are giddy with anticipation, jumping up and sitting down and hurrying out to the lobby. Now they all come to a temporary halt as the M.C. calms the room and asks us to stand while a portly minister intones the blessing.

Still standing, we put our hands over our hearts, face the flag, and say the pledge of allegiance. Then we sing "God Bless America." It has been a long time since I sang "God Bless America" before lunch. It feels good. One thing I will say about the people of Taft: They are not cynical. They do not intend the phrase "Maid of Petroleum" to have more than one meaning. They genuinely want America to be blessed by someone. And though relatively little of the profits from these mammoth oil reserves trickles into town, they are thankful when the fields come back to life, as they have in these past few years, because then Taft comes back to life. The mood on this particular afternoon in Veterans Hall is one of carefully nurtured prosperity.

During lunch—paper plates of fried chicken, potato salad, carrot-and-raisin salad, coffee, or iced tea from pitchers—I talk to the plumbing contractor who moved here forty-four years ago. He wears a rodeo shirt and cowboy hat and has let his beard grow out for the whiskerino contest. Business has been good, but it is a mixed blessing. He complains about the hard time he has finding qualified help. "They all want to go work in the oil fields now. Out there they start at seven-fifty, and move up to nine, nine-fifty right away. Your best workers are going to head for the fields. So I've always got a new man to break in."

After lunch we drive out to the site of the Lakeview Gusher, south of town, on Petroleum Club Road. The distance is ten kilometers, a figure I remember from the program. Early Saturday morning there is to be a footrace, an event called The Lakeview Gusher 10K, starting where the original derrick stood before the gush of oil and gas reduced it to splinters, and ending downtown.

The race is another tribute to that great explosion. The place where those racers will assemble, "The Site," is a built-up pit perhaps forty yards across. Its walls were originally made of timbers, sandbags and dirt. A wetter climate would long ago have flattened these walls, but seventy years from now it will probably look pretty much the same. Sandbags can still be seen, tattered strips of burlap show through the dirt and the grimy boards. In the special edition of the *Midway Driller* there is a photo of two grinning, oil-stained men standing on an oil-encrusted wooden raft floating in a shiny lake of oil. They are poling from one side to the other. This caked and sandy pit Bill and I are standing in used to be that lake.

While we wander to the far side he is telling me the story, one he heard firsthand from an uncle who worked this field in the earliest years. Eventually both of us fall silent, kicking at the shards of oily sand. Something eerie hovers here, something reverent in the breeze across these scarred dunes, in the near-absence of motion or life where once there had been such a swarm, such frenzy.

Between the pit and roads stands a monument, with a plaque affixed, which says, "AMERICA'S MOST SPECTACULAR GUSHER." It's a California Registered Historical Landmark. If you squint, it could be a gravestone. Around here they talk about this gusher as if it had a life and an identity, the great creature who sprang forth, lived its wild existence for a year and a half, and suddenly died, of subterranean causes. Seventy years later there are photos everywhere—in the Oildorado program, in the special issue of the *Driller,* in shop windows downtown, and on permanent display in the new Westside Oil Museum—the lakes and rivers of oil, the oily workers rafting through it, the shattered derrick, the black spurting geyser of oil. They commemorate the early time, which was also the time of wildness, before this piece of earth had been quite tamed, and the sky-high gusher who could not be contained burst forth, made a huge and glorious mess, then disappeared or perhaps just retreated back into its cave.

I don't know why, but when you're driving around in the central valley, the songs from these country and western stations always seem to be providing some ironic comment on the landscape or the general situation. As we pull away from the gusher site, Bill switches on KUZZ, and it's an old Buck Owens arrangement called "Today I Started Loving You Again."

Buck is singing it. Merle Haggard wrote it. They both happen to be Kern County heroes. As we near the oil field village of Maricopa, Bill says in passing that he knows someone who went to high school with Merle in the days before he married Bonnie Owens. Everyone in Kern County seems to know someone who knows Buck Owens or Bonnie or

Merle or all three. "She was married to both of 'em, you know. Of course, not at the same time."

By pure coincidence the one thriving business in Maricopa is called Buck's Steakhouse. No connection. "Best place to eat, for as long as I can remember," says Bill. From the look of things, it is the only place to eat. Taft and Maricopa started even, back in 1910, when they both incorporated. By 1911 Maricopa had its own opera house. In the mid-1970s, when they were filming *Bound for Glory*, Woody Guthrie's life story, Maricopa was chosen as the location for some early scenes set in the wind-blown west Texas town of Pampa during the 1930s. Very little had to be changed. It still has that sanded, worn-down Western patina. Only the cars are new, and some of the pickups outside Buck's.

Maricopa sits near Midway-Sunset's southern edge. We head due east now, along the base of the Temblor Range, running almost parallel to the California Aqueduct, which also swings eastward here, with its long flow from the Delta passing through these lowlands before making the salmon's leap over the Tehachapis and down again, to water Southern California. Along here the aqueduct waters more cotton fields. A few miles out of Maricopa we are driving through one of those tracts so vast your eyes burn trying to see the end of it. And right out in the middle of this small continent of cotton, about half a mile off the road, stands the drilling rig we have come looking for. With no pumps or derricks in view, the rig looks like some intergalactic vehicle that has landed in the wrong place.

It's part of Bill's beat to see how they are doing, how deep the hole is, and whether they've had any show. This is a wildcat well, he says, in a part of the valley that hasn't been drilled before. "There's probably some oil down there, but ten years ago you wouldn't have found anybody drilling that deep."

He takes a side road, looking for access, finds it, and we are easing along a dirt track between cotton rows toward a clearing where maybe half an acre has been opened up to make room for the platform, the caravan of trailers.

Bill has two hard hats in the trunk. We don these and climb the metal ladder. Everything is made of metal and painted battleship gray. The steel platform is thirty feet above the cotton, and rising a hundred thirty feet above the platform is the bolted network of struts and pulleys they call the mast. Climbing aboard you have the feeling of boarding a great vessel, anchored in the invisible waters of the inland sea.

Five men are working, the standard crew, all wearing hard hats and T-shirts, and smeared with grease and oil. Bill introduces me to Terry the tool pusher, the crew leader, who grins when I offer to shake his hand and shows me the palm thick with grease. Something about the way he stands would tell you he is in command, even if you hadn't been told in advance. His face is lean, his hair black and straight. He could be part Cherokee. Early thirties. He wears cowboy boots and jeans, no shirt. Without being muscular, his body looks powerful, whip-like. He stands with one foot forward, like a sailor on a rolling deck.

Bill mentions a man who died a couple of days ago, on another rig in some other part of the county. "I read in the paper that the cable crushed his chest."

Terry laughs and shakes his head, nods toward the draw works, the broad metal drum that winds and unwinds the cable that feeds up to to the top of the mast, then down toward the center of the platform where the lengths of pipe are lowered or raised.

"I read that story," Terry says. "There is no way this cable is gonna crush your chest. If it breaks and comes whipping out of that drum it might knock you around some. It got me once. But it's not gonna crush your chest. What I figure is, they were pulling on the pipe, and it was the pipe broke loose and come free and swung out and got him. That pipe is what can crush you."

Any of this stuff could crush you. This is what Terry is ready to roll with, not an ocean, but the great chunks of moving metal that surround him. The drilling pipe comes in thirty-foot sections. They are slung from the cable on a lobster-shaped hook the size of a VW bus, which hangs directly overhead. Next to us, another large piece of thick steel is hanging loose, about the size of a Harley-Davidson. When I ask Terry about it he says, "All this is here is a great big pipe wrench. We just clamp it onto the pipe there to tighten the fit."

He shrugs it off, makes it simple. And it is simple. You put a bit on the end of a pipe, and you start cutting a hole in the ground. After awhile you screw on another length of pipe, and you cut a little deeper. It isn't the act that's impressive. Like everything else in the oil business, it's the magnitude. This rig down here at the absolute bottom edge of the San Joaquin Valley is running a pipe that is now twelve thousand feet into the ground, chipping and grinding through the next inch or foot of sand or shale or ancient fossil layer. What we have here is a brace and bit over two miles long, which is deep, Bill says. An average well in Kern County runs four to five thousand feet. Lakeview Number One came in at 2,225 in 1910.

Retracing our route through the rows of cotton we head back toward Taft, where I left my car. From there I follow Bill to Bakersfield and our final stop, a Basque place downtown called The Pyrenees, established in the days when Basque shepherds roamed the foothills east of here. The food is served family style, and the folks who run the place pile it on the table as if everyone who walks in is a shepherd just back from a month in the mountains or a roughneck coming off a seventy-two-hour shift.

This is Bill's favorite restaurant. The house beverage, Picon Punch, warms his county patriotism, stirs to life an epilogue for today, a prologue for tomorrow's parade.

"Kern is a kind of headquarters, you see. This is the biggest drilling year in the history of the state of California, and two-thirds of the new wells are here in this county—over two thousand wells. Meanwhile, oil people fan out from here in all directions. The contractor Terry works for has twenty-one rigs like that one we climbed. His main yard is outside town, but his rigs are trucked to Nevada, Wyoming, and into the Rockies where all the new exploration is going on. You take Terry himself. He grew up here in Bakersfield, started out as a roughneck, worked his way up to tool pusher. He just got back from Evanston, Wyoming. Couple of years ago he was working in Alaska. It's typical. Some of those fellows over in Taft, you would never know it to see them walking along the street, but they have been to Peru, to Arabia, Iran and Venezuela, and they wind up right back home again."

The next morning we start out in separate cars, planning to meet at the reviewing stand. I am ten miles south of Bakersfield, whizzing along to Loretta Lynn's version of "I've Never Been This Far Before," and near the village of Pumpkin Center, when I smell the smell of warm rust, glance down and see my temperature needle heading off the gauge.

I pull over, pop the hood open, and gingerly ease the cap loose. Steam pours out but no water. There isn't much left. The top seam on my radiator has split. I make it to a phone and call the first place listed in the Yellow Pages that claims to be open on weekends. I cadge some water from a Freddy Fast-Gas and limp back to this radiator shop on the outskirts of Bakersfield, in the middle of a district that seems coated with rubber dust and filmed with oil, not from wells but from the generations of cars that have moved through its grimy jungle of transmission shops, upholstery parlors, abandoned service stations, warehouses, and wrecking yards.

I pull in with steam billowing around my hood and a trail of what could be diluted blood. The radiator man is sympathetic, a fellow in dark coveralls whose eyes cannot quite open, as if the lashes have been coated with honey. He says that since it is Saturday and he plans to close at 1:00 P.M. he will do the repairs only if I pull the radiator myself and install it again. I agree, making it clear that I am truly in a rush since my friend is going to be the Grand Marshal in the Oildorado parade. I emphasize this, figuring the local reference might enhance our relationship. He stops me right there.

"The what parade?"

"Oildorado."

"What the hell is that?"

Well, I think, this is curious. Here is a fellow whose entire livelihood depends on the internal-combustion engine, the heat it generates while burning gasoline, heat that must be cooled with water, which must circulate and sooner or later spring a leak, which he then is qualified to repair. And this fellow has never heard of the event I have driven halfway across the state to attend, the celebration of an industry that keeps not only this radiator man but a good part of California, if you will pardon the expression, solvent.

"You mean to tell me," I say, "that you work on cars all day long, every day, and you have never heard of Oildorado over there in Taft?"

Something in my tone unnerves him. We are both on edge. For a moment his eyelashes pull apart. I see indignation in there. "Hey," he says, "you want this goddamn radiator fixed?" Before I can reply he says, "Taft is thirty-five miles away. How the hell am I for Christ sake supposed to know what's going on over in Taft!"

I don't argue. It is important for the two of us to get along, at least for the next hour, which we do, working side by side, sometimes eyelash to eyelash, above and below the fittings.

By the time I reach Taft it is mid-afternoon. I have missed the parade. I have missed the Lakeview Gusher 10K Run. I have missed the Fly-in at Taft Airport and the barbecue at The Petroleum Club. Searching for Bill, I stop at Franklin Field, where the World's Championship Backhoe Contest is scheduled. It hasn't started yet. I happen to catch the most intense tug-of-war I have ever witnessed. These are not college kids pulling each other across a mudhole at the Spring Fling. These are some of the largest men in the state—truckers, hay-buckers, roustabouts, and derrick-men—thick men bursting through their T-shirts and playing for keeps.

One team is fully outfitted with matching blue and white jump suits, paratrooper boots for sure footing, and ball caps that say "Duval Sporting Goods." They have a coach, also in uniform, who paces back and forth in a half-crouch, muttering instructions before the match begins. They have some moves worked out, some hand and voice signals. They have prepared for this moment, and it is sad to watch those thick boot soles sliding through the sand as they are dragged across the line in less than thirty seconds by some ragtag group who have evidently organized at the last moment, who wear Adidas running shoes, whose T-shirts do not even match, but whose pecs and biceps would bring tears to the eyes of many regulars at Santa Monica's Muscle Beach. After a few rebel yells the winners swagger off toward the Budweiser truck, while the team from Duval Sporting Goods stand there frowning at each other, gazing at their shoes in bewilderment.

In the middle of the bare acreage called Franklin Field, sixty backhoes are lined up, their earth-scraping bulldozer blades drawn in low at the back, their crane-arms crooked high in front, scoops at the ready, waiting for the championship to begin. The cabs are empty. On one windshield a sticker says "Iran Sucks." In a half-circle a thousand fans wearing cowboy hats stand around sipping Budweiser and waiting too. This is where I finally find Bill. I recognize him by his bare head. He is carrying his hat. I still have not seen him wearing it.

He doesn't take my absence personally. When I explain what happened he laughs and says it reminds him of the old Merle Haggard tune "Radiator Man from Wasco," which is set in a Kern County town north of Bakersfield, up Highway 43.

"Sounds like you've been reliving Merle's song," he says.

I ask him if the parade committee had made him ride a horse.

"Nope, a fellow here in town provided a Cadillac, which would have been real comfortable if the top was down. It wasn't a convertible, though. The roof was so low I couldn't get my cowboy hat on. In that respect I guess I lucked out. My wife, Frankie Jo, was with me, so we all three sat hunched in the front. The fact is, I am weary. Waving to so many people, trying to keep a smile on for an hour and a half, and then not sure anybody can even see you, under a low roof like that."

Bill grins all through this account, amused by the parade, and narrows his eyes as if faced with heavy weather, which at the moment happens to be true. It is clouding up. Warm heavy clouds have filled the sky.

"I'm glad I don't have to do this again," he says. "Five years from now, it'll be somebody else's turn. They only have Oildorado every five years, you know. For a while it was annual. But people were running out of time for anything else."

I have a couple of beers and wait for the backhoe drivers to mount their rigs. I can only guzzle so much Bud, since I plan to start north this afternoon, sooner or later, and there are mountains to climb. I decide on sooner. It is looking more and more like rain, and the backhoes are still sitting like tanks on D day waiting for the signal from Eisenhower. Something has delayed the contest. No one is certain what, and no one much cares as long as the Bud holds out.

I say good-bye to Bill and start out 33 through the Midway-Sunset, making one last quick stop at Fellows, another oil-field village five miles away. Fellows reminds me of the pueblos in New Mexico, the ones you pass driving out of Albuquerque—no roadside billboards in any direction, no pitch to the motorist, no hotels or motels or fast-food neon, no Rotary lunch. It's just a village, a cluster of low buildings a mile or so off the road, out there all by itself in the high desert. Pumping wells dot the slopes beyond town, where the Temblor Range begins to rise. More wells decorate the plains spreading south. There is no main street in Fellows, no grocery store. Where the houses stop, I find what I have left the highway for, another gusher site Bill has recommended, another monument stone, another plaque:

THE FIRST GUSHER

Midway Field 2–6, which made the Midway Oil Field famous. Blew in over the derrick top, November 27, 1909, and started the Great California Oil Boom. At its peak it produced 2000 barrels a day.

Lakeview was the biggest and wildest. Midway 2–6, coming four months sooner, gets credit for being first. The granite block stands by itself inside a low fence. The air and land nearby is strangely quiet under the lowering sky, punctuated by a faint creaking from the nearest well, where the cable rubs once in every cycle. No wind this day, no dogs, no cars. Perhaps everyone who lives in Fellows went off to Franklin Field. In the hills and plains around the monument where the first gusher blew in, nothing moves but the bowing pumps, the silent praying of a thousand mantises near and far across the western San Joaquin.

How Various Large and Small Bodies of Water Move Around from One Place to Another

In the spring of 1979, while the buckeye trees were blooming, a young outdoorsman named Mark Dubois hiked downstream to a remote spot on the Stanislaus River and chained himself to a boulder. Before snapping shut the padlock he hid the key. He hid it out of reach and in a spot known only to himself, planning to stay put until the waters rising behind the New Melones Dam covered him, or until someone assured him that the part of the world he cared about most would not be buried under two hundred feet of new reservoir.

The Stanislaus is one hundred and twenty miles long, with headwaters in the high wilderness, between Lake Tahoe and Yosemite. Thirteen dams had already been built on this river. Dubois felt that fourteen was one too many. On the day he snapped that padlock shut and sat down to wait, he was genuinely prepared to die.

His opponents tried to simplify his cause, saying he was just another bearded romantic who wanted technology to go away so he could have the wilderness to himself. But that was not it. Dubois, like all of us, is immersed in technology. He had to travel over well-banked and federally financed roads to reach Parrott's Ferry Bridge, where he pushed off toward his hiding place, to take his stand. Technology was not the dragon. *Too much* technology was. Overkill.

The following year we drove up there together to take a look at what he had, at least temporarily, saved. It was an education, spending a while with a fellow like Dubois. He is an expert white-water man. During the years he spent looking for ways to preserve what remains of the Stanislaus, he had also become an expert on this state's plumbing system, which is something like the fault system. It is enormous, it fans out in all directions, it affects everything, and most of the people who live here pay scant attention to how it works.

I have lived most of my life on this coast, with never more than a dim sense of how the water moves around. With Dubois you have to talk about all of it at once, the river, the water, the watershed, soil chemistry, flood control, human thirst, federal payoffs, urban sprawl, wildlife, the future and the past.

Talking about where the river has led him, he paraphrases John Muir: "When we try to select out any one thing, we find that it is connected to everything else in the universe."

We leave from Sacramento, heading south into the morning heat of the central valley, which is kept rich and fertile and productive by the water that pours down from the Stanislaus and twenty other bountiful tributaries carrying snow-melt from the Sierra Nevadas into the lowlands. We are crossing some of these—the Cosumnes, the Mokelumne, the Calaveras—as he begins to tell me the story. It is much more than the story of his week alone on a rock watching water lap his tiny protestor's outpost. The Stanislaus has been the center of his life. It has been his teacher, his home for a while, his playground, his chapel, and ultimately his pulpit. He talks about the river's magic. He speaks as if it is alive, the flowing water, the ferns and trees along the banks, the fish and the insects and the play of light through spiderwebs and buckeye leaves—all of that, one intricate organism. Listening to him describe these things, you soon realize that whatever beliefs he now holds —about watershed management, balanced use of resources—came second. What came first was the river. He is more than its friend. He loves every ounce of it.

He walks and sits with the slight hunch of a man who has for years been leaning or bending or dipping his head to talk and listen. For him no car has yet been built with enough head room. His clothes are plain, a green short-sleeved shirt, green twill trousers, shoes scuffed and bursting at the edges. There is something monkish about him, some monk's air of inspired self-denial. His brown hair is short, his brown beard close-cropped, his brown eyes direct and clear. He talks fast, almost nonstop, pausing only for moments, with a small intake of breath, for centering, as I have seen Buddhist teachers do, though when I mention the Buddhist connection he is surprised. He has never thought of it.

Nowadays, at thirty-one, he is six foot eight. As a high school freshman in Sacramento he was already six foot plus. A lean and lanky kid who had grown very fast, he had the size to high-jump or play basketball, but he was too loose-limbed to compete well. He shied away from competition. He was a loner then, uneasy with sports, uneasy with people. He preferred rocks and unspoiled rivers. At age sixteen he started exploring limestone caves along the upper reaches of the Stanislaus, about two hours south and east of his hometown. After he passed his first driver's test he was up there every weekend with friends, or alone, hiking the trails, climbing the rocks, sometimes prowling caves no one had entered since tribal days. He had found a pastime full of excitement yet free of competition, a physical challenge that put him in close touch with the riches of the wilderness. "It was," he says with a grin, "just me and the rocks."

When he started rafting a couple of years later, it took him a while to get the feel. "I broke eight oars the first season," he says. But soon he was spending weekends in the water instead of in the caves. Again there was no competition, just him and the river, the snags and boulders, the flood time, the low time, the power and the flow.

The river gave him confidence and a sport to excel at. Next it gave him a job. He was working weekdays in Sacramento and weekends guiding parties down the Stanislaus, which happens to be one of the most popular white-water runs in the United States. This eventually turned into full-time work as head boatman, at which point, in an unexpected way, the river began to put him in closer touch with unfamiliar parts of himself.

As a guide he was meeting people from many parts of the state. "Taking them down the river," he says, "there is an equalizing factor. You're all wearing the same uniform, or the same non-uniform. The other identities are left behind. Except for the ways people speak, you have no clue where they're coming from. Secondly, you had this incredible fear. You are immediately plunging down the huge rapids, and everyone is hanging on, really wondering if they're going to survive, and all of a sudden you have exposed your emotions to everyone else. All of a sudden we saw that we were human.

"It was exciting, talking to people of every status, as I was slowly learning to dance with this river. There were some surprising dialogues, about fear, and other feelings. You see, prior to that I had not talked with anyone about any of my feelings."

As of 1973 Mark was in his early twenties. He had dropped out of college, one test shy of a degree in anthropology. With two partners he had formed a small rafting group on the river. In between paying customers they were offering free trips to kids, handicapped kids, ghetto kids, free-school kids. By that time he knew his river was in some kind of trouble. Somewhere in the near future a dam was looming.

"I always felt guilty about not doing a little more. As a guide I knew about the letter-writing campaigns. I'd write once in a while myself. Part of my justification for continuing to play on the river was this very backdrop of the idea that its days were numbered. We were having great experiences with these kids, sharing what we knew. We taught them about stars, and edible plants, about the critters who live in the water and on the banks. We talked about where water comes from, so that when they got back home they'd be more conscious about switching off lights they weren't using, turning off the faucets. But gradually it dawned on me that this place was going to get destroyed unless some of us who cared about it went down into the cities where decisions about rivers get made."

When the environmental movement went public in the early 1970s it happened to coincide, or collide in a rather fateful way, with the long-percolating plans to construct this fourteenth dam across the Stanislaus. The New Melones, as it would be called, had existed on paper for almost thirty years. It was authorized by Congress in 1944 as part of the Central Valley Project. No dirt was turned until 1966, when access roads went in and an observation point where spectators could watch the cranes and the Caterpillars. Construction on the dam was scheduled to begin in 1972. But the new consciousness had spawned a counter-move, a plan to preserve two surviving stretches of unspoiled riverscape as Wild and Scenic Recreation areas. The original purpose of the New Melones, back in 1944, had been flood control. A much smaller dam, it seemed, could still impede flooding yet save the upper gorge. A new group called Friends of the River had gathered half-a-million signatures to put this initiative on the 1974 statewide ballot. When someone asked Dubois if he would coordinate the campaign in Sacramento he said yes, and thus he began paddling out of the white water and into what he now calls "the river of politics."

By the end of the campaign he was coordinating all of northern California. The River Initiative was defeated by a narrow margin: 47 percent in favor, 53 percent against. A poll conducted after the election revealed that many of those who voted against the measure thought they were voting against the dam. They had been confused by the issue, perhaps by a heavily financed opposition campaign which ran ads implying that a No vote could "Save the River."

Meanwhile, construction of the New Melones had already begun.

For Dubois it was a short course in water politics. It turned him from a full-time river buff into a full-time river activist. He spent the next four years lobbying, traveling, studying. He became executive director of The Friends of the River. In 1976 he and his colleagues worked for the Behr Bill, a proposal put before the state legislature to preserve the upper canyon. It too was narrowly defeated, even though a third of the legislators had endorsed it. In 1976 they also worked on the Jimmy Carter campaign, moved by his promise to reduce the number of dam projects out West. That year Friends of the River expanded their range to include all of California's threatened waterways. But for Dubois, the main focus for his environmental ideals would continue to be the Stanislaus, his first love, and later on his microcosm.

During his apprenticeship as a water politician he discovered an endless cataract of facts and figures such as these: in California only about 5 percent of the water delivered for consumption goes to households, for drinking, cooking, washing, flushing, watering the yard. Eighty-five percent goes for irrigating cropland. Yet according to a Government Accounting Office report in 1976, over half the irrigation water that flows through the Central Valley Project is lost or wasted. Every household in the state could stuff the toilet tank with bricks and save bath water for a year, and it would add up to a slender fraction of what conservationists like Dubois say is lost through water-costly irrigation methods that continue to be practiced largely because so much agricultural water has been so cheap for so long. For decades federally subsidized water has been available to many users at prices far below actual cost—an arrangement that has not encouraged thrift and efficiency.[11]

Farmers don't appreciate this kind of talk. They will tell you it is already hard enough to make ends meet, without running up the price of water. But then conservationists will point out that great chunks of the central valley are controlled by such venerable farming families as Standard Oil, Superior Oil, Getty Oil, Southern Pacific, and the Chandlers of Los Angeles, who own not only the Times-Mirror Company but 25 percent of Tejon Ranch, which, at a quarter-of-a-million acres, is the largest privately held, contiguous parcel of land in the state.

Mark, standing back and taking a long look at it all, concludes that for whatever reasons, no matter who is the guiltiest of guilty parties, we have a leaky system. He fervently believes it is in the best interests of the state, the nation, the planet and the Stanislaus to begin by tightening up that system. If the demand by current users of the Central Valley Project was reduced by one half of 1 percent, he says, all the new irrigation promised by the builders of the New Melones Dam would be provided for. In a wider context, the heat lost or wasted in California each year through inefficient shower heads amounts to three times the power that would be delivered by the New Melones.

The way he describes it, if the dam was filled, the Stanislaus gorge would be sacrificed not to immediate social needs but to sloppy and wasteful habits we can no longer afford. We may postpone conservation measures for a few more years, he says, perhaps for a few more dams, but sooner or later we will come up against the same limits again, making conservation policies inevitable. So why not start now, and save certain natural wonders that can still be saved, rather than delay the decision and lose something we can never replace? In his eyes, filling the dam to capacity began to look like a crime against nature, as well as a rip-off of all future generations who might otherwise have access to this marvelous streak of landscape. There were already twelve active dams tapping the river's annual average flow of one-million-plus acre-feet. If building another dam could not be stopped, perhaps we could just fill part of it, and save these ten miles of exquisite rafting, wilderness beauty, and unique archeology. Or must this too be covered over in order to deliver water and power we could provide from other sources if we only learned to mend our profligate ways?

During those apprentice years he also discovered some well-placed people who shared his loyalties. It was not just the eco-freaks and bearded mountain hippies who wanted to save the Stanislaus. He found allies sprinkled all through offices in Sacramento, and some in Washington, D.C., people who could quote John Muir and who had been asking similar questions for years, before and after the building of numerous other dams. He discovered a baroque, one might even say medieval, power play in motion, an old-time drama involving states' rights versus federal control, with the jumbo land interests playing both sides to their best advantage. Thirty-seven thousand acres near the new dam, for instance, had been purchased for speculative "ranch-style" development, while farther downstream there was the unquenchable thirst of California's runaway growth, with its underlying premise that the more dams and aqueducts and pumping stations, the greater the volume of controllable water to service the uncontrollable speculation and investment. In this expensive drama, the gorge of the Stanislaus—which can appear to be the entire world when you're floating along between its forested walls—was, for certain players in certain federal and corporate offices, just another tiny point on someone's battle plan.

To reach the dam we head east out of Oakdale, along Highway 108, which follows the Stanislaus, climbing easily from the valley floor, through the first lift of the Sierras, into the Mother Lode country. Among the thousands drawn into these hills from the 1840s onward, in search of riches, were the ferrymen who set up a chain of river stations, surviving now in the names of roads and bridges. At O'Byrne's Ferry Road, ten miles south of Sonora, we turn left, curve a few miles through rolling hills and come out upon the observation point, with a full front view of the New Melones. We are standing on a promontory, a cliff edge some four hundred feet above the river. The dam rises higher, blocks the near horizon.

Mark has all the numbers. I ask him how high it is.

"Six hundred and twenty-five feet," he says. "Fifteen hundred and sixty feet across the top."

"But the numbers don't get it, do they."

"Nope," he says, "you really have to see it."

The gorge is steep and narrow here. Rough, rocky cliffs rise on either side, reddish in color. The dam appears to be a Goliath's tub of stucco that was poured from the sky and dried instantly. From where we stand the surface looks gravelly, a pebbled slope of crushed rock, slate gray, fitting each niche and boulder in the facing cliffs. This was once bedrock, gouged out to make a spillway, then sifted and graded for surfacing the slope. Were it not for the rough and rusty contours of the canyon, the slope would be absolutely featureless. In some unseemly way they define each other, canyon wall against the sifted bedrock, rust on bluish gray. Far below, two white tubes of water gush from outflow pipes, man-made rapids filling the deep canyon with a man-made sound.

Forgetting for a moment the various upstream effects, it is possible to view this enormous sloping wall, this monument, with true awe, in the same light as the Pyramids or the Great Wall of China. A vision is working here, a large, intricate, roaring vision of what humankind can add to the natural shape of things. As dams go, this is a masterpiece, the second largest earth-fill dam in the country.

It was built, as usual, by the Army Corps of Engineers, whose motto tops the sign right where we turned off Highway 108: "BUILDING TO-MORROW TODAY." When the Central Valley Project was set up in 1935, the Bureau of Reclamation was the federal agency charged with developing it. The bureau put the corps to work building the New Melones. It took them five years, and by the time construction was finished they had found out that building it was the easy part.

According to the state's water code, the bureau had to obtain approval for the various uses and amounts of water it had in mind for this dam. In 1972 they duly applied to the State Water Resources and Control Board, who came back with partial and very guarded approval, mainly in the area of "prior rights" related to the Old Melones Dam,

soon to be buried behind the new one. The state board noted in passing
—and this was during the Reagan administration—that the Stanislaus
was "a unique asset to the State and the Nation." The state also reserved
the right to change its mind about water levels in the new reservoir.

The Bureau of Reclamation did not like the sound of this. They sued
the State Water Resources and Control Board for standing in the way
of progress, a suit that went to the U.S. Supreme Court, where it was
decided five years later that a state has the right to approve and control
the uses of its own water, even though a federal agency may have built
the dam. In those five years the state's position had not changed much.
And since the dam builders did not yet have enough contracts from
potential users to justify filling it to the top, there was a strong feeling
in Sacramento—supported by several years of mounting environmental
concern—that maybe we did not really need to gather up 2.4 million
acre-feet of water behind the New Melones.

With the Supreme Court ruling in the background, the Water Resources and Control Board did not want to see any filling until an
operations study could be made to determine how much water was
actually needed and contracted for. But the corps had a problem. Before turning the dam over to the Bureau of Reclamation, it was obliged
to test the turbines. To do so, they needed a minimum of 275,000
acre-feet. This would bring the new reservoir to about 808 feet above
sea level, stopping just short of an old bridge at Parrott's Ferry. Thus
808 came to be a figure acceptable to both the Water Resources Board
and the Friends of the River. In addition to preserving the life of the
upper canyon, it would give archeologists time to study some seven
hundred known sites in the event further filling, at a future date, could
not be avoided. A memorandum to this effect was endorsed by the
President's Advisory Council on Historic Preservation.

In October 1978 the dam was finished. In December Huey Johnson,
the State Resources Secretary, asked the federal government to "act
voluntarily to provide maximum, long-term protection to the Stanislaus
from Parrott's Ferry upstream." This idea, supported a short time later
by sixteen of California's forty-three congressmen, came to be known
as the Parrott's Ferry Compromise.

Through the early months of 1979 the reservoir was slowly filling
toward 808. Friends of the River, regretting the loss of every yard of
riverbank, had begun a series of Witness Encampments, for one last
look at the meadows and beaches and waterways so many had enjoyed,
as well as the wildlife and various archeological sites. Rising waters had
spread some four miles up the lower canyon when they heard that the
corps had plans to fill past level 808. This was never publicly announced,

but there is what Dubois calls the "river grapevine." Corps officials would mention something to project contractors, who would pass it on to their crews, who would mention it to someone in town, who would mention it to a Friend of the River.

One spring day the number 828 was heard. A jump of twenty feet. If this was true, and if they could jump the level twenty feet this month, without any official notice, what would prevent them from jumping it again, and then again? The Corps of Engineers are visionaries, after all, and in their version of the world such a dam should be filled to capacity at the earliest possible moment, not because they themselves planned to do anything with the water, but because they are builders. They had recently finished building something rather spectacular, and who could blame them for wanting to see if this huge piece of equipment really worked? They are professionals. They have just spent five years and $360 million. At the very least, they said, when pressed for explanations, some of our engineers believe they need a few more feet of elevation to give the turbines a test that will really mean something—engineers who evidently had not been consulted when it was agreed to hold the line at Parrott's Ferry.

"Hey!" cried the voice of environmentalism. "You guys made a deal! You told us you wouldn't go past eight-oh-eight!"

"Well, hell," grumbled the inner voice of the Corps. "Eight-oh-eight. Eight-twenty-eight. Is that so far apart? It's just a couple more miles up the canyon. The world is full of canyons. We wouldn't go past eight-oh-eight if we didn't have to. Anyhow, before you know it, the water will drop down again to whatever level you people think is so sacred."

Dubois, watching all this from his backyard office in Sacramento, had about decided the time had come to draw some personal line of his own. The F.O.R. had tried every legal means they could think of, and legality had not worked. Corporate financing had sabotaged the River Initiative. All efforts at legislation had been blockaded. Lobbying had produced allies but not enough power. These stop-gap measures—the Supreme Court ruling, and the provisions of the Historic Preservation Act —had brought temporary hope, but now the corps seemed to be ignoring them.

For all the previous year, as his frustrations ebbed and flowed, Mark had been tinkering with the idea of some kind of "statement." He had thought of taking a shovel down to the foot of the construction site, to dig away at the bulwark in puny defiance. He had considered lying in front of a bulldozer. Now he had a new and bolder idea. He did not yet know quite how to make it happen. A friend had done some welding.

Mark had asked him to look around for some shackles. The friend refused. He thought Mark was losing his judgment, perhaps his mind.

It was Wednesday, May 17, when he learned, via the grapevine, that the water level was only five days from Parrott's Ferry. Five days meant Monday. This news jarred him into action. His idea had been unsettling him and beguiling him, a strange fantasy that suddenly became real as its details started clicking into place.

First he drafted a letter to Colonel Donald O'Shei, head of the corps' Sacramento District Office. O'Shei had supervised construction. They knew each other. They had spoken many times. In the letter Mark talked about the magic of the canyon, the irreplaceable loss. He said the corps' action left him no alternative.

> I plan to have my feet permanently anchored to a rock in the canyon at the elevation of Parrott's Ferry the day the water reaches that elevation. I urge you to do all in your power to prevent the flooding of the canyon above Parrott's Ferry.[12]

The next day, while copies were being mailed special delivery to the White House and to various state and federal offices, Mark paid a visit to the hardware store. He pretended to be a miner with some equipment to stash in the hills.

"How would I do that?" he asked the clerk. "How could I, for example, secure something to a rock?"

You do it, he learned, the way old-time miners did it when they had a hole to bore, with a sledgehammer and a star drill. While the clerk went looking for a drill and a six-inch eye bolt, Dubois secretly wrapped some chain around one ankle, to see precisely how much he would need.

"I didn't want to buy too much," he tells me, laughing now. "This was a very low-budget operation."

On his way to deliver the top copy of his letter to O'Shei's office, he made a brief stop outside the window of Governor Jerry Brown. He wanted to pay homage to a toyon tree planted there nine months earlier by the Friends of the River. In the weeks before the dam began to fill, twenty people had made a pilgrimage, carrying this tree from the lower canyon to plant it outside Brown's office, at the southeast corner of the Capitol building, in the lee of its golden dome. By May that part of the canyon was covered over. Everything formerly living there was dead, except this toyon—two feet tall when they brought it out, and now as tall as Mark. Sometimes called California holly, the toyon has flat, shiny leaves and red or yellow berries in the fall. You find it up and down the Coast Range and in Sierra foothills. The sight of this tree filled Mark with a new exhilaration, a rush of feeling he now calls "the third freedom."

The first—and these are all lessons he thanks the river for—had been the freedom from things, from the idea that the main aim of life is to accumulate more money and more possessions. The second was the freedom from fear of the future and what his later life would be like if he failed to accumulate enough possessions and personal property. "Freedom is not land. It is all up here," he says, pointing to his head. "I carry it with me."

The third freedom poured over him as he regarded the toyon tree that had started life in the now flooded canyon of the Stanislaus. He saw how closely linked are life and death. What he was about to do involved the risk of drowning. With a kind of religious clarity he saw that whether he lived or died didn't make that much difference. Either way, the statement would be voiced. Through the act of heading down the river, or through the acts that would follow, if and when he came back out again, the commitment would be voiced. Making the decision to go ahead with this liberated him from his own fears of dying.

When Colonel O'Shei's reply arrived the next morning, two things about it struck Dubois. Corps officials had never been eager to communicate with him, never quick to return his calls. In their ongoing dialogue, the colonel's letter was the fastest answer Mark had ever received, and this amused him. In the letter, O'Shei listed all the state and federal decisions that mandated filling the New Melones, and this shook him, reminded him just how much ammunition the corps had. The colonel also withdrew permission for any Friend of the River to enter the canyon, a tactic Mark figured could be designed to set him up for trespassing. He dashed off a quick response and called the District Office to make sure O'Shei was there to receive it. The secretary put his call straight through.

"Colonel," Mark said. "There is one thing I want to make clear. I am not doing this on behalf of the Friends of the River. I am only doing it on behalf of myself."

"Do you want to get together and talk about it?"

"No."

"I just can't quite understand why you're doing this."

"I'm sorry, Colonel. I don't trust you anymore."

The colonel, it should be pointed out, is not the villain in the piece. A suitable adversary, but not the villain. He was a West Point graduate, a career officer with degrees in law and engineering, a Bronze Star with oakleaf cluster, an Air Medal, service in Korea and in Vietnam. At age forty-five he was nearing the end of a three-year tour of duty in northern California, during which time he commanded operations in nine western states and had overseen the completion of at least one superb dam. He had not broken any laws. And neither had Dubois. There were laws on the books, along with documents and memos and opinions and briefs, to support both their views. They just did not agree on which documents held the top priority.

Parrott's Ferry was established in 1860 by one Thomas Parrott, to connect two mining towns on opposite sides of the river. It was a flat-bottomed wooden ferry propelled back and forth across the surge via heavy cables. A bridge was built there in 1903, and another, more durable bridge, which still stands, in 1940. To reach it, you follow Parrott's Ferry Road out of Sonora, through Columbia and Saw Mill Flats, winding from twenty-one hundred feet down into the gorge where the green water flows along at about eight hundred feet above sea level, give or take a fathom, depending on the time of year.

Often used as a parking spot and jumping-off place for river riders, this forty-year-old bridge can still handle cars and trucks. Without the F.O.R. it would already be two hundred feet underwater and permanently out of sight. This was the plan. Deactivate the old bridge, and reroute traffic across the new Parrott's Ferry Bridge, about a mile downstream. From here it crosses the sky like a piece of futuristic sculpture seen at the World's Fair. Two concrete pillars a hundred yards high support a thinly convex ribbon of concrete, miraculously thin, as thin as a pair of wings. Built in 1979, it is part of the New Melones system, part of the future envisioned for this ancient gorge. Turn upstream from the old bridge and you are looking into what might be called the past but is really another image from the future. The river here is about thirty yards wide, rushing down from the mountains higher up, around Ebbett's Pass (8,730 feet) and Sonora Peak (11,429 feet). Islands of bedrock keep the water veined and streaked with white. Wooded slopes rise back from the streambed, and here and there rock islands poke through the stands of pine and small oaks, giving the slopes that same kind of streambed definition.

The wildness upstream, the winged viaduct downstream, it is almost melodrama, making it almost too easy to interpret the line drawn here as that choice between wilderness and technology, or, as some accounts described it, between ten miles of primeval whitewater and the pressing needs of an expanding society.

"I saw that the Stanislaus could be in its final hour. People had been telling me it was a lost cause. The dam was built. It was going to be used. So, do I let this river go and start working on all these other issues that are equally critical? Or do I drop all these other issues and focus on the Stanislaus? It was a painful decision, but I really had no choice. My heart had touched that place. I also realized that by concentrating on that one issue, we had a chance to use it as a symbol for what we're doing to all of our land and all of our resources—by saying, 'No, stop, we made a mistake, and we can't afford to go on in this direction!' "

Dubois rode up here that Friday night with a friend from Berkeley named Don Briggs, a photographer and surveyor. Early Saturday they computed the rate of rise, where the water would be by Monday, the precise location of 808, and thus how high above the present level Mark should set himself to carry out his ultimatum. Then he started downstream from the bridge, alone in a kayak, looking for the boulder he could anchor to. He foresaw a rock large enough to stretch out on, and hidden. He had no clear picture of how long he'd be in there, a week perhaps, or two or three. He expected search parties. It was extremely important that he be well hidden.

He was not many yards below the bridge when he began to weep. He had not anticipated this, and he couldn't control it. It wasn't fear. It wasn't grief for the endangered life in this canyon or for the wild things already lost to rising waters. He was weeping for his mother, and then for all the people he cared about. That morning he had called her, to explain what he was doing, and why. She was the kind of mother who worried about her son's exploits. He had expected her to try and talk him out of this, as some of his friends had attempted to do, but she didn't. And he had wanted to convey to her the full measure of what he was feeling—the sense of purpose, the rightness, the inner peace, the joy—but he couldn't. He had not been able to ease her anxiety. He regretted that. Now it overwhelmed him, the pain this voyage might bring to her, the not-knowing. In all other ways he felt strong. It was the one thing he could do nothing about.

Drifting downstream he wept for half an hour. Then his tears subsided. It was a bright morning, with the barest breeze running. He began to note the reflections of the trees that were slowly going under. The water had been backing up about a foot and a half per day.

"Those trees were still alive on top," he says, "not yet dead at the roots. It was some of the most intense beauty I had ever seen, like the canyon was going to go out in a blaze of glory."

He came to a rocky face decorated with petroglyphs left behind by a tribe who had lived here before the Miwok. On the far bank lay the remains of a gold rush mining camp. A quarter of a mile downstream he could see what had once been a wide stream-side meadow. Three weeks earlier he had hiked in to that meadow with a hundred people for a Witness Encampment. Now it was thirty feet underwater, as the petroglyphs and the mining remains soon would be. Originally he had planned to float farther down, into the lower canyon, but the conflu- ence of these time zones, these moments in the river's history, spoke to him, magnetized him. This was where he wanted to stop. He looked around and immediately saw the spot, a shoulder of bedrock, flat on top, surrounded with foliage. A cliff rose behind it, and there was space between branches to peek out toward the water. He stashed a few supplies, then moved out into the flow again, heading downstream. He still had a lot to do.

Near the main reservoir, already dotted with pleasure boats and weekend fishermen, he parked his kayak and composed a longer reply to O'Shei's letter, in which he wrote:

> I apologize for saying Friday that I no longer trusted you. When I calmed down I realized that I now understand you better and realize how different our values are. . . . I admire your ability to take charge, but regret that you don't implement laws protecting the resources as well as construction schedules. Each one of us must do what we most believe is right.[13]

It would take several hours of steady drilling to cut into the rock, and he knew this would add a grating, alien noise to the canyon, with the risk of drawing unwanted attention to his spot. On Sunday morning he rose before dawn and hiked in with the tools, the four-pound sledge, the miner's star drill, and hammered away for two hours before the Sunday river-users came to life.

"It makes an awful sound, but it's interesting the way it works. The bit is in the shape of a star. You hold it in place, and tap it. At first I was twisting back and forth, getting nowhere. Finally I figured out that by turning it slightly, each time in the same direction, it just steadily chips and chips and chips."

That night a small group of friends and supporters gathered near Parrott's Ferry. Afterward Mark met with the fellow who would serve as contact, the only person who would know his exact location and could bring in news. At one point Mark had nearly given up trying to fill this job.

"I made some calls and gradually realized I was asking people to do something far heavier than I was going to do. My plan was to chain myself up so no one could find me. Going in, my feeling was I had a ten percent chance of stopping the water level, a ten percent chance I would join all the critters in the lower canyon, and an eighty percent chance of being found. But I was going to do everything I could not to be found. And I purposely made the chain short so that if they did find me, I would sit all around it and make things as difficult as possible to get me off of there. Now, for me, all this would be easy, but if I joined my friends in the lower canyon, others could feel the pain of that more than I would. It was hard for me to ask somebody to risk taking on that kind of role."

When this longtime river buddy appeared almost at the last moment, asking how he could help, Mark recruited him. He had the time to visit every day, he knew and loved the Stanislaus, and he shared Mark's views about life and death. In the days to follow he came to be known as Deep Paddle.

Mark slept that night in the woods near his hideout. Early Monday he spent one more hour on the star drill, cutting to a depth of four inches. He drove in the expander bolt, then threaded the chain through the bolt's eye-loop, wrapped the chain around one ankle, and snapped the padlock shut. With the key hidden in brush a hundred feet away, he sat down on his slab of bedrock to wait. At that point he had no food, he was planning to fast. He had a sleeping bag, a poncho, some books to read and a cup to scoop drinking water from the reservoir, which was then two feet below his perch and still rising.

He had told Deep Paddle that if the water ever reached his knees not to come back. He did not want anyone but himself to have to deal with that part. Thankfully, no one had to. The water, which had been rising since October, began to level off within the next twenty-four hours, according to Dubois, who was watching it at closer range than any other player in the drama, and according to Jim Taylor, Public Affairs Officer with the Sacramento District Office, who announced on Tuesday that the lake had been "stabilized."

On Monday Colonel O'Shei had received the second letter. Also on Monday Harold Gilliam, an environmentally supportive San Francisco columnist, published the first report on the subject, in the *Chronicle*. A valve was thrown open, and then the corps joined forces with the county sheriff's deputies to search the upper and lower canyons.

While more newsmen followed the action, five boats were deployed, a helicopter, a light plane, and eighteen men on foot to tramp the riverbanks—all without success. Dubois had secluded himself better than he realized. Though the stretch of river they had to cover was only ten miles long, widening waters fattened the perimeter to about sixty miles. There were new bayous, and whole treetops to cut through, and thriving clumps of springtime poison oak. He was in there, but by Wednesday, when the F.O.R. staged a rally outside the state capitol, no one but Deep Paddle knew where.

Jerry Brown appeared at that rally, and drew cheers and hoots of joy when he called the river "a priceless asset to the people of California and this nation." Brown had already sent a telegram to President Carter on behalf of the Stanislaus and the life of its champion. A Carter aide would soon be contacting someone at Interior, and an undersecretary there would soon be calling someone at the corps and then calling Huey Johnson, State Resources Secretary, who would be checking with O'Shei, who would be getting back to Johnson, who would be getting back to Brown, and hopefully one or all of them would be getting back to Dubois, who, though the waters had now stopped rising just short of Parrott's Ferry Bridge, was not going anywhere until he had written assurance that the filling wouldn't resume once they had him out of the canyon.

For the first three days he saw no one but Deep Paddle and, from a distance, the pilots of approaching planes and launches. He discovered a narrow ledge, a body-size niche on the underside of his rock. Each time he heard an engine drone he would pull his poncho over him, camouflage himself with scraps of moss and driftwood and duck out of sight.

"Some of them got close, but they didn't spot me because they were usually going twenty-five miles an hour right down the middle of the reservoir. Helicopters would come zooming by, doing the whole canyon in two minutes."

Once a day Deep Paddle appeared with news from the outside and, on the second day, a small parcel of food. Mark had never fasted before. He soon decided this was the wrong time to experiment with that part of his life. He ate fruit and nuts. At night he slept with a sleeping bag wrapped around him. "The way the zipper works on my bag, I couldn't get into it with my ankle chained."

Though he had planned to read and catch up on paperwork, he spent long hours "getting in touch with the river again." His crusade to save it had taken him into cities, and for most of four years that's where he had stayed. These few days alone at the bottom of the canyon gave him time to rediscover the cycles, the textures, the play of light at dawn and sundown, the chill, the heat, the distant rush of moving water, the profound silence under the rush.

"It took me three days to isolate one tiny sound, to focus on it and realize it was a little shrew, poking under the leaves, skittering back and forth looking at me. I had a river otter who would come and play around in front of the rock. Beavers were working across the way. Every kind of insect. Spiders. I was right under a buckeye tree in full bloom. Once I was sitting there and felt this movement right behind me. I turned and saw this huge snake slithering past. It had the coloration of a rattler, but it was just a big gopher snake. Sorry, my friend, I said as he made his exit, I didn't mean to trouble you."

While Mark waited, while planes and launches buzzed the reservoir, while reporters queried Friends of the River and friends of Dubois, and while six more chained-up protestors appeared on the rocks near Parrott's Ferry Bridge, Jerry Brown sent his chief aide, Gray Davis, to confer with Colonel O'Shei. On Friday a letter, a pledge, arrived at the governor's office. After that it was only a matter of a few formalities. The following Monday, a week from the day he drove in the expander bolt and looped chain through its eye, a letter from Gray Davis made its way south and east from Sacramento to Sonora, along Parrott's Ferry Road and downstream into the hands of Dubois. The letter noted the corps' renewed commitment to elevation 808, together with a promise from the state to police the water level until the courts and Congress could decide that matter once and for all. Given the ways of the courts and Congress, this could mean months, a year, maybe more. He had bought the river some time and bought its friends time and space to pursue new legislation. Sitting underneath his buckeye tree, he read Davis's letter carefully, then he revealed the whereabouts of his key. He unchained himself and floated back to dry land.

Over a year later we stood on the old bridge watching the river flow under us. It hadn't changed much, yet, though many of the players had. Soon after the showdown, Colonel O'Shei, in the normal course of his career, had been transferred to Israel. A few months later, the Corps of Engineers, with a collective groan of relief, officially transferred control of the New Melones Project to the Interior Department.

Behind us, on the roadbed that crosses the bridge, there was a hand-lettered list of rivers that gush down out of the Sierras, painted in blue during the weeks when this bridge had been the battle zone, the final line of defense:

FEATHER

YUBA

AMERICAN

MOKELUMNE

RUBICON

COSUMNES

STANISLAUS

TUOLOMNE

MERCED

KINGS

KERN

WHAT'S LEFT OF THESE WILL ALSO DIE,
BURIED BY THE CONCRETE WORSHIPPERS,
IF WE DON'T STOP THEM HERE.

SAVE THE STANISLAUS

Had they been stopped? Mark still did not know. In May of 1979 Representative Don Edwards of San Jose had introduced a bill in Congress proposing that the nine miles from this bridge eastward become part of the National Wild and Scenic Rivers system. It seemed to be the last hope. For a year it had been in committee, and for a year Mark had been lobbying for passage. He had just returned from a week in Washington, D.C. This bill had to make it through by the end of 1980, he said, otherwise Interior Secretary Cecil Andrus would be obliged to fill the dam and flood the river. The various restraining orders were running out.

An apprehension hung in the air that day, a film of suspense coated the mountainsides. This could have been an effect of the afternoon's cloud cover, or it could have been the shadow thrown back across the canyon from those concrete wings a mile west. By the altitude of that winged viaduct, floating atop its long skinny legs, you could see the plan, you could see how high the water was intended to rise.

Mark leaned against the bridge rail, gazing in the other direction, upstream.

"Look at this place," he said. "There used to be twenty-five thousand miles of rivers, streams, and wildlife habitat in the state of California. You know how much we have left?"

"I would guess a few thousand."

"More like a few hundred. We've got thirteen hundred major dams, thousands of minor dams, we've got polluted streams and dried-up streams and reservoirs and irrigation canals and aqueducts and levees, but in the whole system all we have left is maybe four hundred miles of relatively pristine river that people can get to and use and enjoy, and anyone you talk to will tell you that the ten miles from here to Camp Nine is one of the finest canyons anywhere in the U.S."

"Mark," I said. "What are the chances of the river bill getting passed in time? I mean, in your personal view, being absolutely realistic."

He turned, gazed at me with his gentle smile, and said, "I don't like the use of the word 'realistic.' I hear it, and my guard goes up. It is a word politicians will use when they are getting ready to try and talk you out of something. 'Okay, let's be as realistic as we can about this,' they will say. 'Here are the realities we're faced with.' Well, the fact is, we create our own realities. If we bring *enough* creative energy and imagination to a situation, we can make it happen. In the past ten years I have seen things happen that no one ever believed would happen. Why? Because certain people refused to believe that they *wouldn't* happen. This is my definition of what is realistic."

Another year and more had gone by, when I happened to be passing through Sonora again and decided to swing down the old road to Parrott's Ferry. During that year the Wild and Scenic River proposal had been defeated in Congress. Secretary Andrus had ordered the reservoir to be filled to 818. Though the Friends of the River protested, the order was upheld by the Ninth U.S. Court of Appeals. For a while water had risen for half-a-mile above the bridge. In the early days of 1981 the F.O.R. petitioned Jimmy Carter—on his way out of the White House—to declare the upper Stanislaus a national monument. It was thoughtfully considered, and denied. A group of handicapped protesters made headlines when they chained themselves to rocks as Mark had done, saying this was the most accessible stretch of whitewater in the country. Then Cecil Andrus was replaced by James Watt, who soon announced that he intended to see the New Melones filled to capacity as soon as possible.

Meanwhile the old battle between the state and federal government was still being waged. In 1977 the U.S. Supreme Court had ruled in California's favor, but a federal district court later excepted decisions regarding hydroelectric power. The state in turn had challenged this part of the ruling. Prolonged court action had helped to postpone any final decision on the river's fate, so that when I stopped again at Parrott's Ferry Bridge, politics and a shallow snowpack had collaborated to drop the water level actually below what it had been during my previous visit. The reservoir's spread was out of sight below the nearest bend.

"We create our own realities," Mark had said.

I looked upstream. Standing there, I could easily believe the truth of that remark. The evidence was right in front of me. By numerous other definitions of what is real, that piece of riverscape should have long been dead and buried. That it had survived for more than two years past what so many had assumed would be its date of execution was in itself a kind of miracle. No one could then predict how long the river would continue to flow. None of the key ingredients could be measured in advance: court decisions, public awareness, snowfall, rainfall, human thirst.

Winding upward out of the gorge, I remembered something else Mark had said. We were climbing this way, back toward Sonora, toward Modesto, Sacramento and the city offices where the fates of rivers are discussed. This Mother Lode hillside had started him talking about his family.

"They've been in this part of the world for four generations now," he said. "On my mother's side, since right after the Gold Rush. My grandmother was born in Carson City, Nevada, then grew up in California, like my mother did, like I have. It's interesting, you know, how the perspective shifts from generation to generation. A few years ago I was hiking along the Yuba River near the site of the Marysville Dam, when the corps was really pushing that project, and we were researching it from our side. I came across all these old dredge fields, great mounds fifty feet high and a mile long—tailings that miners had left behind— and I remembered that my grandfather had worked for the Yuba Dredge Company. It was fascinating, because here I was working to stop the building of another dam in this area, and my grandfather had worked to dredge and to mine that very river we were trying to save, which in his day was the right thing to be doing, the best thing he could do. It just struck me how each generation discovers how to do what is right for its time."

El Pachuco and the Virgin

Following Highway 1 I curve around Monterey Bay toward Watsonville, cut inland there, through the lettuce fields, the fertile delta lands of the Pajaro Valley where sedans and pickups stand in crazy patterns along the roadside, left by the pickers who drove out early this morning to park and move down the rows after romaine, chicory, onions, whatever is in season.

According to Luis Valdez, this is one important difference between the Mexicans and other immigrant groups. They have not ceased pouring into the United States to take these jobs.

"If we had all come in as one group," he says, "within a certain period of years, like some of the groups through Ellis Island, people would be able to say, 'Oh yes, there they are, now they're at stage two, now they're at stage three, now they are becoming lawyers and doctors.' But the farmworkers keep coming across and staying visible, and the whole process of acculturation and integration which has been continuous on this continent for five hundred years stays *in*visible. You know, when *Zoot Suit* was playing in New York, we had Chicanos flying in from all over the Southwest. There are Chicano millionaires around. There are Chicano doctors and lawyers, and they've been around for a long time. It's just that the most visible groups have been the farmworkers, who keep coming across, and the low riders. Any time of the year I can be driving through California and look out into a field and see the image of my parents, the image of my grandparents, the image

94

of myself. I drive by an apricot orchard and there I am, thirty years ago, a little kid still up in the tree picking apricots."

Heading eastward through the mountains, toward the valley that lies beyond, I cross the San Andreas Fault again, as usual, then take the overpass above four wide lanes of 101, the refrigerated rigs and the compacts speeding along beneath me. From the overpass, looking across the valley, I can see the very top of the mission's bell tower and the low buildings through the oaks and eucalyptus groves that screen the town. I am barely out of earshot of that continuous north-south hum and rumble of the twenty-four-hour freeway, when I walk into his office, his den of cigar smoke and posters. While exhaust fumes still hover around my car outside, while technology still quivers in my temples and my wrists and legs, he is telling me about his grandfather from northern Mexico, who was part Yaqui Indian, and the sounds he would make, not songs, not words, yet sounds made by a human voice.

"Duh—HAAAAAAY—dah, duh—HAY—dah, duh—HAAAAAAY—dah!"

Luis's voice is rich and nasal, rising from the chest and suddenly warrior-like, full of authority as he fills his office with this chant. The Yaqui in him is blazing at me through the black, luminous, steady eyes. He is talking about three things at once—his grandfather, his Indian background, his view of theater.

"The theater has got to do more than talk with words. There are many elements that speak. The body speaks. Movement speaks. Rhythm speaks. I remember songs that came through my grandfather. The hey-yuh, hey-yuh sound was part of reality for me. Sometimes he would be telling us stories about his childhood in Mexico, stories of the Yaqui, and he would imitate the sound of calling from one hill to another. He would stand up and the sound would be, 'Duh—HAAAAAAAAAY—dah, duh-HAY-dah, duh—HAAAAAAAAY—dah!' That is my grandfather talking to me about some of my people. There are certain sounds that have something to do with no-words-at-all. It's *sound*. What I'm saying is, that is part of my cultural experience. As a Yaqui I still feel the drumbeat. As a playwright I cannot dismiss the part of myself that is a savage."

This makes him laugh. His eyes are often on the verge of laughter. Valdez is a deadly serious man who seems endlessly amused—by his own foibles, by Americans, by Mexicans, by incongruities large and small. In 1977 he received a writing grant from the Rockefeller Foundation. In 1979 he took a play to Broadway. A few months from now his road company will commence a six-week tour of Germany, Italy, Switzerland, and France. Today he is laughing in his smoky office in San Juan Bautista, saying he cannot dismiss the part of himself that is a savage.

The grandfather who voiced that Yaqui call—his mother's father— fought in the Mexican Revolution, then worked his way north toward Arizona as a *vaquero*, a cowhand. The grandfather on his father's side came north working on railroad crews. He too carried Yaqui blood and also ended up in Arizona, where Luis's parents met.

"The whole Yaqui connection on both sides was very strong," he says. "The pride, the stubbornness. Everything that was strong and powerful and lasting was Yaqui. That was bred into us, how courageous you were. This is generally true of the Yaqui as a people. Even within Mexico, they have never relinquished their pride and their independence and their sense of identity."

His parents speak Yaqui as a third language. Luis figures if his family had stayed around Phoenix and Guadalupe he'd probably speak it too. But in the years before he was born they left for California.

"My father's life might have been different if his father hadn't died of pneumonia. At twelve my dad became the man. He had to go to work in the fields. And that was his life. He supported his family for fourteen or fifteen years, until he got married. The path they followed has been a general path traced by thousands and thousands of people who took the same route, from Mexico, through Nogales into Arizona, then across to Brawley and the Imperial Valley, sweeping north into the San Joaquin, following the crops, through valley towns like Delano, where I was born."

Luis was in the fifth grade when his father decided to stop moving and try to settle in San Jose, so his kids could have some regular schooling and better opportunities. It was a risky choice. Fieldworkers made their money by moving from harvest to harvest, being ready to pick at picking time. Hoping there would be enough work in the fields and orchards within range of San Jose, they moved into the east-side barrio called "Sal si Puedes" ("Get Out If You Can"). The first step out for Luis, as his father had hoped, was education. With the help of a Bank of America scholarship he entered San Jose State College in 1958. The year he graduated, his first full-length play was produced: *The Shrunken Head of Pancho Villa*. William Saroyan, California's original prize-winning dramatist (also born in the San Joaquin), saw the production. The story is that he took the chewing gum out of his mouth, threw it into his program, leaped onto the stage at the end of the show and proclaimed, "This is a brilliant play! It is the work of a genius!"

When the Grapeworkers' strike erupted in 1965, Luis was living in the Haight-Ashbury and doing some work with the San Francisco Mime Troupe. For a young writer interested in radical theater, the Bay Area seemed like the right place to be. But he could not stay away from what was happening in Delano, where the strike was centered. There was a blood tie: some of his relatives were involved. There was a movement underway: this labor struggle, led by Cesar Chavez, had given focus to a new, emerging consciousness of what it meant to be Chicano.

There was also a very personal challenge. "It was a real fork in the road for me," he says now. "I felt it was important to go to Delano, as much to help other farmworkers, as for myself. I needed to deal with my own personal fears and insecurities. All that time my father was in the fields, there was a humiliation, a fear of poverty, a feeling of displacement for all of us. As a kid I never really understood why sometimes the work stopped and no provisions were there for us. I blamed my parents. I needed to go back to Delano and face the monster."

The guerrilla theater he started that year was called *El Teatro Campesino* (The Farmworkers' Theater). His first actors were striking pickers with time on their hands. He gave them simple lines to speak or signs to hang around their necks, homemade masks to wear. They climbed onto a flatbed truck and drove out to the picket lines and performed short *actos*, skits, sketches, broad quick strokes of social and political satire, designed to teach, to organize and also to entertain. "Our use of comedy," he later wrote in his book *Aztlan*, "originally stemmed from necessity—the necessity of lifting the strikers' morale. We found we could make social points not in spite of the comedy, but through it."[14]

Valdez has described these plays as "somewhere between Brecht and Cantinflas." It was an extraordinary kind of theater. He mixed language—English, Spanish, and the street slang called *calo*. He mixed modes—pantomime, slapstick, commedia dell'arte—stirring up a spontaneous, gutsy folk art, aimed at working people, and always community oriented, communally produced.

When he moved to San Juan Bautista in 1971, he brought with him the idea of communal theater, gathering together an extended family of performers and technicians committed to drama rooted in Chicano experience and cultural heritage. Artistically and emotionally it was a healthy move, coming to San Juan. This is a small, bilingual town surrounded by fields and ranches, where nothing much has ever happened since the mission was founded in 1797. "A good place for raising a family," Luis says. There is space and time here, to go inward, to tap downward. Professionally, it was a very risky move, as risky as his father's move to San Jose. Novelists and potters are the ones who can afford to live in out-of-the-way communities. Theaters need the ongoing live audience. People hoping to have a voice in contemporary theater are expected to go to Los Angeles or the Bay Area or New York. Yet, since that move, his teatro, in addition to playing regularly for Chicano audiences throughout this state and the Southwest, has won awards in all those cities, with works developed here in San Juan. In 1973 they won an Emmy for *Los Vendidos* (The Sold Ones). In 1976 they sent a play to Europe as an official American bicentennial event. It was called *La Carpa de Los Rasquachis* (The Tent of the Underdogs).

In a dozen years, under the corporate heading of Menyah Productions, they also cut a record, published writings, produced a prize-winning film, and revived some traditional Mexican religious events which they keep alive locally through annual pageants at Easter, Halloween and Christmastime. With a sound studio, films to store, a small jungle of filing cabinets and a year-round production schedule, they were about ready to burst through the back wall of the converted warehouse that was serving as headquarters, when the success of *Zoot Suit* brought in enough cash for the company to buy a much-needed new building. Actually it is an old building near the center of town, which they were just beginning to refurbish on the day I called.

"Hello," said the woman who answered the phone. "New Space."

The space is so new, uncovered studs and joists are still showing. It used to be a packing shed. "Potatoes probably," says Luis, showing me around. The huge interior has been partitioned to house a generous rehearsal room, props, costumes, various offices. In the costume department, suits and dresses hang on the racks, above rows of shoes for every occasion—a costume department like any other, except that here and there you see evidence of this company's uncommon character, serapes, Aztec robes. On a long shelf, in with the fedoras and the cowboy hats, there are sombreros, feathered helmets, the silvered helmet of a conquistador. Next door in the prop room stands a giant skull with a sign above the mouth that says *El Mundo* (The World). Facing the skull stands a sign used in his play *Los Vendidos:* "HONEST PAN-CHO'S USED MEXICANS."

On the way to his office we pass through a small workroom with typewriter, taping machine, a wall board covered with clippings and various photos and drawings of Tiburcio Vasquez, the notorious nineteenth-century bandit and the subject of the newest Valdez drama. Valdez is a man intensely involved with images, personae—human pictures that work in his own imagination and connect to his current writing interests, as well as public images that work in the public mind.

From his earliest days on the picket line he has been a master juggler of masks and stereotypes. Typically, he will conjure up a role-player such as El Pachuco, El Revolucionario, El Bandido, or the lazy *campesino* dozing against the archetypal saguaro cactus—then he will pull the rug out from under some hazy or lazy preconception.

While he relights his cigar, I sit down on the new sofa, facing him across the polished wooden desk, and have a moment to glance around the office. On the rack hangs his wide-brimmed chocolate brown charro hat. Across one wall hangs a woven serape. On the wall behind me, two posters have been hung, one that features a Mayan stone emblem with the words "TEATRO CAMPESINO" underneath; the other advertises *Zoot Suit*, with a lean, black-clad pachuco set against the L.A. skyline.

Next to his desk hangs a black-and-white photo of the San Francisco Cliff House from around the turn of the century. At first glance it seems out of context, since there is no apparent connection with theater or farm labor or *la raza* or the nation of *Aztlan*—matters Valdez has been often associated with. On the beach below the Cliff House, a horse-drawn carriage is standing in the sand. Men in dark suits and bowler hats are posing next to the carriage, with women in wide-skirted traveling dresses. It's a sunny day in 1900. The waves are breaking. Above the photo a card has been tacked to the wall with the hand-lettered word CALIFORNIA.

I say, "That's the original Cliff House."

"I think it's the second," he says. "After the first one burned down. I found that it an antique store and had it framed. When I lived in San Francisco in the early sixties the Cliff House was one of my favorite haunts. You remember the old Sutro Baths next door? And the crazy museum they used to have up there? You could wander around and look at the cases, the old clothes. It was like plunging back into the nineteenth century."

"I remember seeing Tom Thumb's underwear in that museum, when I was a kid," I tell him, "his tiny shorts and little undershirts getting moldy and yellow under the glass."

"Yes, that's right." He grins broadly. "Tom Thumb's underwear."

We break out laughing. He loves these incongruities. He savors them. Earlier, when he told me that this former warehouse had once housed tons of potatoes, he pulled the cigar from his mouth so he could spend a moment chuckling. We had just been talking about the play his company will be rehearsing here tonight, part of their annual Christmas cycle, reenacting the miraculous appearance of the Virgin of Guadalupe.

I am still looking at the old Cliff House photo, knowing there is more to this than nostalgia for the sixties. The sign above it is the key. I have never before seen the bare word CALIFORNIA tacked on someone's wall. I ask if this imagery is here to keep him in touch with some other facet of his writing.

He wants to talk about it. "That connects to everything I'm working on. I have started to think of my work as outlining one part of California history. The play about Tiburcio Vasquez, for instance. He was born in Monterey."

"*Zoot Suit* is a slice of L.A. during World War Two."

"Of course. What I have finally managed to understand is that one thing I have been doing all these years is defining reality for myself. I felt alien in Delano, and I had to understand why. It was my birthplace, after all, and why should a person be an alien in the place of his birth? The whole process, particularly since I've been writing, has been to understand it historically and psychologically and culturally. It has helped a lot to understand the waves of people who have come into the central valley, and how it took shape as a place, and how that relates to the rest of the state. I have spent most of my life traveling up and down California, so I feel pretty much at home here now. This is my stomping ground."

I ask him how long this has been going on, this sense of region. From the way he talks it sounds more recent than other features of his identity —the ethnic, the artistic, the political.

"Three or four years," he says, "perhaps even five. In the mid-seventies I felt something fundamental changing in the so-called Chicano movement and in the country. It was a time to reappraise reality. I found that the whole idea of California was very real to me, and it was a continuing reality, something that did not go away. And I saw this as a positive thing, something I wanted to relate to as a writer. You can't tell the story of the whole world, though I know some people who try. I prefer to concentrate on California. If I can explain this much, it is something. There is a lot to explain, you know. It's a huge story and I think it is an unfinished story. I really get the sense that there is a lot more to happen, very basic stuff, in this state. In a very funda-mental way, we are still pioneers. East meets west here in a very fundamental way, and we are still pioneers at that. The whole Chicano experience is a part of the pioneering thing. You just barely begin to relate to the land, then you stake a claim, then you find it gets to be a reality, a place, a state of being. Of course that has been going on for a while, in terms of Spanish California and all that. But it is still in its first stages. What's a hundred years? What's a hundred and fifty or two hundred? It's nothing."

Two hundred years of Hispanic presence in California. "If I can explain this much . . ."

I know of no one before him who has tried, in quite his way, to convey the range and uniqueness of this experience from what you might call "the inside." Perhaps only a Yaqui with a lifetime supply of cigars would attempt such a thing. It is bold and ambitious, yet not an improbable vision, considering the ways in which his life and his work, in some ongoing interplay, are already giving shape to it. The very fact that he has located his home and his theater company in an old mission town puts him in touch with the original artifacts of Mexican California. They are physically right around the corner, and he uses them. He stages plays in the chapel and on the mission grounds and in the streets of the town.

Earlier Luis had told me how his first impressions of the legendary bandits came from men like his father, sitting around the labor camps in the agricultural valleys, swapping stories, bits of lore passed along through the decades and the generations.

"There was still a fairly strong oral tradition while I was growing up. The young kids would be invited to kind of listen—not speak, just listen —and the older people would be constantly discussing the history. So they'd be comparing notes about Joaquin Murietta and Vasquez and others. We were working in areas where these men had ridden. It was a historical region. The farmworkers gave that as a bonus to their kids. At the very least, they could talk about the history of the area."

Now his workroom is filled with pictures of the mustachioed and fierce-eyed Tiburcio Vasquez. He is immersed in a play about this man whose life began at the very end of the mission period and in many ways epitomizes the Chicano predicament in the years before and after state-hood. Born in Monterey in 1835, Vasquez came to maturity while California was entering the Union. His flamboyant career, like Murietta's, was linked to a time when landed families were losing everything— power, dignity, self-respect—to the inexorable tide of manifest destiny pouring toward them over the Sierras and sailing around the Horn. On the run from the age of sixteen, Vasquez has been variously described as a public menace, a splendid horseman, a daring and romantic outlaw, and a symbol of resistance against the Anglo takeover of his homeland. He roamed this state from Los Angeles to Mendocino, from San Francisco to the Sierra foothills. When he was captured for the final time, and imprisoned in San Jose, thousands visited his jail—friends, enemies, curiosity seekers, admiring women. On the day he was hanged, in 1875, he carried a small crucifix to the scaffold. As the rope was slipped around his neck he spoke his final word, *"Pronto!"*

On the day we talked, the Vasquez play was still in progress. Luis, like any good writer guarding his material, wouldn't say much about how he was handling it. *Zoot Suit*, however, was another matter. At the Mark Taper Forum, where it opened early in 1978, and later at the Aquarius on Sunset Boulevard, *Zoot Suit* had broken box-office records in Los Angeles. Now the film deal seemed set, and he was hoping for the funding to put a company on the road. His most successful and prominent work to date, it is also the work that most explicitly bears out his commitment to the history of his people in this region of the world.

The numbers in L.A. were unique because the crowds attracted to the show were unique. In addition to the seasoned theatergoers from Westwood, Beverly Hills and Santa Monica, there were cab drivers and factory workers from East L.A. "We had a hell of a lot of Chicanos come in to see it," he says, "because they were ready to dress up and go to the theater. It's just that a play *for* them and *about* them had not been put there before."

Like the legend of Tiburcio Vasquez, the actual events this play is based on have not until recent years been widely discussed outside Chicano circles. Thus they too have assumed a kind of legendary quality. Just as the World War II internment smoldered for decades in the communal memory of Japanese-Americans, the Zoot Suit Riots of 1943, and the Sleepy Lagoon murder case which preceded them, have smoldered in the communal memory of Mexican-Americans. Every Japanese-American in California knows someone who spent the war years inside a fenced camp like Manzanar or Tule Luke. Every Mexican-American seems to know someone who fought against the carloads and truckloads of sailors and marines invading L.A.'s barrios in the summer of 1943. At various times both events have been written off as sad examples of panic and frustration. What they both revealed is how quickly and easily such goads as wartime panic and economic or military frustration can transmute into blatant racism. When the pressure is on, we look for scapegoats.

In 1942 in Los Angeles the Mexicans were unfortunately very handy. And the Sleepy Lagoon case was a very handy launch pad. A murder had, after all, been committed—near a gravel pit in east L.A., where a small pond had inspired a reporter to label the region and the incident with the name of a recently popular song. Moreover, two rival Chicano gangs had been involved. But what emerged from this was a kind of persecution far in excess of the crime. Though the basic facts of the killing were never determined, twelve young men were sent to prison as co-conspirators in the murder, and five others were convicted of assault. The L.A. papers used the case to stir up and then to prey upon anti-Latino feeling. Certain passages of courtroom testimony from city officials sound like something out of seventeenth-century Salem. In one version of his play, Valdez in fact tried to take some dialogue directly from trial transcripts, and early readers found it incredible. "They thought it was propaganda," he says with a grin. "So I had to change those scenes, to make it more *believable.*"

After the trial a defense committee was quickly formed. Though all the convictions were eventually reversed, the matter was still unsettled, in fact was still very much alive in the volatile racial atmosphere when the Zoot Suit Riots erupted. As with the murder that triggered the trial, the actual details of the event that sparked the riots have never been pinned down. Some say it started in a barrio saloon where Anglo sailors had come looking for women. It mushroomed into a week-long street battle, involving thousands—servicemen back from overseas or waiting to embark, and young men of Mexican descent, many of whom sported zoot suits, gaudy hipster outfits first made popular in the late 1930s by the great black bandleader Cab Calloway. In the eyes of the soldiers and sailors, zoot suits became the uniform of the enemy. As each battle raged, the police kept their distance. When the smoke cleared, only Chicanos were arrested. Meanwhile the L.A. papers cashed in again, sounding at times like a cheering section, announcing such details as the time and place, even the precise street corner, where the next collision could be expected.

The media, Valdez says now, covered these events so luridly that a national stereotype was forever imprinted in the public mind. "I really do believe," he says, "that the Sleepy Lagoon case and the Zoot Suit Riots were the starting point. *Time* magazine, *Life,* the national papers all ran big stories about pachucos, and the readers said, 'Oh, *those* are the Mexicans. They're street punks, hubcap lifters.' And that image has persisted. So I thought, hell, let's take it to the root."

Zoot Suit begins with a blown-up front page from the Los Angeles *Herald-Express* dated June 3, 1943. The headline cries out, AMERICAN BOMBER VICTIM OF JAP RAIDER. Down the right-hand column runs a story titled, GRAND JURY TO ACT IN ZOOT SUIT WAR. A knife blade slices a six-foot hole down the center of this enormous page. The sound of the slice, of thick paper tearing, and the look of the oversize blade under stage lights, is startling, a theatrical shock. For an instant that sound is allowed to hang in the air. The timing is perfect. Then a lean figure steps through the slice. He wears black shoes with riser heels, black trousers pegged at the cuff, a long gold pocket chain, a knee-length black coat with wide shoulders and fat lapels, a black wide-brim hat, and a loud pink shirt. At a cocky, defiant angle he tilts back on his bent left leg and begins to address the audience, to set the stage and set the tone.

He is El Pachuco, the voice of this drama but not the hero. The central character is Henry Reyna, caught up in the events of his time and his barrio, caught between conflicting loyalties—to family, to a code of manhood—and conflicting affections—for his Chicana sweetheart, for the Jewish woman who leads the defense committee. Reyna is the dramatic hero, while El Pachuco is a specter, a lurking presence, a dark angel. On stage he is amusing, beguiling and sinister, with a mysterious power that I begin to comprehend as Valdez peels back yet another layer of his work and thus his own life.

Luis's ethnic roots are Yaqui, mestizo. His politics began in the fields and the orchards. His home region is California. His beliefs, meanwhile, have been shaped by a long and thoughtful study of Maya and Aztec imagery, language, the surviving documents. (Menyah, his company's name, is the Maya word for work, derived from two shorter words— men, meaning to believe, to create, to do; and yah, meaning love and pain. Working, then, means believing and creating with love and pain.) El Pachuco, he tells me now, is a Mexican-American character out of the 1940s who can also be seen as an avatar of Tezcatlipoca, a figure from Aztec mythology.

With his cigar he gestures toward the poster above my head, where the pachuco strikes his pose against the concrete backdrop of L.A.'s downtown buildings.

"He is the figure of darkness," says Luis. "In Mayan, a similar figure is called Ixpalanque. According to the Mayan calendar, he is the ruler of our age right now."

"You mean, like Mephistopheles?" I ask. "Or Satan?"

"Something like that. Except that in Christian mythology, sooner or later God is supposed to triumph once and for all. The Native American mythologies are closer to the Asian view—things flow in cycles."

In the Aztec myth, Tezcatlipoca is the dark brother of the feather-headed serpent god, Quetzalcoatl. In the play, El Pachuco slides and weaves across the stage, with body language that seems expressly serpentine, speaking with what could be called a forked tongue, a slinky tempter who encourages the beleaguered young Chicanos to turn their pride and their loyalties into a self-destructive vengeance.

In the cast of mythic figures who populate Valdez's theatrical world, El Pachuco/Tezcatlipoca looms large. Standing right next to him, looming just as large, is the star of the drama they will soon be rehearsing here (for half an hour now, crews have been moving stage furniture around in the hall beyond his door)—a sixteenth century miracle play called *La Virgen de Tepeyac.* This will be the ninth year the theater company has staged the story of her four apparitions. She too has her counterpart in Aztec myth.

Again, there is a legend to be dealt with. Immediately after the Conquest in the 1520s, Spanish priests were dispatched to convert the native peoples to Catholicism. The Indians, however, were not taken seriously as human beings. They were asked to believe in the Church and also to accept their role as unenlightened and inferior underlings in the eyes of God. On December 12, 1531, an Indian named Juan Diego, only recently converted to Christianity, had a vision. He met and spoke with the Mother of God. But she was an Indian. She had all the qualities of the Virgin Mary, but her face was brown and she had come to save Mexico's Indians from spiritual annihilation, to reveal that they too were worthy in God's eyes. This vision occurred on a hill called Tepeyac, where there had once stood a shrine to Tonantzin, Aztec earth goddess, mother of mankind as well as of the sun, moon and stars. As the Virgin Mary had borne Jesus, so had Tonantzin, via a miracle of divine conception, borne the sun-god, Huitzilopochtli.

According to the legend, the Mother of God instructs Juan Diego to take the news of her appearance to the Spanish bishop and request that a temple be built in her honor. The bishop refuses to believe the story. Twice more the Virgin appears to Juan Diego, and twice more he goes to the bishop, who finally announces that if Juan has truly seen the Mother of God he should be able to prove it. The bishop makes what he thinks is an impossible demand, a bouquet of roses, which are out of season in December.

Before his final meeting with the Holy Mother, Juan Diego returns to his village, where he finds his uncle, Juan Bernardino, near death with smallpox. He tells the villagers the story of his vision, which they too refuse to believe. They grow angry because he has abandoned their traditional gods. Soon, however, the Holy Mother appears to Juan Bernardino and restores his health. Then, in her fourth appearance to Juan Diego she gives him the roses, which he joyously delivers to the bishop, who is thereby persuaded of the truth of this miracle.

In Mexico La Virgen is still the reigning saint. Her image can be found as well in many thousands of households all over California and throughout the Southwest. When Cesar Chavez and the Farmworkers' Union made their famous march from Delano to the state capitol in 1966, drawing national attention to *la causa,* the march was led by a picture of the Virgin of Guadalupe. Much more than a religious deity, for many she nourishes a complex ethnic pride. For Valdez and El Teatro, as they have incorporated her legend into their annual cycle of mystery and miracle plays, it is the story of an oppressed people finding a voice, a guiding spirit, a renewal of dignity. In the history he hopes to chart and dramatize, her legend is surely a fitting prologue. She is both saint and goddess. She is European and Indio. She is Mediterranean and she is Aztec. She is the embodiment of a uniquely mestizo energy that has been flowing back and forth across the so-called border all these years like continental holy water.

Before we leave his office, I ask Luis why the pachuco on his poster is wearing a cross around his neck. "How does this fit in, if he is the figure of darkness?"

"It is on the pachuco because he too is quasi-religious, you see. He may have been a lot of things. But at the very basis was a belief in, if nothing else, *La Virgen de Guadalupe*. There is a root to it that is really fascinating. It's a contradiction. But contradictions are real."

He reflects a moment, gazing at the poster above my head, at the gold cross around the neck of the zoot-suiter. Then he explains how this universal emblem in itself can work as the touch point, where cultures and symbologies merge.

"Remember too that the cross can be seen in so many different ways which attach to reality. The four seasons. The four directions. The tree of life Christ was hung on. In Nahuatl, the Aztec language, the cross is called *Nahui-ollin,* which means four movements. It is depicted as two horses that are hooked like this"—he holds up index fingers interlocked —"making the four points. This symbol is at the very heart of the Aztec calendar. It is the New World version of the interlocking yin and yang."

The rehearsal is called for seven o'clock. The hall is the size of a basketball court, plenty of room in here to work out choreography, block a procession. Two rows of old padded theater seats are right-angled into one corner. Sitting back in one, I watch performers wander in from the dressing rooms, a brown-robed friar, a muscular barefooted Aztec warrior wearing cape and head plumage. A handsome young fellow sits down next to me and asks if there is anything he can help me with. He carries a Polaroid. In a while he will be creeping around behind one of the scenes snapping pictures. His name is Mark, he's eighteen, and he tells me he is Luis's nephew, the son of an older brother, living here in San Juan for about six months and doing odd jobs around the teatro. He is one of half a dozen Valdezes among the gathering crowd. Luis's younger sister, Cindy, is performing the title role in the play. Another sister, Socorro, is directing. Two of his sons, Anahuac, age nine, and Kinan, seven, are playing on the theater seats, laughing, jabbering. At one point Socorro the director has to become Socorro the auntie and order them outside. You don't usually see kids scampering around before a dress rehearsal starts, yet no one is much troubled by this. It happens most nights, a little family ritual. Thirty minutes later the boys are back. Their mother, Lupe, has arrived, and they are sitting in the seats, behaving themselves, like kids in church, just barely holding it in.

Earlier, talking about his family, Luis had said, "The little kids growing up are a very important point of reference. They're innocent, they're just starting out. If you're having some kind of personal crisis, they know nothing about it. They're just in there laughing. That really puts the correct perspective on things. We're all living life here, and no single day is any more important than another, really, when you get down to it."

For Luis, living life in the family context is extremely important, the extended family of theater people, as well as the blood kin who are nearby. His parents both reside in San Juan Bautista now. His wife, Lupe, helps manage the company's business. It was she who handled the purchase of this one-time packing shed, talked to the agents, negotiated the price. There are cousins around, nephews and in-laws. Luis's younger brother, Steve, is musical director for the Virgin play.

His sister Socorro is walking toward me now. We met briefly in the office, and I've been waiting for the chance to talk. This is the third season she has directed the play. Last year she toured Europe as artistic director with the overseas company. Now she has a few minutes before the rehearsal starts. She's a small woman, under five feet, wears spike heels for the extra altitude, walks and sits with an urgent momentum, supple as a leaping trout, with that kind of compact energy. Her skin is dark and glows with a charged vitality that makes me recall what Luis said about his father's lessons in Yaqui pride. She carries a cigarette, puffs frequently, while her eyes dart toward the performers assembling around a wooden platform, dancers, musicians with hide drums, the chorus of village women.

I ask how she got started in theater, what her background has been.

"You're looking at it," she says. "When I was in high school in San Jose, I started traveling down to Fresno on weekends to work with the teatro. By the time I finished school Luis had moved to San Juan so I came straight here. That was almost exactly ten years ago. Anything I know about theater I learned right here, working with Luis."

In this annual show there are slight variations from year to year. With a grin she tells me that this time more women will be featured. "It's a play about *La Virgen*, after all. She's a woman. I feel that adding more women to the cast fits in with that."

This December, for the first time, they are playing two nights in

English. "So more people can understand what's going on," she says. "Not just the Anglos, but the Chicanos who don't know Spanish."

She and a translator have brought it over from the Spanish-language version Luis wrote several years back. That version, in turn, grew from a four-hundred-year-old Mexican play based on the legend.

"One year," Socorro says, "we tried a few speeches in Nahuatl. People in the audience got such strange and bewildered looks on their faces, we stopped doing that. It's a hard language to learn, so many variant dialects. I'm not even sure now that we had it right." She laughs and takes a puff. "An Aztec in the audience would probably have been the most bewildered person of all."

The room is thick with performers now. She looks at the clock and tells me to be sure and come back to see this play at the mission. "We have done it in other buildings," she says. "But it never is the same. Inside the church there are the chandeliers, the old altar with the religious figures up behind the action. One scene is set in the bishop's house in Mexico, which would have been made of adobe. You don't have to create a set for that. The whole church is made of adobe. It all fits. You couldn't design a better setting for this play."

She is striding toward the company, who have gathered around a stepped platform. Socorro climbs to the top step, again for the altitude, sits there with her hands on spread knees, her cigarette smoke floating, and takes command of the waiting throng.

"All right, all right. Tonight is the night we run through this whole thing in English."

There are half-serious groans from those with speaking parts.

"I still have lines to learn."

"I don't even know it in Spanish yet."

With a challenging glint in her eye Socorro says, "All you people with your highly developed bilingual skills shouldn't have any trouble speaking the English language. . . . Then tomorrow night we'll see if we can do it in French."

"*Sacre bleu,*" mutters one of the Aztec warriors.

"*Sacre bleu,*" echoes Socorro with a husky laugh.

Five nights later I come back to see the production, which is preceded by an invocation on the brick patio outside the mission church. In the frosty air, Indian women and feathered warriors dance around a goblet of incense that stands burning on the bricks. The men wear capes, high headdresses, loincloths, no shoes. One carries a cross decorated with flowers. The women wear short-sleeved woven tunics of red and purple stripes. Tom-toms, gourds, and mandolins provide a pulsing music for the dance, which Luis tells me is of Aztec origin.

"*Danzas de la conquista,*" he says. Dances of the conquest. "Which of course means, *Danzas de la reconquista.*" By blending native forms with Catholic ritual, the Mexican Indians were able to blend their power with the invaders' power, recover some identity, and not be conquered in spirit.

"Of course the reconquest," he adds, as the dance ends and the audience starts to troop inside, "is really the conquest of oneself."

I have to leave him then and join the crowd, which is about half Chicano and half Anglo, filling up the long rows of old, wooden, movable pews. Whether by accident or by design, we have ten minutes to sit here before the play begins. I suspect it is by design. Something about the waiting prepares us for what's to come. I am here, I think, to watch a drama—which means, at one level or another, an entertainment. Something about sitting in a church stirs other expectations. The coolness and the quiet, accented by low mutters and the shuffling of feet across the bricks, this stirs up reverence, a buzzing revery. I am not a Catholic. But the inside of a Catholic church will always work its sensory magic, especially these mission churches that carry a two-hundred-year layer of prayers and worshippings, and also resonate of Mexico and Spain and the Moorish cities farther east where certain curves and arches come from. Mass has been said on this site every Sunday since the mission was founded a hundred and eighty-two years ago. The floor beneath us is the original brick, polished by thousands of knees and feet and sandals and shoes. The outer walls are a yard thick. Square pillars of plastered adobe, connected by arches, line both sides of the center aisle. Above the pillars the ceiling is supported by dozens of parallel hand-hewn beams. At the rear, above the weather-eaten entrance door, there is a wooden balcony with a balustrade where the Virgin will make her first appearance. At the front, above the altar, carved wooden figures of saints are set in backlit alcoves. The walls of the church, recently restored, are painted with earthy rusts, sandy yellows, pale blues. These colors tint thin floral garlands twining up the pillars, across the arches, twining along beneath dark oils that depict the twelve shadowy stages of the cross.

Two miles away, on Highway 101, the double-truck diesels are thundering along, hauling cable reels and engine parts from San Jose south to Oxnard, from Santa Barbara north to Marin. On their way to the next Travelodge or Howard Johnson's, high-speed travelers listen to the talk shows and KCBS News, as I will do on my high-speed journey home to Santa Cruz later tonight. But here in the cool peace of this adobe interior, the very shape of the place takes us quietly to the eighteenth century, while the play could take us even farther back, into the Middle Ages, and the early days of European drama, when it was staged in the churches, at the altars, the priests acting out high moments in the lives of Jesus Christ and his disciples.

The prologue of quiet is broken by a burst of voices, two dozen of them, entering from the rear. Villagers and warriors fill this space from bricks to ceiling beams with fervor and exuberance. This is a tribute, after all, a celebration. It starts and ends with joyful praise. The song, in Spanish, is long and purposely repetitive, casting a spell for the audience as well as the performers. They use this song for charging up the atmosphere, and then commence a slow, intense procession down the main aisle. It is like a wedding, or a coronation. In a second grouping, twenty paces behind, come three friars and the Spanish bishop, played by Abel Franco, a Chicano actor from Los Angeles who had a key role in *Zoot Suit*. He recently finished performing in *Death of a Salesman* with another Latino theater group, and he has come to San Juan for this production. Franco is very good. He is a veteran. In his very carriage he makes this bishop a man of power, who is awesome, yet vulnerable. Watching his entrance I know he is an actor, I can enumerate his credits and admire his craft. At the same time, as I watch his brown robes, and the slow procession with his friars toward the crucifix and its field of saints, this all begins to slide toward some other kind of ceremony.

When the entire company has reached the altar, a few lines are exchanged—this happens to be a night when the dialogue is all in Spanish—then Juan Diego, bearded, sandaled, dressed in peasant whites, hurries back to the center of the church, as if on his way home. The audience surrounds him here. This is theater-in-the-round, or more precisely theater-in-the-shape-of-a-cross. Where the main aisle and a transverse aisle intersect, he falls to the bricks as if struck down. When he looks up, we all look up with him, discovering as he does that an apparition is hovering above the balustrade on the balcony behind us, backlit so that the entire figure is framed by a bright aura. Then full light from the front illuminates the shimmering gold robe and white mantle of the Holy Mother with the brown *Indio* face. The circular aura has become a large halo of woven straw. She is luminous, stands with hands clasped like a statue of the Madonna, and she speaks gently to Juan Diego, telling him who she is and why she has appeared.

When she appears the second time she is much closer to us, on a pedestal set up in one arm of the transverse aisle, six feet from where I sit. Lit only by candles, dressed in her silky garments, she possesses an irresistible radiance, which is not the result of makeup. The lovely, dark-eyed mestizo face seems lit from within, so lovely, so beatific, at this range so strangely real and physical yet ethereal and afloat with saintly grace, it would take no effort at all for me to join Juan Diego and throw myself at her feet. The effect she creates is echoed by the chorus of village women. Carrying candles, they have circled this platform to sing in homage. Their voices are strong, full of reverence, with that haunting, gripping note you hear in blues and flamenco and in ranchero songs from Mexico: the deep lament, the near-breaking in the voice that runs like counterpoint against the other note which is the deathless yearning of the spirit and the appetite for life.

The play follows the legend scene by scene, most of them staged where the aisles cross. The climax, when the Virgin makes her fourth and final appearance, is staged at the altar, where the whole cast has gathered. Juan Diego is there with the miraculous out-of-season bouquet of red roses, which he presents to the astonished clergyman. Someone cries, *"Los indios tambien son hijos de Dios!"* (The Indians also are children of God!) Instantly the scene explodes with sound and light and color, a song of triumph, a dance of joy. Surrounded by men and women of the village, *La Virgen* is lifted high by four feathered warriors. Directly behind and above her, among the old wooden statues, is the crucifix—for Christians, a symbol of sacrifice and redemption; in Aztec imagery, a symbol of the world's interlocking opposites.

It brings to mind El Pachuco, who wears that cross on the *Zoot Suit* poster because he believes in, "if nothing else, *La Virgen . . .*" I am thinking that, although he has no role in this miracle play, if La Virgen is visible, El Pachuco isn't far away. He is the archetypal character who coexists with her in the mythic theater of Luis Valdez like yang and yin —Tezcatlipoca, brother of struggle, figure of darkness; Tonantzin, mother of compassion, figure of light.

A cloth painting of the Virgin has appeared at the altar, and all the performers—the clergy, the warriors, the villagers—are backing down the aisle in a slow, reverse processional paying homage before it, chanting, *"Adios, adios! Adios, Santisimo Altar!"* (Farewell, farewell. Farewell, most holy altar.)

The words are European. The gesture, the stepping backward, is Indian, out of a tradition that says you don't turn your back on an altar until you have left the place of worship.

Cindy Valdez, who played *La Virgen*, has removed her mantle and joined the others. Socorro Valdez is among them too, Director, singer and dancer in the chorus, she now reveres the Holy Mother with her full voice, her humble bow. It is a powerful moment, a dramatic moment that is much more than drama. I came in here expecting theater, and have seen them take theater back to its origin, and beyond—to a Catholic ritual that predates the arrival of Catholicism on this continent, tapping into a source of ancient power at large in North America for many centuries and contained somehow, carried into modern times, carried into the middle of high-tech California through this simple holy legend of the Virgin of Guadalupe.

When they reach the entrance of the church the performers stop and form two lines inside the doorway, so that we members of the audience must pass between them on our way out. The triumphal chant continues, backed by tom-toms and mandolins. *"Adios, adios! Adios, Santisimo Altar!"* Again it is hypnotic, again it casts a spell, or extends the spell cast when they first danced in. I pass Socorro. She is dressed like an Indian woman from some village in central Mexico. Her eyes are blazing with a spiritual rush. She stands next to her brother Luis, who has joined this reception line made up of blood kin and the theatrical family. All their hands are joined. His baritone is booming out. His eyes too are blazing, with that same rush, which is partly the thrill of drama, and partly the ritual fire this miracle ignites, some kind of Mexican American Christianity, or pre-Christian fire imported from Mexico, that rekindled Aztec and Maya wisdom mingling in there with the grandfather's Yaqui pride.

Three Women
in the North Country

North of Sacramento and its suburbs the world thins out. People thin out, while the mountains get thicker, gradually merging up around Enterprise and Whiskeytown to make the Trinity Alps and the Lower Cascades. Above Sacramento you don't hit another major urban zone until you cross all of Oregon and reach the Columbia River, six hundred miles away. It is the part of California the Spaniards barely reached and never settled, and it is still a stronghold for pioneers and ranchers, dope-barons, survivalists, renegades and wilderness buffs, folks in search of their numerous versions of elbow room.

The Sacramento *Bee* carries a daily section of news from this region. The section is titled "Superior California," meaning that part of the state which, if you are looking at a wall map, lies above or higher than the rest. Roughly, the northern third. People up here savor the double meaning in that word "Superior." Either way you take it, when you are traveling through this country it is not hard to understand why petitions circulate from time to time demanding that California be divided in half. Across the middle of the state you will hear citizens worrying about where to draw that line. Up this way they have no such problem. Wherever the mythical line might be, we are unmistakably north of it now, and the distance to the palm-lined boulevards of Beverly Hills and Santa Monica can't be measured in miles—unless perhaps you are measuring miles of water pipe. There are northerners who say water pipe is the only possible connection between these two dissimilar realms.

It happens that I know three women who, for their various reasons, have chosen to live in Superior California. I am looping through the northern counties to visit them one at a time, to see what their lives are like and talk to them about this part of the world. They do not know one another. They arrived here from different directions, and they each live in a singular spot, *a place* with its own mystique and microclimate.

I am stopping first in Sierra County, where Marlea Berutti lives, and she will tell me about a symbolic battle waged not long ago when the people who own Disneyland picked out a prime slice of wilderness—a virgin lake and an unspoiled mountain—as the site for a new, high-country entertainment empire. It would have brought wealth to the county's coffers. It would have been to Sierra County what the Pipeline has been to Alaska. But the planning commission was troubled by the Environmental Impact Report, and the Board of Supervisors, against formidable lobbying, decided that some things are just not worth the price. By a narrow vote they rejected the plan.

"I saw it as a life-and-death struggle," Marlea says. "There was a large group of citizens who were ready to take torches in there and burn the whole area down before they'd see Disney get their hands on it. I wouldn't go that far. But I wouldn't want to continue living here either if Disney came in."

She has spent her life in these mountains. Her world—this county —in look, in spirit, in density, is far closer to Oregon or Nevada than it will ever be to the city-states farther south. Most of the county lies above five thousand feet. In square miles it is slightly larger than Orange, down in the subtropics below Tehachapi Pass, where Disneyland is located, and where the county population is close to two million. According to the 1980 census count, the population of Sierra County is 3,069, a number that is slowly rising, like every other number in the state. It will never become an Orange County, if only because winter temperatures here can drop to forty below. But old-time residents can be heard grumbling about real estate adventurers, thickening traffic, strange sounds in the night, and a steady decline in the size of deer herds that have for uncountable centuries used Sierra Valley as a stopping place and watering hole.

"When I was a girl," Marlea says, "we made a yearly trek to see the deer migrations. In the early spring they pass through the valley. A few will stay, but mostly they move on up into the higher mountains. In the fall they come down, stay in the valley awhile, then head across Long Valley and down Red Rock and the Pine Nut Range, on out into the deserts east of here. In those days there would be three, four, maybe five hundred deer at a time moving through. This spring the most any of us saw was forty. Hunters have taken a lot of them. And then, of course, those three years of drought took an enormous toll. But you know, the road-kills account for a great many more than what the hunters take. It's not unusual for John and I to drive from Truckee to the ranch and see nineteen or twenty deer on the road at night. I drive thirty-five because I don't want to kill one, and I don't want to *get* killed. I don't want to have my car destroyed hitting an animal that size. And then, in the dark and on a curve, here will come some guy in his pickup truck whipping past us at sixty miles an hour."

At Donner Pass in early April the snow is heaped along both sides of the road, thrown high and cleanly edged by plough blades. Elevation at the pass is seventy-two hundred feet. From there you drop down to Truckee, a weather-battered and venerable railroad town, where the snow is scattered and murky with tire-scum. Ski-laden cars on their way to Squaw Valley and Lake Tahoe turn south at Truckee. I turn north, through twenty miles of unbroken pine forest, over another high pass with its road banks of newly plowed snow, curving down, until the white ridges open out into this astonishing Alpine pasture called Sierra Valley.

In eons past it was a companion lake to Tahoe. Now it is a broad field some thirty miles long and fifteen wide, surrounded by peaks that catch and fend off the heaviest snows, so that even after one more late and unexpected storm, the fields are clear, green, and grassy—a bowl of springtime in the midst of the prolonged mountain winter.

Villages dot the valley—Beckwourth, Sattley, Chilcoot, and Loyalton. Outposts is what they are, small clusters with Victorian-style ranch houses, metal roofs built steep for snow, new barns next to elderly and eroded barns, horse trailers, and lots of cattle.

Most of the valley is semimarshy grassland where cattle roam and graze. A corridor of pine trees sticks out into this meadow, like a long pier into what used to be the lake. Marlea tells me the trees grew from a tongue of alluvial soil, topsoil, and half a mountainside that spilled down into the lake from the nearest canyon. In amongst these trees stands the house she and her husband, John, designed. They worked on it together, and continue to work on it. The knotty pine siding still glistens. Their talk is filled with the plans of what remains to be done inside and out—the finishing work in two upstairs rooms, the turkey yard, garden fencing, the new corral with its narrow run for funneling cows toward the squeeze chute.

John is a burly bear of a man, ruddy in the face and thick all over. Marlea's skin is fair, and her bones are small, like a deer's. Next to John she seems that much smaller, and more delicate, though "delicate" is not the word to describe her. Or, not the only word. She is both delicate and hardy. Slender and tough. In one breath she will talk about her sense of stewardship, her desire "to nurture some small piece of this land I live in and let the cycles of nature keep flowing." With the next breath she will be laughing about the steer that nearly ripped her open.

"Almost everybody has war wounds if they've been in the cattle business for very long."

"How about you?" I ask.

"I have a shirt that's torn across the belly where a horn just came *that close*. I wasn't hurt. But I save the shirt as a souvenir."

With John she works this ranch, the chickens and the rabbits they raise to eat, and the small herd of commercial cattle they raise to sell. She wears jeans and long-sleeved shirts and rides a palomino quarter horse. She can train horses, and she can school dogs to work with horses when it's time to move the cattle. We are hiking out through the long stand of pine trees toward some of their grazing land, beyond the house and out-buildings, and she tells me about the animals they have bred.

"We work with a three-way cross," she says. "Hereford, Angus, and Durham, which gives us the best incidence of hybrid vigor. Genetically you want the hardiness of the Hereford. But in the summer you want the black skin of the Angus. They don't have the fly problem, and they don't have the frost-burn on their udders in the winter. The shorthorn gives you more milk than either the Hereford or the Angus, and with more milk you can raise stronger calves."

When I ask her how many cattle they have at the moment, she gets cagey. Though she has already described what a pleasure it is to ride out every day and check the herd, she now says she isn't quite sure how many cows are there. Later on, with a laugh, she will tell me that this is a question a cattle person never asks. You may have a very good idea about how many animals your neighbor owns, but you would never pin him down on the subject.

She says, "Oh . . . somewhere between fifty and seventy. Unless I sat down and counted up each little group, I wouldn't know for certain. Somewhere in there. We are going to build up to between seventy-five and a hundred, which by the way is the size of most herds. Raising cattle is still the biggest industry in this state, and you will find that most of the ranches have under a hundred head. . . ."

"What's that?" I say, surprised, even mildly alarmed. "Did you say biggest? You mean, bigger than oil? Bigger than real estate?"

"In the area of farming and ranching . . ."

"Agriculture? I thought cotton was the biggest. . . ."

"Check it out," she says.

I do. Later. Back home. And she is right.[15] More than right. State-wide, calves and cattle comprise a $2 billion crop. If you add beef and dairy cattle together, you have roughly 25 percent of California's rural produce—bigger than cotton, grapes, and lettuce combined—a good part of it parcelled out among small herds like the one Marlea and John are gradually building up. If you add in the hides sold for leather, the manure sold for fertilizer, the pasture leasing, the slaughtering and butchering, the feed that pours through the great feed lots down near the border in Imperial County, and a couple of thousand vets on hand to keep the animals healthy and alert, you have a formidable industry that plays almost no part these days in the public imagery, either outside, or inside, the state. Why? The usual reason. Most of us live in towns and cities near the coast, where cars and tourists far outnumber every form of livestock.

Marlea knows that other side of western living well enough to know what works in her life and what does not. She has lived in San Francisco ("Six weeks was all I could take"). She has lived in Sacramento ("I didn't last much longer there"). She has lived in Reno. And she lived in and around Lake Tahoe during the years when it transformed from a summer resort to a year-round recreation area.

"For fourteen years I worked in motion picture theaters there. I worked up from usherette until I owned four theaters of my own. For a while I was very intensely a businesswoman. The fancy clothes, the fancy house, the fancy cars. But it didn't work. Pretty soon I couldn't get away from it. This is what happens. You become what you do."

Tahoe is where she started life, on the Nevada side of the lake, just forty miles south of where she lives today. Incline Village, her home-town, is now a major ski resort. When she was a child it was literally a village, with few all-year residents. Her father had bought some land there, after leaving Wyoming and the huge Mormon clan his parents had spawned. The family renegade, he came looking for space, and found it. Marlea remembers that her closest neighbor, in the winter-time, was seven miles away. "Where they have the main lifts now and the big downhill runs, my brother and I used to walk up and watch the beavers building dams."

In the world of her childhood there were more animals than people —beavers, coyotes, wolves and mountain lions. She fed raccoons off the back porch. Black bears tipped over the garbage. Mule-tail deer made trails across her father's property.

There was the unforgettable winter of 1951–52 when they were snowed in for twelve weeks, without electricity or phone.

And there was Tahoe.

"I really value the fact that my father trusted me implicitly on the lake. I'd paddle around in a canoe or a kayak. I was all by myself from the time I was real little. And he trusted my own judgment to dictate when I had gone out too far. He never seemed to doubt it at all, and I never got into trouble. It would have bothered me enormously if he had hovered over me. He just taught me what to watch for, the blue line across the lake that indicates the waves are going to start. He taught me that it normally comes up at three o'clock. If you're not in by three, be close to shore where you *can* get in if you need to."

She sees some inevitable link between the waters of Lake Tahoe—which was in her youth a kind of mentor, teaching her to honor all natural forces—and the waters that surround her now, some visible, some not so visible, in the onetime lake-bed where she and John have their house and ranch.

"I need water nearby, and there is no year-round stream through here. When we first moved onto the ranch, I felt very lost. Then I discovered these springs, and that made all the difference. I walk out here nearly every morning. It is my own form of meditation. We learned, you see, that these springs were sacred to the Washo. This was their territory, through here and all down through the Tahoe basin. The last of the Washo medicine men, a fellow named Herman Sams who was a friend of John's, used to walk across Sierra Valley every full moon to drink at these springs."

We have stopped, past the pines, where the fields open out and you can see for miles across the broad silent grasslands. The ground is so wet on this side of the valley that John and Marlea, in order to keep cattle at this altitude through the winter, have to find pasturage for most of them on the warmer, eastern side. So today there are no animals nearby. Just these two mossy ponds each the size of a small swimming pool, green with algae and gently bubbling.

"These springs," she says, "had meaning for a whole race of people who are now gone. It's a sacred place for John and me too. We keep this whole back acreage as natural as we can. The only thing we do is take out the dead or beetle-infested logs. Otherwise it's still the way it has always been. The Queen Anne's lace that the Washo used to eat bulbs from, in order to stay alive in certain years, and the wild onions—everything that has ever grown still grows. I can feel them out here, the people who came before us. And I can feel the waters that filled this valley before the Washo came. Up on that mountainside you can see the waterline where the level of the lake used to be. It's a rusty line, like iron, etched right into the granite, four hundred feet up the slope."

She talks reverently about the cycles of things, the seasons, which are specific and extreme up here, and those longer mountainous rhythms through geological time.

"It is easy to get lost in the day-to-day busyness of life. Up here on the ranch I can stay in touch with the things that are most important to me. There's a lot of hard, physical work. It's one of those jobs you have to love, in order to do it, because you don't make that much money. The beef prices you see in Safeway do not reflect what the small rancher gets, at all. But raising cattle, it allows you to live a certain kind of life."

This idea, or ideal, is still talked about a lot out West—the yearning for some authentic contact with land and landscape. It was not invented in California, but it is central to the California dream. Marlea of course is not just talking or dreaming. She has found a way to do it, and in that sense she is a good deal more Californian than many of the people I know. So I am rather startled, when I ask her if she thinks of herself as a Californian, and she immediately shakes her head.

"Why not?"

"I'll give you an example of why not. I took a trip through Texas and Oklahoma and Missouri and part of Arkansas one year with my step-mother, and I found myself quick to tell her relatives that I come from Nevada. California had such a negative connotation."

"For them? Or for you?"

"For them. They really look at you askance. 'Why aren't you driving a Cadillac?' they say, or, 'Do you really spend all your time surfboard-ing?' In their eyes it is all frivolity, it is Hollywood, and I didn't really care to start explaining it."

"So you still identify with Nevada?"

"California is too big. There is too much of it. I'm not sure I can relate to anything that size. But I'll tell you what I do have—a very strong regional identification that has nothing to do with states or politi-cal boundaries of any kind. My region is this mountain range, the Sierra Nevada. This is where I come from. I go down to Sacramento or San Francisco, I can't wait to get back up here. I need this elevation. I feel best when I'm at this altitude. I have lived essentially all of my life at over five thousand feet. Most of it over six thousand."

I have never heard anyone say this before. I don't know many people who *could* say it. I look at her, at the steady blue eyes, and I see that I was wrong when I said she resembles a deer. She is small-boned, but not that gentle. Her size is deceptive in the way the size of certain trim and vigorous mountain creatures can be deceptive. A puma, for example. She writes poetry. She also thrives on dry, cold mountain air. She keeps a pistol in her car and in her saddlebag.

We leave the old springs bubbling quietly at the bottom of the invisible lake and start back toward the house. You have to stay right on the path. Anywhere not packed down by steady use, you would sink in up to your ankles.

"Silt," she says. "Be careful. This time of year there's no bottom to it."

The Feather River curves along Sierra Valley's upper edge, and Highway 70 follows the river, first the Middle Fork, then the North. I soon leave the snow country behind, swinging down through Twain and Rich Bar, through the Feather's magnificent gorge, on my way toward the central valley, the eternal flat place, the long skillet in the center of the state. But this time, before I reach the true lowlands, I turn north again. Where the Feather empties into one of the lakes backed up behind Oroville Dam, I start climbing again, toward Paradise.

I am climbing one of the long ridges that finger down beside the Sierra foothills, parallel ridges that are partly of the forested mountains and partly of the arid, unforested valley floor below. As you near the town, pines and firs begin to mingle with the thriving fruit trees. Ellen Ferber tells me that the difference in altitude makes all the difference in climate. Summers can be intolerable in the valley, where she works, and actually balmy up here at seventeen hundred feet, where the town is set.

"I figure that's why they call it Paradise," she says, with a wary grin that tells me not to make a comment about the name.

"If you want to know the truth," she tells me later, "I have had it with Paradise jokes. When I first moved out here, I used to write to my friends back East and tell them where I was living, and here would come this barrage of what they thought were original gags."

"For instance."

"Okay. How about, 'Gee, I didn't know Paradise had a zip code.' "

"That's not funny."

"Of course it's not funny. If there is a curse on Paradise, that is it. Dumb jokes."

The name goes back to the late days of the Gold Rush, when so many names carried the high hopes and the big promise. Nowadays it does not promise gold and riches. It offers shade, and altitude, and cooler air. This has become a popular retirement town. Many mobile home communities are clustered up and down the ridge, along with bungalows and cottages. No buildings can be seen above the treetops. Former engineers and sales reps from L.A. mingle with college students who drive down the hill each day to the campus in Chico, twelve miles west, where Ellen teaches.

Into this world she has brought an uncommon history. The typical point of departure for someone moving to Paradise is Southern California. Ellen came here from Connecticut. What's more, she moved from the East directly into a rural district. Most Easterners heading for this coast move into San Francisco or Berkeley or L.A. or San Diego. If they are drawn to more open country, the urge is usually a few years taking shape. Ellen bypassed the cities. From Storrs she moved to this two-acre spread on the outskirts of Paradise. That was eight years ago, and she is still making discoveries, still surprised by the look and feel of the sky, the space, the foliage and the soil.

"When I first got here I was amazed that I could actually see the soil. For you that seems crazy. But remember, I grew up in Manhattan, where the streets cover everything. And in New England, where I went to school and started teaching, I never saw soil. It rains so much, everything is covered by some sort of vegetation. So I get here to Paradise and I see soil for the first time in my life. I mean, large bare places in the ground. And it looked wounded to me. I was asking myself, What have they *done* to this place? The earth was so exposed, so dry and seeming to cry out for water. I was reluctant to step on these places, or walk on them."

"Like some raw patch on a dog's coat," I offer, "where the skin is showing through."

She cringes, then laughs. "Oh, that's awful. But, yes, exactly. And you want to pat around it, not *on* it. Those spots needed to heal. They were wounds in need of healing. That is how it looked to me. I had never lived without rain, you see. In New England it rains all the time. People who have never been West really do not grasp what it means to be without rain. There is so much in the Northeast, no one needs to irrigate. Until I came to Paradise, I had never seen a rainbird sprinkler."

"You can't be serious," say I, who have never visited New England; say I, after a lifetime in this region, where the rainbird sprinkler is an unquestioned feature of every lawn and public park.

"I am totally serious," Ellen says. "Until I came to Paradise I had never seen a hose that was permanently attached to an outside faucet."

Now here, I am thinking, is a fresh and necessary perspective. Who else in California would ever look to the lowly garden faucet for an insight into Western living?

Water, I soon learn, is often on Ellen's mind. Len Fulton, the man she lives with, is president of the local water district. He also owns a press called Dustbooks and publishes *The International Directory of Little Magazines and Small Presses*, which he and Ellen edit together. But up here in Paradise, people don't pay too much attention to little magazines and small presses. He is known locally as the renegade voice of the Irrigation District, the man who prefers underground aquifers— rather than more and larger dams—for water storage, the man who voted against a move to increase board members' pay from $35 to $50 per meeting. I suspect that the number of people in town who have actually read one of his publications would fit comfortably into this living room, where we sit surrounded by shelves and heaps of antholo- gies and quarterlies. They spill over onto stacks of irrigation pamphlets, dam-site proposals, bulletins on state flood-control policy, and back issues of *Western Water*.

At the university, Ellen's field is literature. She can get passionate about both subjects. Rhetoric, or rainfall. She throws her hands around, and her eyes flash. She is a small, energetic woman with dark curly hair and an explosive smile. As we talk about the differences in water tables, she is living evidence that there can also be a clear and vivid difference between people from the East and people from the West. She is capable of a passionate expressiveness you seldom hear among Westerners. To the subject of water or the lack thereof, she brings more vocal anima- tion than you are ever likely to hear expressed out loud by a native.

"Before I came out here," she exclaims, "I thought all of California was one long beach!"

With a broad sweep of her arm she describes the size of this beach.

"I thought anywhere I landed I would be able to see the Pacific. But I saw more ocean when I was living in New England than I have ever seen since I moved to Paradise. The fact is, California is not one long beach. It is one big desert! The whole state! And, like a desert, at certain times of the year you get rainfall. Then it pops out with all this marvelous green you're seeing on the hills right now, and all these massive colors."

Her arm flies out again to describe the hillsides, and from her sud- den smile you could believe the rain-fed colors are right in the room with us.

"But don't let that fool you," she says. "The basic condition is desert."

Then she laughs. A sly, conspiratorial look comes into her eye. Her voice softens. "Up here in northern California, people get very upset if you tell them they are living in a desert. But it's true."

"Hold it," says Len, whose home state is Vermont and who reached

Paradise a dozen years ago, by way of Wyoming and Berkeley. "Hold on now," he says, with his ironic grin. "Up this way, we are thought to be living in the *wet* part."

"Not to me," says Ellen. "The other thing about the Northeast, not only does water fall from the sky, instead of having to be forcibly extracted from somewhere, the air itself is full of water. Humidity is a fact of life. You never feel dried out. People who go East from this region find the humidity oppressive. They will find it hard to breathe, like they are being put through that water torture where you're perpetually having to breathe through wet handkerchiefs. Out here I am still very conscious of the fact that if I breathe through my mouth three or four times, the whole inside of my mouth turns dry."

"Does that mean you want to go back?" I ask her. "Could you go back, say, to New York City?"

"Oh God," she murmurs, with a sigh of genuine ambivalence. "I keep thinking I could say yes. I always love it when I'm there. I still have violent emotional ties to New York. I am one of those people who goes to see Woody Allen's *Manhattan* just for the opening scenes. Then I can get up and leave.

"And I cry," she says. "Just show me Central Park in the snow. That is why I know I could never live in San Francisco or L.A. I would always be comparing them to New York. Paradise is so totally different, it doesn't compete, because it doesn't compare. It is a whole other kind of life. And I long ago opted for one or the other extreme. Here, you see, I can roll out of bed and into the outdoors, naked, if I want to, it doesn't matter, because there's nobody around. I can go roll in the grass. I have a kind of privacy that I love. Although I confess this is another thing that has been a little hard getting used to, the whole difference between indoor and outdoor consciousness. In California you can really plan on spending a considerable amount of your time outside. Even if you are not athletic. In New England, and certainly in New York, you take for granted that outdoors is something between one building and another, and you plan to spend most of your time enclosed. Inside spaces are designed to hold people for long periods of time, together. Here, they are designed as spaces you move through or come back to, to do something before you go somewhere else. It is more than climate. It is a whole way of thinking that exists here because of the climate."

She talks fast, and I am listening closely, don't want to interrupt, because she is catching hold of something here, positioned as she is, a woman from the East, in the heart of the West, in an old high-country town called Paradise, with a sense for both the East and the West, and still loving both.

"The truth is," she says, "I am still somewhere in between. Years ago it occurred to me that the world is divided into two kinds of people, those who see the way Eliot Porter does, and those who see the way Ansel Adams does. Most Californians are congenitally Ansel Adams. Now, I love what he can do with the contours of a whole mountainside. But meanwhile I move one little vinca plant into one little hole in a brick in the retaining wall, and it makes me extremely happy to do that. I love the way plants respond to sunlight here. Plants you would have indoors and hover over and worry about all the time in New England, for instance a fuchsia that you would always be moving into a more favorable light—here you watch it grow ten feet tall. It's nice. It's still a bit like science fiction to me. I am still a putterer in the New England sense. I can't envision changing my environment in large ways, only in small ways. I have what I think of as a sort of Eliot Porter consciousness. I think of taking this one wild flower and placing it in this one spot."

I am tempted to suggest that the town is like that for Ellen—a wild flower in a desert landscape. I don't. It would be overstating the case. The town is not quite as lovely as a wildflower, and the surrounding terrain is not nearly as forbidding as the word "desert" makes it sound, especially at this time of year, when the early rains have covered the pastures and hillsides with a skin of bright green. While I was driving up here I passed a herd of Angus cattle grazing on one such emerald hillside, under a low and misty sky, and I could not help but think of the Scots Highlands, where those particular blacks and greens and muted greys prevail.

But still, in this part of the world the town does have the quality of an oasis, an image that is sharpened for me by a story Ellen tells the next day, as we are driving down the long slope toward Chico.

On both sides of the road we can see the buttes that give this county its name—broad and flat-topped formations, their sides cut away by centuries of river action pouring through from the higher peaks. The buttes too are coated with green, the tops and sides, during this short season when rain happens to be pelting the foothills and the wide valley below. She begins to describe the layer of smoke that hovers above the valley, the upper Sacramento, several times each year, when stubble is being burned off the enormous rice fields.

"It's a dark gray layer," she says. "It actually looks solid when you're driving into it, especially if it's combined with winter fog. I was driving down like this once with a friend of mine who had flown out from New York for a visit, a black woman my mother had as a housekeeper all during the time I was growing up. We started into Chico one day when smoke from the rice burn happened to be covering the whole valley.

When she first saw it looming in front of us she grabbed my arm, afraid we were going to hit it. She had spent her whole life in Manhattan and had never seen anything quite like this. She made me stop, and we both had to get out of the car and walk down to where the wall began, so she could see it wasn't solid. I knew how she felt, because I *still* see it that way. I still find myself catching my breath—not from the smoke, but from preparing for the impact.

"When you work all day in something that thick, you sometimes forget the world can look like anything else. Then at the end of the day you climb back out of it, up the grade to Paradise."

Ellen was right about the distance to the ocean. It takes me most of a day to cross the state, since the east–west roads up this way are not nearly as handy as the north–south trunk routes. The traffic flows from Sacramento to Portland, from Eureka to San Francisco. If you want to get from Paradise to Mendocino you have to cross that grain and surrender your timetable to roads that still hug the old contours of lakes and riverbeds and eventually the rippling ridges that typify the Coast Range.

The cape called Mendocino was sighted and named by Juan Cabrillo in 1542. Three hundred years later a town was founded south of the cape, a logging town, then a fishing town, nowadays a cult town and weekend haven. Some of its calluses still show, but there are north coast veterans who look upon the renovated version as a suburb of L.A., connected by air and by boutique packaging.

The first road inland from this stretch of the coast was cut through dense forest in 1873. A few more years went by, and a homestead was established some two miles beyond the road. The farmhouse is still there, on a knoll, out by itself, and about as far into the woods as anyone can get these days, in California. The nearest neighbor is a mile and a half away as the crow flies, says Eva Yee.

"That is northeast," she will tell me. "If you go directly east, it is thirty-five miles to the next house. South, it's twelve."

The last mile in is so overgrown I begin to glance again at the map she sent, fearing I have turned onto some abandoned track. *No sign,* she scribbled in among the arrows. *Turn right at gate. It looks locked. Slide lock through loop.*

I did all that. Now the limbs of bay trees intermingle a few feet off the ground. Brush hangs so close across my hood, twigs and leaves scratch at the windshield, sometimes blocking all sight lines. My radiator has been acting up again. I am certain that if something goes wrong with my car, this is where it will happen, at this altitude, in this forest, on this road which is not a road at all but the bad memory of one. A moment before I lose all faith in Eva's map and in my own sense of direction, the last limbs part and I pass an ancient barn.

I take a little rise and break out onto a hilltop where weather-eaten lumber lies scattered about among relics of farm machinery. Great circular saw blades lie rusting in the grass outside what must once have been a sawmill. Logs that would have been cut into board feet are stacked, bleached, still waiting. Where the road passes the mill, heading toward the farmhouse now visible on the next knoll, a circular blade has been propped against a two-by-four that is propped against a stump. Painted on the blade is a rustic announcement:

OLD MILL FARM

ALL PARKING

I learn later that Eva does not like traffic dust falling into her vegetable garden, which follows the slope just below the old mill, so visitors park here and walk the last quarter-mile to the house.

When I turn my engine off, not a sound can be heard, and not much movement catches the eye. The house, from this distance, looks inhabited but, in mid-afternoon, empty. It is white, two stories, with a split-shingled roof and wooden siding. On one little patch of hillside, sheep are browsing. Near a pond, in a meadow at the bottom of the garden, three sleek and muscular draft horses seem to stand like cutouts, bronze on green. Then a breeze comes up. In the garden, leaves flutter around snow peas climbing one side of the high wire enclosure. Farther into the garden, near the ground, something blue moves. It is Eva's down jacket. She is shifting her weight, where she squats next to one of the built-up beds, cultivating onions.

The breeze is moving across the slope. She didn't hear my car. I hike down and unlatch the gate. She hears that click and turns and laughs when she sees me.

"What happened?" she says. "I thought you were going to be here for lunch. Did you get lost?"

"For a while there, I thought I was. The road . . ."

"I like the road that way, don't you? Makes it a real hideout here. Where's your stuff? You want to go over to the house and find something to eat?"

"I want to look around your garden. Tell me what you're doing. How did you get this dirt to look like that? You must have trucked in tons of something."

Her hands are dark from the potent soil. Crumbs of it cling to her trowel, and to the knees of her jeans. She tells me about fish guts hauled up from Noyo Harbor, and sawdust from the Fort Bragg lumber mills, mixing in with manure from the dozens of animals here on the farm, mainly from the chickens and goats. She shows me the careful fencing to keep deer out, the compost bins, and some of her favorite crops— Jerusalem artichokes, Chinese chive, elephant garlic, and four kinds of beans just now getting started, Scarlet Runner, Kentucky Wonder, Cuban Black and Romano. Everything is thriving, bristling with nourishment and obvious signs of full-time loving care.

I ask about gophers, the affliction, the pox and bane, the curse on all growing things west of the continental divide. With another laugh Eva says, "We don't have any. I think because we're so far away from everything else. Why would a gopher crawl that far through the trees?"

Watching her laugh, I am thinking back. I happen to know that she finished college twenty-five years ago. If I didn't know that, it would be difficult to guess her age. She could be thirty-five. In this garden, with the favorable sunlight slanting over redwoods to add rich color, she could be thirty, or younger. Her skin seems to be glowing. Her smile is wide. Her eyes are clear. She looks at ease, in this place of endless toil, as if she has found her spot. And if that is true, she has come full circle.

She was born down in Fairfield, grew up on the family fruit ranch in the Suisun Valley, north of Berkeley. Her father had immigrated from China and settled there soon after World War I, sending for her mother a few years later, a picture bride, from the same village, near Canton. When Eva went off to school, she left the family ranch behind. She got married, raised two kids, taught second grade for a while, became an expert at sandal-making and all forms of leather work. She owned an art gallery and crafts shop, managed rentals, and made a life, a living, in and around the cities of central California. Now her kids are grown. Those earlier lives are . . . were . . . earlier lives. And she is here, with an acre of vegetables and eighty chickens, twenty goats, two dozen sheep, assorted fruit trees, turkeys, ducks and geese.

She digs out the parsnips we'll be having for dinner, snaps a lettuce head, then walks me down to the chicken house to show off her silkies. In the barnyard, as in the garden, she has her favorites, her firm opinions. Among chickens she prefers the Japanese silkie, for the meat, which is succulent and tender and black.

But chickens, as a class, do not rank as high as ducks.

"One of our chickens hatched five duck eggs," she says. "And look at them. They're only two weeks older than those little chicks and look how much bigger they are. They're almost big enough to eat. Ducks grow faster, and they give bigger eggs. I am not going to fool around with chickens anymore."

Among all hoofed creatures she prefers the goat. "Cows are too stupid," she says, almost with anger. "Cows break down the fences. Goats are smart, and real obedient. They come home on time. They sleep where they are supposed to sleep. Right around five-thirty you'll see them come parading across the pasture."

On this farm goats provide the milk, which becomes the base for cheese and yogurt. In the kitchen she unwraps a chunk of fresh cheese, smooth and creamy and delicate on the tongue. This she makes to eat. Most of the yogurt she sells in town, along with excess eggs. The goats are essential, and the loss of a goat is felt in the heart as well as in the accounting, in the careful balance between ecology and economy she is maintaining here with Chuck Hinsch, her companion and partner.

"We were starting into town one afternoon," she tells me, "when I saw a nanny out in the pasture, on her side. I figured she was giving birth. All the nannies were pregnant. So we stopped and walked over there and saw blood all around her throat. She was gasping. We threw a blanket over her and took her into town to the vet's, but she didn't make it. She died with three kids in her belly. When we got back home we counted the animals and found one other nanny missing. So we went looking for her and found her body still warm. Her throat had been chewed open, and two perfectly formed kids in her belly had died with her. Dogs did it. Sometimes packs of dogs from town roam out this way."

Chuck wears a beat-up straw cowboy hat and jeans, a Levi's jacket, and a plaid shirt. His cheeks are ruddy, almost rosy, giving his lean face a youthful smoothness under the thick beard he sports. He comes from Cincinnati, drove out to the coast a dozen years ago, to look around, and stayed. In his eyes there is a shine of wildness, of some fierceness he is keeping under close control.

Joking, he says, "We're just a hippie commune here."

He knows they aren't. He knows the difference. Years ago he was part of a wilderness experiment farther north, in Oregon. "There weren't any limits," he says. "No matter what went on, no one would ever say stop. Anarchy never says stop. I got lost in the anarchy."

With a loud laugh and that wild glint he adds, "Maybe that's why I had to get my own land, where I could be the dictator."

He and Eva both arrived in Mendocino County, on their separate paths, in the early 1970s, during the heyday of the great migration outward from the cities into these mountainous regions of northern California. Counterculture historians link that exodus to the collapse of the Haight-Ashbury as West Coast headquarters, sometime around 1968. The movement bred a thousand communes and backwoods adventures of one kind and another, and most of them have come and gone.

"Ten years ago," says Eva, "everybody wanted to go back to the land. Now a lot of them have moved the other way again, in toward town."

Former hippie carpenters or plumbers who once worked just enough to maintain the mountain life-style became builders and contractors, with offices and small fleets of pickups. Some who bought wooded acres in the early days sold them off at huge profits and moved on. Others found that even bigger profits could be made in these hills with the right kind of crop. Thanks to the county agricultural officer, who decided to call a spade a spade, Mendocino became the first West Coast county to announce officially what everyone had long known unofficially: in 1980 he put marijuana at the top of his annual report to the state. His honesty raised such a stir, he was advised to take early retirement. But meanwhile the facts were out there. Grass was grossing an estimated $100 million a year, replacing wine grapes as Mendocino's first cash crop.

Given the look of the road and the distance to the nearest house, no one would be surprised to find a stand of the tall stalks and pointy leaves at Old Mill Farm. But it soon becomes clear that Eva and Chuck aren't doing it that way. They are secluded but not on guard. Nothing is hidden here, none of that moment-to-moment wariness, the suspicion of strangers, the moonshiner's paranoia, with the weapon near at hand. In this old farmhouse, which was a homestead in the 1890s, they are homesteading again. Subsistence farming. Organic. No chemicals. No vitamin pills. No indoor plumbing. No public electricity. Minimum dependence on urban systems and energy-devouring equipment. Reaching back. Reaching back. The goal is self-sufficiency. What it takes is follow-through. That is why so many of the earlier communes and high-country expeditions folded. High on anarchy, low on follow-through. These two are loaded with follow-through. You can see it in the look of the animals, the sleek hides on the goats and the draft horses, the full black coats on the sheep.

They run a kind of school here, in conjunction with the gardening and husbandry. They take in apprentices, people who will exchange work for the chance to spend a few weeks or months on the farm. Right now a young couple from New England are living in the cottage across the slope from the main house, sharing chores, picking up some basic skills and crafts. One of them recently finished four years in the Marine Corps, and he is rethinking his life.

A few times each year busloads of kids drive out from the cities, usually from somewhere around San Francisco Bay, with their teachers and their counselors, sometimes inner-city kids who have never seen a goat up close, or bees, or compost. They hang around the farm, take hay rides and sleep outside, they shovel manure out of the goat corral, or look for excuses not to. They help Eva weed and gather, and listen to her talk about the silkies and the onions and the artichokes.

She has two stoves in her kitchen. One burns wood and the other gas. She prefers the wood burner. "I like the way the whole top heats up, so you can use all of it at once. But in the summertime it makes the house too hot, so then I switch to gas."

She cooks in the Gothic half-light cast by kerosene lamps. The oven doors screech every time she opens one to peer inside. The food she puts on the table is all from the farm: young snow peas, steamed parsnips, crisp salad greens, and lamb chops from the animals they raised and butchered. On the stove, still cooking, is the goat's milk that will appear at tomorrow's breakfast as cottage cheese, to go with the nectarine preserves.

I haven't sat down to a meal like this since I visited my old cousin Jocie back in Tennessee in 1969. She was seventy-five at the time, born on Cumberland Mountain, where she stayed, and she had never known any other way of life. She and her husband were the last in a long line of subsistence farmers who took great pride in filling an entire table with food they had raised, grown, canned or cured. The main difference between Jocie and Eva is that Eva is not here by unbroken family tradition, but by choice, or by process of elimination. She and Chuck have agreed with each other to put in the time, the ten or twelve hours a day that it takes. It wears them out, and it buoys them up.

"How are those lamb chops?" Eva says.

"Great," I tell her. "Best I've ever tasted."

"I didn't put anything on them."

"Meat like this, you don't need to put anything on it."

"Wait till in the morning," says Chuck. "When you taste the eggs. People eating off the Alpha Beta racks really forget what eggs can taste like."

"What happens around here at night?" I ask.

He is still wearing his scruffy straw hat, shoveling in the food and grinning across at me. "This is what happens. We eat dinner."

"I mean, after dinner."

"It's dark. The frogs croak. We're tired. We go to bed. I'm really tired. Aren't you tired?"

He is absolutely right. It is very dark, and everyone is tired. I myself traveled all the way from Paradise today. He walks me up the slope to my cabin, a wooden shack that used to travel around on skids, in the days when loggers worked these woods and brought their housing with them. We say good night and he disappears into the darkness, his hat brim showing once, against the kitchen window.

Inside I light my lamp, roll out my bag and look for a place to plug in my tape recorder. Conditioned reflex. There aren't any outlets, of course, and I tell myself it is just as well. If God had meant for everything to be enshrined on magnetic tape, he wouldn't have given you a memory.

I wake to a scene you will only see in northern California: a mountain meadow, bordered by second-growth redwoods with a low mantle of coastal fog right above the treetops. In the foreground, along the fence around Eva's duck pen, little mirrors send back the pearly glow of morning fog. These are abalone shells taken from the low-tide reefs fifteen miles away. At the edge of the meadow, next to redwoods, one doe is grazing.

When Chuck lets his sheep out, the doe glides away. He and Eva are already up and at it. Another day. She has water on to boil and biscuits in the oven. In the kitchen we sip coffee and talk about toast, how it's too much trouble when you're cooking with wood, so you skip toast and bake biscuits, using the whole wheat she grinds in the old-fashioned grinder.

When I fell asleep last night, electricity was on my mind. Now I ask them if they miss it. They look at each other, and Chuck answers first, with a laugh.

"Hell yes. I miss it all the time. It's wild when you think about that. All those centuries, people never even imagined electricity. Then, in really less than a hundred years, we have created this unkickable addiction. I have been living out here for seven years. But I had electricity for thirty-one years. Every day I feel that yearning to be able to just reach over and switch on the light."

"Not me," says Eva, peeking in to check her biscuits, here in her kitchen powered by wood and kerosene, some two hundred and forty years after Ben Franklin ran the famous key up his kite string to change the course of history. As she speaks, Pacific Gas and Electric Company executives in San Francisco are preparing the largest rate increase ever proposed by a utility ($1.7 billion). It will add $17 a month to the average household bill in California, which in turn could dig a big hole in Eva's profits from the egg and yogurt sales down in town—that is, if she and Chuck were wired to the system.

"Not me," she says. "I *hate* electricity. If you have electricity then you have to have a telephone. If you have a telephone, then people are calling you up all the time and you can't get your work done. Before you know it you have to have a television set, and then . . ."

Her Asian eyes spring wide with amusement, and a hint of impatience, and perhaps a sense of prophecy.

"And then?" I ask.

"It's all over."

II

SOME REGIONS
OF THE MIND

Going to California! It is only three thousand miles nearer to Hell.

> HENRY DAVID THOREAU
> from his *Journals* (Feb. 1, 1852)

I'm going to California
Where they sleep out every night.

I'm leavin you, Mama,
Cause you know you don't treat me right.

> JIMMIE RODGERS
> from *California Blues* (first
> recorded in Atlanta, Ga., October 1928)

Everything is deemed possible
except that which is impossible
in the nature of things.

> Section 1597
> *California Civil Code*

Voices in the Afternoon

I was on my way to the thirty-second floor of Number One Embarcadero Center, arriving by cab, and I was late. The way the city is laid out now, with all its Right-Turn-Only streets and Left-Turn-Only and No-Through streets and No-U-Turn streets, I told the driver he didn't have to pull up right in front of the glassed portico that guides you toward the arcade and the escalators. I persuaded him to drop me at the corner of Battery and Sacramento, and I would walk the final forty yards.

I soon found myself walking backward, not forward, bumping into shoppers, becoming my own traffic hazard on the sidewalk as I kept retreating, trying for a fuller view of this amazing structure, trying to count my way up to floor thirty-two where I was now supposed to be. I used to do this when I was ten, when the downtown buildings were not nearly this tall. I still do it, and I never succeed. I always lose count. The rows of windows slide and overlap, and soon I am simply standing on the sidewalk, a mindless gawker, still astounded that human beings can get it all together and mount the girders and the concrete in such a way that something this long and narrow can stand there without keeling over.

Never mind that this is San Francisco, home of the century's most infamous earthquake. Never mind that geologists are quoted weekly in the papers telling us it is only a matter of time, etc., and never mind that some vast gamble is on display here, not merely the high-stakes gamble of super-construction, but the decision to take that gamble in the very cradle of one of the world's most active fault zones. Set all that aside for a moment and simply stand with me and gaze up at the spectacle of Embarcadero Center Number One, a plane of stepped surfaces, like a flat and sleek up-ended layer cake, and next door its sibling, Number Two, and next to that Number Three, then Number Four, and finally, what some call the climax, or the icing on this row of cakes, the Downtown Hyatt Regency, with its indoor elevator capsules exposed, and its indoor gardens climbing up from the lobby, fifteen tiers of hanging vines and tendrils.

These are not the tallest buildings in San Francisco. At forty-stories-plus they may not be tall enough to qualify as skyscrapers. Cloudscrapers might be closer, or high-fog scrapers. But taken together this five-block city-within-a-city is the biggest, the boldest, the most ambitious piece so far in the ongoing downtown transformation. If this were 1925 and I were Hart Crane, I might try to see Embarcadero Center as he saw the Brooklyn Bridge, as another gleaming symbol of the great advance. It is hard these days to summon that kind of exuberance, knowing all we now know about city living, knowing of the multitudes who have fled in search of calmer lives. San Francisco happens to be the California city hardest hit by that trend, the state's only major city actually to lose population during the 1970s. This fact, however, can't be read in isolation, any more than the city can be thought of as a domain unto itself.

Each working day other multitudes come pouring north along the freeways and on the Southern Pacific commuter trains. They come car-pooling south across the Golden Gate and west across the Bay Bridge or on the subterranean BART tracks into highrises like Number One here, adding a daily surge some ardent San Franciscans call a daily invasion. I feel it, this afternoon, as part of the great urban buzz, and admittedly that is sometimes difficult to interpret, when you are used to smaller towns and fewer decibels. Desperation, for instance, can be misread as vitality. Contained fury can be misread as hustle-and-bustle.

At midday, when you have just stepped out of a taxicab at the corner of Battery and Sacramento, the air is thick and noisy with a dozen moods at once. But as I sprint through it, on my way to the portico, through little sidewalk pockets of anxiety and paranoia, I can still feel the keen edge of faith. I am always looking for signs of faith, and I swear that it is palpable right here, in the midst of all the rest, and in the very lee of Number One Embarcadero Center, a continuing belief in what this city is, or can be, its fabled possibilities. I am surprised to be feeling this (what you get from afar is the picture of an embattled danger zone) and yet I am not surprised, because it has always been a city that calls forth loyalty, affection and enthusiasms, and I have in fact been hearing some of this in the voice of a woman I am about to meet. That, quite literally, is why I am here—a voice, which is broadcast throughout northern California from the thirty-second floor, and which, to my ear, conveys a certain attitude toward this part of the world.

Her name is Lila Petersen. The first time I heard her I was crossing the Bay Bridge, fooling around with the dial, trying this station and that, keeping one eye on the Yerba Buena Tunnel up ahead. I always have an ear out for what I think of as "a radio voice," one that is inherently compelling, that will hold you even though you may not know who is talking. Sometimes you may not even know *why* this person is talking. But something in the voice itself keeps you listening instead of reaching for the knob.

Lila Petersen has that kind of voice. It is both quick and sultry. If she were a late-night disc jockey she could keep an audience of hard-rock insomniacs alert and believing in tomorrow. If she were doing the weather report, you would feel better about the weather after listening to her describe it, even though hailstones might be battering your windows and frightening your dogs and cats. She has the kind of voice that can surprise you too, when those beguiling tones are wrapped around a question such as I once heard her ask Mayor Dianne Feinstein.

The mayor appears on this show regularly, once each month, to talk to Lila about San Francisco and take calls from listeners. The subject happened to be downtown growth, raised by a rather irate man who called in to ask how the mayor could continue to support unrestricted highrise development, "*. . . given the great demand for housing and rental housing, which is driving up the cost thereof.*"

After explaining that she did not support unrestricted growth—noting the city's height and density limits—the mayor went on to say that during 1980, new construction, new millions of square feet of office space, had produced some twenty thousand new jobs for the city.

"*In the previous ten years,*" Mayor Feinstein said, "*we've only produced forty thousand new jobs—which means we've had half a decade's growth in one year.*"

She wanted to be proud of these statistics. But Lila had others on her mind.

"*There are plans on the drawing board now to build several more highrises in San Francisco,*" Lila said. "*For starters, that would substantially change the city's skyline. If they are approved and completed they would add over ninety thousand people to the city's work force.*

Rush hour traffic by 1983 would increase by about thirty percent. Housing in the city is, as you know, terribly tight. There are 528,000 jobs in the city now, and there are about 306,000 houses, apartments, and condominiums. What's the answer? Where do you go? How do you decide which building goes up and which one doesn't?"

At such moments Lila has my full attention. Here is a woman with a compelling radio voice, who is also equipped to ask the toughest and most necessary question. At such moments the details at her fingertips tell me she understands this city very very well; and something in her tone, and in the quickness of reaction, tells me she is not the kind of call-in host whose covert or not-so-covert motive is to keep listeners propped up by gouging at fears and uncertainties. She genuinely cares about the answer.

Mayor Feinstein was quick to acknowledge the housing crunch and the transportation crunch, topping Lila's figures with crises figures of her own. Then she outlined one possible, perhaps pace-setting, solution —a new policy that requires developers to create housing units equal to the demand their highrise adds to the city's load. Her voice leaped with excitement when she said, *"It has resulted in one corporation coming forward and saying they will rehabilitate 450 vacant, vandalized, and unused units of public housing—which is a first in America."*

The mayor also has a good radio voice. When she makes a statement like this on the air, answering Lila and the citizen who called, you can hear the human being in there, in and around the politician's words. You can hear the native San Franciscan wrestling with this unwieldy tangle of demands. That is something you cannot always catch when you see the words in print. If radio is making a comeback, as they say, this has to be part of the reason. It is more intimate than television. And the voices tell you things that pages often don't, especially when the show is live and the calls unpredictable.

Here in California there is one more thing to consider. Radio may well be this state's most indigenous or characteristic medium of communication. There is a radio in every car, and we have more cars and more cars per capita than anywhere else in the world or in the history of the world. In the zones of thickest traffic—the San Francisco orbit, the L.A. orbit—it often seems as if every car is on the road at once, which wears down the nerves, but it has been good for radio. I myself have logged thousands and thousands of radio hours behind the wheel. This is how I discovered Lila's show, sitting in my car alone and looking for some company. I tuned her in by chance, and then kept listening, first to the voice itself, wise and shrewd and feminine, and then to the voice as it addressed the many layers and permutations of this bursting

Bay Area where most of her listeners reside. From moment to moment, from interview to interview, her show conveys an abiding concern for the way her listeners think, how the city works or fails to work, and, by extension, how this larger region works, this sub-region of the West for which San Francisco is namesake and bank vault and emblematic center. It is not her voice alone that conveys all this, of course. It is the range of voices she gathers in, the panelists, the experts, the mayors and the callers who call from Ukiah, from Salinas, from Vallejo, from Tomales Bay.

By the time I reach floor thirty-two, pick up my I.D. tag from reception/security, and walk down the long corridor past the newsroom, today's show has already started. I am ushered into an engineer's cubicle where a man and a woman sit at a broad console fulls of knobs and gauges, both of them peering through an even broader pane of glass, into the sound studio where Lila sits.

I have been vaguely dreading this moment, with a dread that goes back to my younger days, before television came along to give us an image for every sound we hear. Radio stirs the imagination in its own way. When I was growing up, here in this city, many of my heroes were radio performers I would listen to week after week. I would have a picture in my mind of how each character looked, and everything would be fine until, by accident, I would come across a photo, in something like *Life* magazine, of four people standing around a boom mike with scripts in their hands, and there would be one of my hero/voices —just another balding guy in a sport shirt. I would groan inwardly, thinking, "Is that *him?*"

What a relief to see that Lila and her voice suit each other remarkably well. She is thirty-one and looks younger, tall, trim, and striking, with blond hair that spills out toward her shoulders. At the mike she wears wide-rim tinted glasses and a bright red blouse that is the single splash of color in an otherwise color-muted studio made of acoustic paneling, with gray drapes behind and a formica table filling most of the room. Sun leaks around the edges of the drapes, backlighting the red blouse, burnishing the hair.

Rising from the table, five adjustable boom arms carry foam-wrapped condensor mikes. Only two are in use, Lila's, and the one hanging in front of Charlie Haas, a Bay Area writer and student of popular culture. It would not be exaggerating to say that Charlie is an aficionado of popular culture and thus, inevitably, an aficionado of trends and tastes all up and down this coast. At the moment they are having some fun talking about barbecue, which happens to be a growth market in the Bay Area.

Charlie once did a personal and stomach-challenging survey of barbecue joints for *New West* magazine. If you could hear the salivation in Lila's voice as she reads a paragraph from this article describing the sauces and the basic cuts of meat, you would know why I listen to her show. Her tastes run the gamut, from the reapportionment debate to the spiciest ribs in East Oakland.

"What's the best advice," she asks Charlie, *"for someone who goes into a place that has a reputation for having really good, spicy barbecue? What if the owner or cook says, 'Well, I don't think you should try this, it's pretty hot'?"*

With a grin Charlie says, *"Give 'em my name."*

"And then?"

"Just hold out. Don't eat at any barbecue place where they don't try to talk you out of ordering the hot sauce."

A smoky laugh from Lila and she says, *"We have a caller on the line from Burlingame. Hello, Burlingame, you're on the air."*

Here in the tiny cubicle, on this side of the glass proscenium, a five-line phone is flickering. Bob, the engineer, is stacking up commercial cartridges for the next break, checking them against his program sheet, while producer Diane Keaton (no relation to the actress) screens the calls. Though Lila's voice has lured me to the studio, I soon discover what an intricate partnership this show requires. Diane is the unheard but indispensable off-mike juggler. The range of these daily conversations reveals her tastes as well as Lila's, the range of interests they both share. Diane is the one who schedules the mayor's visit, then gathers the reports and articles that give Lila ammunition for an on-mike dialogue. When the subject is something like water rights, Diane rounds up the necessary voices: the small farmer, the state senator, the salmon expert from Fish and Game.

"Conducts" might be a good word to describe what she does. Or "orchestrates." She spends her mornings lining up the guests. Afternoons she's on the multi-phone, where each voice appears first as a lighted button. Sometimes four or five light up at once, and then Diane is talking fast.

"Will you hold, please?" she says, pressing button One.

And again, pressing Two, "Will you hold, please?"

Then to number Three, "Hello. Where are you calling from?

Petaluma? What's your question? . . . I'm sorry. We only take questions. Have you listened to our program before? Please stay on the line. I'll get back to you in a moment."

Pressing Four she says, "Will you hold, please?"

Then it's back to One. "Hello. Still there? Thanks for waiting. Where are you calling from? Oakland? What's your question? Okay. Okay." She is scribbling now, Magic-Marking big words on a sheet of eight-by-ten. "Okay, you'll be on next, right after the break. As soon as Lila says, 'We have a caller from Oakland,' you go ahead."

She sticks this page to the pane of glass, with the words facing Lila, then presses Three again. "Thanks for holding. We haven't forgotten you. Have you thought of a way to express that in a question? Okay. Okay."

Again she's scribbling with the Magic Marker, and now two sheets of eight-by-ten are fixed to the pane. Sometimes three or four hang up there in sequence, each one naming a town and a topic, stuck to a permanent stripe of tape across the glass.

Bob has been shoving cartridges into his bank of tape decks. In here we're surrounded by decibel dials and stacks of cartridges, each with a thirty- or sixty-second spot for Grand Auto, Armstrong Paint, Rochester Big and Tall, West Coast Federal Savings. When the last commercial is looping through, Bob raises one arm, like a racetrack starter. As the loop ends, his arm drops, shooting a forefinger at Lila, who says, *"Welcome back to the KCBS News Magazine,"* as if we have been gone for two years instead of two minutes. With a glance at the first page on the big window she says, *"We have a caller from Oakland on the line. Hello, Oakland."*

The subject now is Reverend Moon and his Unification Church. Lila's guest for the second hour is the sister of a woman who is apparently being confined by the Moonies against her will. This sister and the mother flew all the way from New Zealand to San Francisco hoping for a reunion. So far, she says, they have had nothing from the church but barricades and double-talk. A Moonie is on the line to offer another point of view.

"Good afternoon. I am curious about the frame of mind you and your mother were in before you came across. I have been a member of the Unification Church for five years, and I went and visited my parents after I was in the church for six months. I stayed with them for over a month after I'd been in the church for a year. I never experienced any negativity on the part of the church toward my family. I have always got my mail."

This sister is one of nine children from a huge New Zealand farming family founded by her grandfather, who had immigrated there from Ireland. You can still hear a strong Irish edge in her voice, and the fierce allegiance to clan and kin.

"We came here to see Mary Lee because Mary Lee's letters had been stopped, because Mary Lee had spoken on the phone to my father and was crying. She said she wanted to come home but she couldn't. My father sent three urgent cablegrams and she didn't receive them. Naturally, we were concerned. Mary Lee, we knew, had little money. We knew she was here, had come in on a tourist visa, had been on her way home, and yet had been here for some months, and we knew something was absolutely wrong. So that was our mood before we came over, that was the sort of knowledge we had about the Moonies before we came. . . ."

Lila says, *"Are there other New Zealand families in the process of coming to this country to find their family members?"*

"There certainly are," the sister says. *"Some cases have had incredible media coverage at home."*

It seems odd that a woman from New Zealand should be getting air time at the top of Embarcadero Center to take issue with a religious order founded in Korea. Odd. Yet typical. In a region that has long attracted every type of adventurer and runaway and drifter, this church/cult/boot camp/monastic order finds fertile ground for converts. Everyone within broadcast range knows someone who knows someone who has been affected, or afflicted, if not by the Moonies then by some other mind-managing system. The buttons on Diane's telephone flash wildly now. Calls are stacking up, more than they'll be able to handle this afternoon. Moonies. Anti-Moonies. A pastor calls from San Jose, perhaps a Methodist:

"I have two people with a daughter who was in the Unification Church. And they would just be willing to support you in any way they can, monetarily, or whatsoever. I was just wondering if you were in need of something along those lines."

The last time Lila discussed this church a trucker somewhere on the road between Livermore and Fairfield came to a screeching halt and rushed to the phone. She was talking to two de-programmers, who had mentioned a sort of halfway house for ex-Moonies. This fellow knew a young woman who could use their help, and he had pulled off the road to get the address and phone number. It was a poignant moment—a ten-hour-a-day workingman standing in a booth somewhere. You could hear the freeway traffic in the background, and you could hear two things in his voice: the distaste for Moonies, and the press of his schedule. It was a heavy risk, cutting into his road time to wait his turn on the call-in line.

Such moments, they add that third and fourth dimension to the news—which can be one of the pleasures of any good talk show. But this "News Magazine" is not quite as loose as a talk show, nor is it as formal as a press interview. With Lila at the mike and Diane sifting callers, it comes closer to a forum, in the true sense of that word. Voices meet here from all parts of California, but mostly from the northern half, swapping facts, opinions, theories, and queries. Sometimes I hear it as a concert of voices, or as an opera of conversation in the afternoon. You hear the Moonie talking to the farm family sister from New Zealand. You hear a de-programmer talking to the trucker. You hear a bus-rider talking to the head of the Transit District, and a welfare caseworker talking to Governor Jerry Brown. You hear prisoners from San Quentin and traffic cops and shop stewards and high-school kids and Chicano travel agents and state congressmen on the newsline from Washington and economists from Standard Oil—five blocks away—and pong-game engineers from Sunnyvale:

ALAMEDA MAN
I have two daughters in junior high, and their boyfriends spend all their time in these video parlors. I'd like to ask your fellow from Atari two questions. One, can overuse of these video games permanently damage the mind? And two, are there any games around that are suitable to have in the home that might have some kind of educational value?

PACIFIC HEIGHTS WOMAN
Good afternoon. I am seventy-four years old. I have been listening to your debate about whether or not this state should have a public lottery, and I do not think it is an immoral idea at all. Why is it any different from a church raffle, or a bingo game? I am a good Catholic, by the way, and a lifetime resident of San Francisco.

SAUSALITO MAN
I am an identical twin. My brother is straight, but I am gay. Have you run across anything like that before?

SEXUALITY EXPERT
Well, it certainly makes it clear that being gay is not genetic. One thing we do know is that twins will often maximize their differences.

CONTRA COSTA COUNTY SUPERVISOR
*Many constituents in the Martinez area will call periodically
and say that they have a yellow substance like a powder on their
porches or on their automobiles. No one knows exactly what it
is. Mr. Judd, from Chevron U.S.A., says it's acacia trees. The
people who live there think it's sulfur. . . .*

Diane says that where she comes from, a radio show like this wouldn't
last a month.

"Where is that?" I ask.

"Indiana. Indianapolis is the city I'm thinking of."

"Why wouldn't it last?"

"There isn't enough variety. People tend to think the same, act the
same. If you're not the same, then you've got a problem. It would take
about a month there to exhaust the possibilities."

I hear no condescension as she says this, no sneering at the old
country. If anything, there is a touch of wistfulness for what she left
behind, along with a sense of wonder for what surrounds her here. She
still calls it "never-never land."

"I am one of those people," she says with a laugh, "who discovered
California at the Rose Bowl."

Diane is in her early thirties now, small, slim and brown-haired, still
reserved in a Midwestern way. She grew up in a little Bible-Belt town.
During her student years she happened to be enrolled at Purdue the
one season they sent a football team to Pasadena. She scraped up the
money and traveled out to the game. A year later she was enrolled at
Indiana University when *they* sent a team to the Rose Bowl. On that
second trip she passed through San Francisco and was taken with what
she saw. She came back to stay in 1974. By that time she had earned two
degrees at Indiana, one in journalism, and one in law. Though she had
interned at a law firm, she never really intended to practice. Studying
law, she says now, was a way to broaden her range as a journalist.

She had been producing the "News Magazine" for a year at KCBS
when Lila was hired to host the show, in 1979. Lila too had come to San
Francisco by choice, but in her case she was not leaving home, she was
coming back. "I didn't have a job here, when I first moved to the city,"
Lila says, "I was just real tired of being away from California. I had been
gone for ten years."

Born in Utah, Lila was eight when her family moved to Stockton, in
the central valley, sixty miles east of the Bay Area. She attended high

school there, then went on to the University of Missouri's School of journalism, where she earned a B.A. and an M.A. In lieu of a graduate thesis she did fieldwork with National Public Radio in Washington, D.C., then landed a broadcasting job in upstate New York. It was during the hard winter of 1976–77 that her memories of West Coast living began to rise to the icy surface.

"That January and February it was twenty below, plus the wind-chill factor. There wasn't any social life. You just couldn't go out. I said to myself, 'This is for the birds, this kid is going home.' "

She was missing the climate, the Pacific Ocean, the Spanish look of certain neighborhoods, the more easygoing Western manner—and missing this city some too. Though she had never lived here, it held a potent place in her memories.

"When I was a kid," she says, "my mom used to get us all dressed up, and we'd come over on Saturday, and I loved to be coming to the city. She would take us to dinner and a movie, which was really a special treat. That was big time, putting on our best Sunday clothes to come over here. I remember the ladies with their white gloves on and their hats. I would have given my right arm to wear white gloves like that, but Mom thought that was a little extreme."

The sound of Lila's voice in person is the same as her voice on the radio, with the added advantage that you can see her green eyes shine with this memory of what the city was, at times still is.

"I loved it. We all did. We were all charmed by it. I remember how it was, long before all this stuff happened in the financial district. . . ."

We are sitting in their tiny office now, sitting, standing, leaning where we can, since stacks of books and magazines and newspapers far outnumber chairs and desk tops. From here we can look out upon what she means by "this stuff"—the downtown's steady transformation into a tourist-oriented, white-collar headquarters. I remember the sound in her voice the day she questioned Mayor Feinstein about the heavy price tags on this economic stronghold: short housing and choked transportation. In the distance, beyond all the buildings, a bright curve of freeway can be seen, thick with cars banking south toward the airport and the Peninsula. Directly below us is the site for what one day will be a twenty-three-story highrise, the Daon Building. It made the news in mid-1981, when a workman punched a hydraulic drill through a sixteen-inch gas main one afternoon, shortly after 1 P.M. People close enough to hear said it sounded like a jet aircraft taking off, right down there at the corner of Battery and Sacramento where that cabbie let me out. A brown and gaseous whirlwind was spewed up with a roar and then a prolonged wail. Some saw it as mere accident, another human error. Others heard that wailing as a siren from some distant early warning system.

In this city where they joke about apocalypse, it was nearly the classic moment. The whole financial district and redevelopment zone was brought to the border of The Big Event. At one point the gas-to-air mix reached 14 percent, well above the level at which it will ignite. An early fear was that fumes collecting in the lower reaches of Number One, the closest major building to the leak, might explode. Within half an hour forty thousand workers, from all these nearby buildings, were heading for the street in the largest forced evacuation here since 1906.

Lila recalls that she was interviewing Senator S. I. Hayakawa at the time. The conversation had turned to World War II and the forced evacuation of Japanese Americans from the three West Coast states, a subject in the air again that summer because a congressional committee was holding reparations and redress hearings in the coastal cities. The senator had just remarked that the internment camps had actually been a kind of prolonged vacation—an opinion not widely shared by the Japanese American community, which is large and vocal in the Bay Area. "We were right in the middle of that," Lila says. "Every one of the phone lines was lit up, and when I got the word to evacuate, my first thought was there had been a bomb threat, because Hayakawa was here in the studio."

"What did *he* think?" I ask.

"We didn't have time to find out," says Diane, remembering how it looked from her perch inside the engineer's booth. "His bodyguard ran into the studio and hustled him out of there before I even knew what was going on. He had been out in the hall and heard the announcement on the intercom. By the time I got the word, Hayakawa was on his way down the stairs."

"From the thirty-second floor?" I ask, envisioning a scene both ludicrous and awful. "The man is seventy-five years old."

"They turned off the power, I guess for fear of something igniting all that free-floating gas, so the elevators were out. Then Lila was announcing that the station was shutting down, and we were all on our way to the stairs. Her voice must have caught the feeling of the moment. Friends told us later it sounded like the station had been invaded and someone was holding a gun to her head."

The air up here had the smell of a kitchen where the stove's pilot light went out half an hour ago. By the time they reached the stairwell it was filled with people moving down from the dozen floors above.

They joined the throng. The smell of gas grew stronger floor by floor as they descended.

"Everybody was deadly serious," Lila recalls. "And all the time this really authoritarian voice is coming over the intercom saying, 'Please evacuate the building'—telling us at one moment to take the stairs, then telling us to take the elevator. But every time we tried to open one of the fire doors to get back in to an elevator the doors were locked. Finally, on the twentieth floor someone pried open one of the fire doors, and this whoosh came through, this smell that made us all jump back. It was *Towering Inferno* all over again. I could see those scenes in the film where they were trying to get down the stairs, and I thought, Well, if anything happens, this is it, we're dead. . . ."

One of their three telephones starts ringing. Diane answers. It is someone from Sacramento calling back about a panel Diane is organizing for later this week. The subject is statewide cuts in welfare benefits. She has to take the call, and in this same moment an urgent message comes down the corridor for Lila. KCBS is an all-news and information station, and she puts in a lot of mike-time doing straight reporting. With a quick apology, a wave, and an enormous smile she is off toward the newsroom, the burnished hair suddenly gone, around a corner.

Diane is gone too, immersed in one of today's fifty conversations. Flanked by pillars of newsprint and magazines, she has scooted in close to her note-filled desk, with the receiver in one hand, pen in the other.

I step out into the corridor to see what else there is to see up here. I am thinking that somewhere in that gas-leak story there lurks precisely what I came looking for today. Call it A San Francisco Feeling. What drew me up to the thirty-second floor was something I have heard in Lila's voice, that abiding belief and enthusiasm for this part of the world, that it can and should work better than it does, and that something can be gained by gathering all these official and unofficial points of view.

I see now that this combines, in strange union, with one more ingredient: the readiness for imminent catastrophe. Some people see these as mutually exclusive states of mind. But they are not. Not in San Francisco, particularly when you are working on the thirty-second floor. Take Lila and Diane. Harrowing as that gas experience was, it has not dimmed their affection for the city or their work. They thrive here, as so many do. They are energized by this environment, the busy flow of news that never ends, by the flux of life in the region of their choice, and surely by the panoramas that hit you up here every time you turn around. Two of these vistas, as a matter of fact, make a fine split-screen depiction of what I am talking about. The building here is so narrow, you can almost see them simultaneously.

Looking south from the "News Magazine" office, you are peering into an open mouth, filled with huge architectural teeth that have been worked on by many dentists, with here and there a block-size hole like a half-extracted molar. These are the newest highrises going in. The unbuilt Daon still gapes below, surrounded by paralyzed rush-hour traffic and construction fencing. Two blocks away, at 101 California, a skeletal and half-raised tower of steel dwarfs the Swinerton and Walberg crane, which happens to be the color of the Golden Gate Bridge. This view is very expensive and very ominous.

Meanwhile a few steps down the hall I take a turn into another office, empty at the moment, and catch a view to the north, which is also expensive, but spectacular. It is one of those astonishing views for which the city is famous—across the water toward Marin and Angel Island, with Sonoma County's foothills in the far distance, and in the foreground the fan of piers that gives this district and this row of towers its name, *embarcadero* (the sailing place, the point of departure). One glimpse like that, while a late sun sprinkles the bay, with maybe a few sailboats cavorting on the water, their white sails like little shouts of glee, and you are shouting too, within, thinking, "My God, it's true! This *is*—or was—still could be—or damn well should have been—the New Byzantium!"

Byting the Apple

The San Francisco Civic Center is noted for its pigeons and for its restful, prewar architecture. Pre-First World War. The high rotunda of the city hall has a cathedral-like serenity that can put the mind at ease. The pigeons swarm and swoop in the bright sunlight, in the granite bowl these buildings make. Sitting there watching them, and watching the winos positioned knee to knee in the April shade, as they pass back and forth the poorboy of muscatel, I would never have guessed what was going on some ten or fifteen feet below my bench. If I had not paid my $10 to pass through the door of the Civic Auditorium and then descend by escalator, I would never in my life have envisioned the menagerie of equipment on display in the underground extravaganza room called Brooks Hall.

"The biggest event of its kind in history," the organizer told me later. "Not as big as the NCC next month in Chicago, but the emphasis there has always been mainframe, the big federal and industrial stuff."

"Of its kind" meant equipment that brings computers down to the individual human scale. "Biggest" meant five hundred booths and over thirty-two thousand people—a record that eventually stood for several months. "In history" meant since 1976, when fairs of this type began.

As he said that date, '76 did seem a long way back. History is so compressed—in the accelerated world of electronics technology—that this morning's breakthrough is already old news. The spring of 1981, when the Sixth Annual West Coast Computer Faire took place, seems now as ancient as Rome. But it happened to be my first computer fair.

It had for me the shine of the Ringling Brothers Barnum and Bailey Circus that came to San Francisco when I was twelve. And I was not alone. I saw many that day who gazed in wonder. I saw grizzled computer veterans whose eyes were filled with true surprise. Excitement was in the air. A sense of discovery filled Brooks Hall, because in those days the personal computer was still a rather recent idea. Moreover, many of its basic features had been invented or developed right down the Peninsula there, forty miles south, in Silicon Valley, and this was the season when it was being introduced in a big way to the public at large.

The main hall was a blizzard of light, a blur of toaster-size screens humming and busy with numbers and rolling print and here and there little robot people acting out stories for kids. Under the steady *ack-ack* from the printout machines, you could see gorgeous full-color butterflies, a perfectly reproduced dollar bill, a ticking watch, a sinuous mountain of topo lines. Rapid-fire eighth and sixteenth notes followed the honky-tonk tinkle of a computerized player piano doing "The Muskrat Ramble."

After my eyes and ears stopped jumping—actually it was during my second tour around the hall—it dawned on me that every other booth at the faire featured the same piece of equipment. It was The Apple II. No single booth was selling the Apple by itself. But dozens, hundreds sold components that interfaced with Apple—graphics programs, tax accounting programs, music readers, war games. It was impressive. I made a third trip around the hall, to look closer. It went beyond electronics. In those days—back in early 1981—the TRS-80 out of Texas still held the nationwide edge in sales. But Apple was clearly running first in something else. Call it pizzazz. Or mystique. In a juggler you might call it style. In a religious leader it would be charisma.

A cult had formed around the Apple. In Vacaville, California, a retail outlet called itself The Apple Orchard. From Burbank you could order a text-editing program called APPLE P.I.E. (Programma International Editor). From Lake Havasu, Arizona, programs were being sold in packages called Apple Sacks. In Aptos, California, a college biologist was offering a course called The Biology of the Apple. In San Francisco there was a computer club, The Apple Core, with a publication named *The Cider Press.* In Venice there was another club, The Original Apple Corps, and at their booth you could subscribe to *Applesauce.* Meanwhile, everywhere you looked the T-shirts were visible. Large, medium, and small, light tan in color, with no words on the shirt, just a big juicy red apple across the chest, and one bite gone.

Should I have been startled by the sight of a lovely young woman at the computer faire walking around in her clogs and her jeans and her snug-fitting Apple T-shirt, with a big bite chomped out of the apple?

Does that suggest anything?

What about Eve?

Is Eve too traditional? The Garden of Eden?

That is what she brought to mind, there in the basement, with the monitors winking and the printouts chattering. Eve. The Garden. The Tree. The Original Apple. The question is, When Eve sank her teeth in to take that first karmic bite, what was she after? She wasn't after vitamins and minerals, as I understand the story. She was after more knowledge, more information. The eternal human quest. And the more forbidden, or forbidding, the information, the more urgent and attractive that quest becomes.

I looked again at the front page of *Applesauce,* at the exuberant members of The Original Apple Corps, at the battalion of components that interface with Apple II, and I remembered a full-page ad someone had sent me from the *Wall Street Journal,* which begins like this:

What is a personal computer?

Let me answer with the analogy of the bicycle and the condor. A few years ago I read a study—I believe it was in *Scientific American*—about the efficiency of locomotion for various species on earth, including man. The study determined which species was the most efficient, in terms of getting from point A to point B with the least amount of energy exerted. The condor won. Man made a rather unimpressive showing, about one third of the way down the list.

But someone there had the insight to test man riding a bicycle. Man was twice as efficient as the condor! This illustrated man's ability as a tool maker. When man created the bicycle he created a tool that amplified an inherent ability. . . .[16]

Now, there are not many places in the world where you will find this particular gathering of images. A bicycle. A condor. An apple. And a personal computer. Something more than circuitry is going on here, I thought. A sense of poetry. Perhaps even a sense of history. I decided then that when the fair was over I would have to find and talk to whoever could think up a computer with such a name, and such an ad for the *Wall Street Journal,* and such a T-shirt.

A while back someone wrote to the San Jose *Mercury News* complaining about the way the term "Silicon Valley" turns up more and more often as a synonym for Santa Clara Valley. "They are not the same," this citizen cried out. And I agree with him. The valley called Santa Clara has been here in its present shape for many thousands of years—a flat and fertile basin, in times past a submerged and southerly extension of San Francisco Bay, and still bordered by parallel ridges of the Coast Range. Silicon Valley is a very recent event, and it exists much more in the mind than it does in the landscape.

Physically it is a collection of low buildings that have been added, laid into various niches and cleared spaces like a scattering of heat-resistant ceramic tiles, around and among the various towns that now contain it: Palo Alto, Los Altos, Mountain View, Sunnyvale, Cupertino, Santa Clara, San Jose. The four long, low buildings that house Apple Computer—sand-colored, with red roof-tiles in the mission manner—are so new, green plastic nursery tape still flutters around the saplings staked outside. They have to be new. Six years ago the personal computer industry did not exist. At the moment, according to the fellow I am about to meet, it is the fastest-growing industry in the history of American business. "In six years," he will soon be telling me, "from zero to a billion dollars."

His name is Steve Jobs. Together with his partner, Steve Wozniak, he developed the first Apple when he was twenty-one years old. Now he is twenty-six, lean and purposeful as he comes striding toward me through the lobby of one of his buildings. He wears jeans, sandals, a plain checkered shirt. His dark brown hair is collar length, his dark beard trimmed. Behind the rimless glasses his eyes, very shrewd and watchful eyes, show a glint of amusement as he says—and this is his opening line—"I have to walk down and draw some money out of the bank. How's that for an introduction to Silicon Valley?"

He is flying out tonight to Boston, to a gathering of some ten thousand people who use his company's equipment, a gathering called The Apple Fest, where he will be the keynote speaker, and he has run short of cash. So we walk two blocks to the nearest Bank of America, another new, low building that presides over a recently completed shopping plaza. From the way Steve prowls around looking over the tellers' fences I figure that whoever usually handles his accounts is not here. Finally he steps into the long line of customers waiting for service.

I am struck by the humbleness, or perhaps it is the sheer youthfulness, of this move. Here he is, vice chairman of a company that, in recent months, moved $250 million through the securities markets, a company that, according to *Time* magazine, enjoyed "one of the biggest and most successful stock launchings in the history of Wall Street," here is Steve standing in line at the neighborhood bank waiting to get some spending money for his trip to Boston.

This is not, as I quickly discover, an uncharacteristic moment. *Loose* is his middle name. He is loose of limb and loose on formalities. At the corporate headquarters he has no parking slot of his own. In his office, which is the size of a small kitchen, the desk is right-angled into one corner, more like a tinkerer's workbench. On the wall above it, there is one embellishment, a small frame around the red and vibrating word:

THINK

We have come back to his office to talk about the history of Apple —which is really the history of his relationship with Wozniak and with these two coexisting valleys—and when we sit down at the round, breakfast-sized conference table in the center of the room, he slips off his sandals and puts his bare feet up there next to the table's one decoration, a small transparent apple made of solid glass.

"I first met Woz when I was thirteen," he says, "in another friend's garage. He was four years older than me and had just graduated from the same high school I was about to go to. He was the first person I met who knew more than I did about electronics. I started hanging around him after that, soaking up all I could. We became friends and have been friends ever since. I've known him now for thirteen years. That's half my life."

Jobs was still in high school when they teamed up for their first collaboration, which he begins to describe, then hesitates.

"I don't know if I can tell you this."

He turns to look out the window. "What's the statute of limitations, seven years? Woz and I . . ." Another pause. Then he laughs.

"Did you ever hear of a blue box? You know how when you make a long distance phone call, you hear these tones that go"—and he sings the bleeping rise and fall—"doo-doo-doo-doo-doo-doo? Well, you can make a little box that goes doo-doo-doo-doo-doo-doo. And you can basically make free phone calls all over the world. And we made the best one ever. We put a note down in the bottom of each one, it was our little trademark. It said, 'He's got the whole world in his hands.' You could get on a pay phone and get over White Plains, New York, and take a satellite to London and cable to Tokyo, and another satellite back to Paris, and take a cable back to White Plains, and call the pay phone next door."

I ask Steve if he was taking any electronics courses back in those high school days.

He shakes his head. "There really weren't any. You just got it by osmosis."

"Osmosis?"

"It's in the atmosphere."

Some kids grow up on the ranch and become cowboys. Some kids grow up in Beverly Hills immersed in show business and become studio executives. Steve Jobs grew up five miles from where we're sitting, in what appears to be a suburban neighborhood like thousands across the land, but you talk to him for a while and you see that he and Woz came of age in this new realm called Silicon Valley just as its headlong energy reached full acceleration. Neither of them holds a college degree or any of the other emblems of formal training. Wozniak's father was an electronics engineer at Lockheed, who had his son designing logic circuits by the time he was in the fourth grade. A few years later he was already building his own computers. Jobs in turn learned a lot from Woz, and from belonging to local computer clubs, and from hanging around the neighborhood garages.

He is the first to acknowledge that Apple could only have happened within the unique support system this Valley has to offer. He feels a sense of lineage that goes back at least as far as the 1930s, and he feels immersed in an environment he is eager to talk about. He calls it the culture of entrepreneurial risk.

"You do not get penalized for failure here," he says. "You are expected to try things. If you go out on your own and try something and fail, your career isn't over. You can actually be more valuable to the next person you work for, because of what you have learned in the process. It operates at every level. There was a point, when Woz and I were working on the first Apple, we needed ten thousand dollars' worth of parts. So we went to a parts distributor and asked him to help us out. And he did. He lent us the parts on a twenty-nine-day loan with no credit, because there is a role model for doing things that way. And you need that infrastructure. You need the engineer who is willing to go out on his own, and you need the parts distributor who is not going to say, 'Well, I want you guys to sign over your house.' He has to be able to say, 'Okay, I'll tell you what. You don't have a house, but I'll take a gamble anyway.' So he lent us the parts, and we went off and built the equipment and paid him back in twenty-nine days."

Adventurous risk is all around you, along with the legendary results, the breakthrough devices that keep this atmosphere charged up and ever challenging. Steve's voice rises with urgency and fills the office when he exclaims, "Look what's come out of this valley. Basically, the first integrated circuit. The first micro-processor was invented ten miles

from here. The first personal computer. Now, the first genetics companies. Probably five out of the top ten things we're going to look back
fifty years from now and say, these are the ten things that impacted the
world the most, five of them are going to come from right here in this
valley."

The passion in his voice almost has the ring of patriotism, making it that
much clearer to me that Steve is talking about his true homeland and
native surroundings—this volatile mix of microchips and circuit boards
and commerce in the fast lane. He grew up in the midst of it, with a
native's grasp of how it all works.

The more he talked, the more I began to wonder where this new
valley had actually come from, this little country unto itself where,
among other things, a new kind of apple had sprouted. What was it
doing here? When I finished high school in Santa Clara Valley back in
1951, the word "silicon" was still something you maybe heard mentioned once in chemistry class and never remembered. By the time
Steve finished high school, twenty-one years later, an entirely new type
of valley had made its appearance, superimposed upon the original. But
why? Why here, in a sunny basin that for a hundred years had been
cherished for its apricots, pears, walnuts, peaches, and prunes? The new
industry did not require any of the things the old farms and ranches
required, unless it be vision, and hustle, and a gambler's nerve. The
basic ingredient is a crystalline substance that can be processed in labs
anywhere but happens to be processed in large quantities here—in
some of these low buildings spread around among the suburbs, often in
the shade of surviving walnut trees.

It is strange. It is almost out of character in a state where most of the
industry and so much of the fame has been directly tied to the physical
endowments. Gold. Oil. Soil. Harbors.

If you add climate to that list, electronics too might be said to have
a regional and earthly anchor. Climate explains a lot of what goes on
in California, and has helped keep this industry centered here. But
climate is not where it begins. When I started asking around, everyone
sooner or later mentioned Stanford University and a two-way flow of
brain power between New England and the Bay Area. The phrase
"critical mass" also came up several times: a gathering of ingredients,
which acquires its own magnetic effect. A clustering begins, and breeds
more of itself.

The earliest name you hear is that of Lee De Forest, who was living
in Palo Alto in 1912 when he invented the triode, key component in the

vacuum tube, which made it possible for the first time to modulate or amplify electric current. De Forest, who had studied at Yale, was working for Federal Telegraph, a company founded in 1909 by a Stanford graduate, with some help from David Starr Jordan, Stanford's first president. Today, in one of Palo Alto's tree-lined, vintage neighborhoods, a small plaque near the corner of Channing and Emerson marks "The Birthplace of Electronics."

The next name you hear—and this one lurks right at the center of the critical mass—is that of Frederick Terman. He graduated from Stanford in 1920 with a degree in chemical engineering, went to M.I.T. for a doctorate in electrical engineering, then returned to Stanford, where he eventually became a department head and later provost. Two of his students in the early 1930s were William Hewlett and David Packard. Both received electrical engineering degrees in 1934. Five years later, with Terman's support, they founded Hewlett-Packard in Palo Alto, now one of the world's largest electronics firms, with annual sales over $3 billion.

Hewlett and Packard are the archetypal Silicon Valley pioneers. The way they started—in a garage—has become the classic way. This is where Apple got started. According to Steve Jobs, this is where some of next year's discoveries are already in the works. "There are guys in garages all over," he says. "I could show you thousands." This is why Jim Warren, who organized the West Coast Computer Faire, has special booths available called micro-booths. "They are smaller and priced more economically per foot," he told me, "so that some fellow with an original idea can come in here and try it out on the public. We have people who started out on a shoestring two or three years ago, renting a micro, coming back this year in a full-size booth."

After World War II Terman promoted a number of ideas that put Stanford on course toward its present position in the forefront of innovative technology. He advocated top salaries to draw scientific talent to the campus. He worked to bring in federally funded projects. He encouraged the collaboration with private industry and supported what has come to be known as the Stanford Industrial Park, some six hundred sixty acres from the university's eighty-two-hundred-acre holding, which was an early home for Hewlett-Packard, Varian Associates, and the Shockley Semiconductor Lab—all within easy biking distance of Stanford's research facilities.

In the legend of Silicon Valley the name "William Shockley" is heard over and over again, usually accompanied by a raise of the eyebrows and a dip in the voice. He is another figure at the center of this critical mass, which had truly begun to exert its magnetic powers by the time he arrived in 1955. Shockley later joined the Stanford faculty and embarrassed everyone there by advancing the idea that blacks are genetically of lower intelligence than whites. But that came toward the end of his long career. And I.Q. testing, as some apologists have pointed out, was not really his area. He was a physicist, with degrees from Cal Tech and M.I.T. In 1947, while employed at Bell Labs in New Jersey, he co-invented the junction transistor, which launched the modern age of electronics and won him a Nobel Prize.

In 1955 Shockley left Bell and moved to Palo Alto, a return, in fact, to his boyhood town. Beckmann Instruments had offered him a higher salary and a free hand with his own researches. A number of talented young specialists were soon drawn West to work with Shockley, among them Robert Noyce and Gordon Moore, two men whose careers have been almost perfectly joined to the boom times.

Today Noyce is vice chairman at Intel Corporation in Santa Clara, while Moore is chairman of the board. Noyce is a native of Iowa. In 1956 he had recently completed his doctorate in electrical engineering at M.I.T. Moore grew up twenty-five miles due west of where his office stands today. By the age of twenty-four he held a Ph.D. in chemical engineering from Cal Tech. In 1957 they were among eight men who left Shockley's firm to found Fairchild Semiconductor in nearby Mountain View. Silicon Valley was officially ushered in, it has been said, with the development of the first practical integrated circuit at Fairchild some three years later. Shockley's transistor had miniaturized the process for controlling current flow, reduced it down to a small chip of semiconducting material, usually silicon. The integrated circuit is a multiple transistor, whereby ten or a hundred or a thousand circuits are squeezed into something the size of your little toenail.

Fairchild, in turn, was soon to become the industry's most prolific breeding ground, or launch pad. At least fifty Silicon Valley companies have been started by former employees.

"This is an extremely flexible technology," Gordon Moore told me, remembering his ten years at Fairchild, where he had directed research and development. "You can do a lot of different things with it. And Fairchild wasn't able to pursue all the ideas that were coming around. Engineers would see opportunities and take it in a slightly different direction and maybe set up an important company."

One of these spin-off companies was Intel, formed by Moore and Noyce in 1968. In 1980, *California Business* listed it as the fastest-growing corporation in the state. Among its main products is the microprocessor, developed at Intel in 1971 (while Steve Jobs was a junior at Homestead High School, five miles away: see *osmosis*). A chip that can actually execute instructions, the micro-processor was another giant step forward, or rather a leap downward and inward, since this happens to be an industry where you advance by getting smaller.

These tiny, miraculous and infamous chips—the memory chips that can store information; and the chips that work like minuscule computers—they are no bigger than shirt buttons and they have spawned and spurred this runaway industry with all its components and interfaces. The firms that have clustered in and around the critical mass now number in the hundreds—some say six hundred, some say a thousand, some give up trying to count. The technology proliferates around the world. But for the time being the center remains here, in this valley of the mind that has traded in walnuts for circuit boards and traded the name of a Spanish saint for the name of, according to my dictionary, "a nonmetallic chemical element found always in combination and more abundant in nature than any other element except oxygen."

Until the mid-1970s the main applications had been industrial, federal and military. Bell was computerized, and the IRS, and the Jupiter space capsule. But the common home owner, the trimmer of lawns, or the woman waiting for the stoplight to change, had only heard about computers from a distance, had seen computer-villain movies like *The President's Analyst* and *2001*, and had seen the effects on mail-order offers from the *Reader's Digest*, where a name had been added to what appeared to be a typed letter, beginning *Dear Mr. and Mrs.* with only a faint discrepancy in the shadings of ink to tell you that your pen pal was really a room-size machine somewhere in the Midwest.

When Steve Jobs and Steve Wozniak met up again, after a few years of going their separate ways, when they began to tinker again in the family garage in the summer of 1975, the home computer, the classroom computer, the computer for the small partnership and the backyard businessman, the preassembled, personal, and affordable computer you could unwrap and plug right in was an idea whose time had come. Like one of those radiating lightbulbs above the inventor's head in the old-time cartoons, the idea was hanging in the air above the entrepreneurial garage door, which from the street still looked much like any number of garage doors between San Jose and Daly City.

After high school, Jobs spent a year and a half at Reed College in Oregon. When he ran out of money he came back and worked a while for Atari, the Video game company, in Sunnyvale. They sent him to Europe, and not long afterward he was off by himself on a six-month trek through India. Wozniak in the meantime had been to the University of Colorado and had done a few quarters at Berkeley. He had designed a computing calculator and a low-cost hobby kit. He was working at Hewlett-Packard, designing hand-held calculators, when he and Jobs began thinking their way toward a new kind of machine.

"We had designed—mostly Woz, actually, but a little bit on my part —a little terminal you could hook up to another computer to use cheap. And we thought, well, we don't just want a terminal, we really want a computer."

They spent six months designing the prototype. Now, from a cabinet below his desk he pulls out an uncovered circuit board and casually tosses it onto the table, in the same way I have seen writers showing the galleys of a first novel long out of print, a thin packet of ink-filled pages that represent a year of one's life. It is the size of a small hand-tray, packed tightly with rows of dark blocks. In one corner I see the stamped letters *Apple I.*

"Only two hundred of these were ever made," he says. "That was the first computer we designed together, and we basically designed it because we couldn't afford to buy one."

When they showed their idea to a local retailer, he immediately said, "Great! I'll take fifty!"

In a matter of seconds they had gone from zero to a $25,000 order. All they lacked was a company, and some start-up capital, and some merchandise to sell.

Making what some Californians would consider the ultimate sacrifice, Jobs sold his VW van. When Woz sold his HP-65 calculator, they had a total of $1,300. They borrowed some parts, and while Woz worked overtime perfecting Apple I, Jobs got on the phone to organize the fledgling corporation.

"What was your feeling at that point?" I ask him. "Did you know you were on to something very large?"

"Yeah. But not this large. Woz and I had done a lot of stuff together, the blue boxes, and other ideas. At that point 'large' meant, Boy, if this really flies, maybe we can afford to buy a house, or get the car back."

By the summer of 1976 they were designing Apple II. Simultaneously, as Steve says, "We had to learn about marketing and distribution. And so we did. I wrote the first ad myself. And we got it placed. We wrote a technical article. And we got that placed. We started finding dealers. We called up Intel and asked who their ad agency was, and they said Regis-McKenna, so we called up Regis and went over there and said, 'We want you to do some ads for us but we don't have any money to pay you.'"

Regis-McKenna is a Palo Alto agency that specializes in high-tech

Silicon Valley companies. On the day I visited Apple, Rene White, the fellow supervising their account, had spent the morning with a writer from the *Wall Street Journal* briefing him on the mechanics of gene-splicing. Five years earlier, when Jobs and Woz came asking for ads on credit, Regis-McKenna said, "Go away."

"They told us 'Go away' four times," Steve says, smiling. "Finally they said, 'Okay, we'll do it.' And we became their largest account."

Call it brass. Call it moxie. Call it self-assertiveness. Or call it, as Steve does, "the entrepreneurial risk culture." Whatever its source, Jobs and Woz were never afraid to ask for what they wanted, or to go right to the best people they could reach to find answers to whatever they needed to know next. In Steve's case, he seems to have discovered it early in life, perhaps by osmosis. "When I was thirteen," he says, "I called Bill Hewlett on the phone and asked him for some parts I needed to build a little piece of electronic equipment I was working on. And he helped me out." With another smile he adds, "I actually got a summer job at H-P too."

From other Silicon Valley firms they hired away some top management people to help orchestrate the company's growth. Healthy sums of venture capital soon followed. In 1977, the year Apple II was introduced, sales hit $2.5 million. In 1978 the gross was over $15 million, and in 1979 it had jumped to $70 million. By the time I talked to Steve that annual figure had increased fivefold, eighteen hundred people were on the company payroll, a quarter of a million Apples had been sold, and there was no end in sight.

It had been a triumph of timing and superb design, together with a brilliantly simple packaging idea. Something about the Apple catches the imagination in a way that the equipment inside—the integrated circuits, the micro-processors—never could. The name, it turns out, was Steve's idea, along with the condor and the bicycle.

"I thought it up," he says. "But Woz and I talked about it for a long time. We wanted a name that wasn't so harsh and didn't have such a heavy connotation. For a lot of people, 'computer' is still a scary word. Apple is sort of warm and takes the edge off it."

"It's earthy," I say, "organic, nonthreatening . . ."

He interrupts me, bristling slightly, and I see that his sense for connotation is carefully tuned. "'Organic' is probably the wrong word," he says. "We just wanted something simple and friendly."

"What about the bite?" I ask, still thinking of Eve, at her fateful moment. "Who decided to take the bite out of the side?"

"Oh that." He laughs lightly. "A fellow at the agency is the one who designed our logo. He did it sort of for fun. It's a pun. *Byte* is a computer term. Technically, eight bits of information. I guess the main reason, graphically, was he wanted to make sure everyone knows it's an apple."

"What else could it be?"

"A cherry. He wanted to make sure no one would mistake it for a cherry."

Hmmmmm, thinks the writer, deflated. So much for biblical symbols. I have been ready to ask him about my Garden of Eden theory. At the mention of puns and cherries, I decided against it.

Steve is getting restless. He takes his feet off the table and slips them back into his sandals. He has things to do before catching the plane to Boston. A writer from *Fortune* magazine is waiting to talk to him. Then he has to pick up a suit. "All my suits are either in a state of disrepair," he mutters, "or at the cleaners. And they close in an hour."

There is time for a final question, and I am relieved to hear that his reply answers the one I did not ask. In an oblique way he confirms my reading of the logo. Eve bit into the apple and opened whatever secrets had been locked inside The Tree of Knowledge. It is Steve's belief that a bite into Apple II, or Apple III, is a 1980s way to liberate some new resources of the mind.

I ask him if he actually foresees the day—the one we so often hear predicted now—when every home owner will have the console and the personal keyboard.

"They are going to be in every school and office first," he says. "Eventually in every home. We think there is a revolutionary process going on here, which is the integration of personal computers into the society at a very individual level. That is going to take about ten years to happen, and we want to be a driving force behind that."

He leans forward and his voice accelerates, with the same fervor I heard when he summed up this valley's history.

"It's my belief that each time there has been a new source of free energy, civilization has taken a step forward. We are living now off the wake of the petrochemical revolution, based on petrochemical energy, which is still basically free, relative to the energy inside. And look at the impact *that's* had! We have very rarely had things that free *intellectual* energy. Language was a big breakthrough. And mathematics. And printing, to some degree. But this thing"—pointing to the twelve-pound, typewriter-sized Apple II sitting on his desk, with video display terminal attached—"it takes about a third of the power of one lightbulb, and it saves me two hours a day. That is basically free intellectual energy. In a very limited way. But it is going to get much more interesting in the next decade. I think the revolution is going to come through free intellectual energy. It is going to dwarf the petrochemical revolution, and I think it is going to happen in my lifetime."

At Brooks Hall the various shapes this revolution might take had been visible everywhere. Signs and portents. It had been half carnival and half window into the near and distant future, and you could not afford to dismiss any of it, since you never know when or where next season's Jobs-and-Wozniak will emerge to make their unannounced debut. It had ranged from the awesome and dazzling to the zany and absurd.

Back in one corner I came across a game called Interface with Fiction. A long-haired fellow was getting up the nerve to add some of his own dialogue to a novel that had been programmed onto a storage disk. The novel was called *Wheeling and Dealing: A Gripping Tale of Skullduggery in High Places.* The story line was incomplete. Spaces had been left for the viewer/writer to add whatever came to mind.

The fellow at the keyboard was giggling. His two pals were giggling too, wisecracking for the small crowd. When the rolling print stopped, four words appeared at the bottom: PRESS ENTER TO CONTINUE. Then the name *Henry* appeared. Long-hair made his move. He typed in, *Do you like rock and roll?*

His friends cackled loudly as the words popped onto the screen. Instantly the next line emerged from the programmed narrative: *Lorraine does not answer.* PRESS ENTER TO CONTINUE.

Henry reappeared, and long-hair typed, *I want to get better acquainted.*

To which Lorraine replied, *Have you ever been to Seattle?*

Five more programmed lines rolled across the screen, leaving the next line to Henry: *It looks like the sun is going down.*

The computer replied, *Lorraine: The bank is only four blocks away.* PRESS ENTER TO CONTINUE.

Upstairs in the meeting rooms that surround the civic auditorium, other personal computer stories were being told, in the seminars and forums scheduled throughout the three-day weekend. I heard an attorney describe how one can be used in an anti-trust suit. I heard a nurseryman talk about growing flowers out of season. I heard a math teacher talk about how it works in his high-school classroom. He looked about fifty, crewcut, light-gray suit. "We're trying to utilize this thing that has been against us all these years," he said. "The tube. The screen. Kids nowadays, they are questioning more and more, and yet they are believing less and less. Let me give you an example of what I mean.

"I can take a math problem involving a lot of calculations about, say, velocity and speed, and I can work it all out on the blackboard, and half the kids in the class won't believe me. They just do not believe I know the right answer. But if I program that same information into a micro-computer, and they see that same answer come out on the screen, then they believe it. And so they learn it. I am not saying I like that situa-tion. But this is the world we're living in, and we may as well confront it right now."

He paused then, to let that sink in, and I slipped out the door.

It was getting late. In the main hall the booths were shutting down. Sales reps were listening patiently to the last questions from lingering browsers. Over the sound system a firm voice informed us that the auditorium was closed for the day. Anyone who did not hold an exhibi-tor's pass was now invited to leave.

Stepping into the Civic Center plaza, I was slightly amazed to see that the world was still there and that the sturdy granite buildings had not moved or changed their shapes. It was six o'clock. The sun was out of sight beyond Twin Peaks, but the sky was rich with color, adding russet hues to the stonework and the domed City Hall across the square.

I moved in next to the wall of the Civic to pick up some of the heat the day's sunshine had stored there, and I noticed then the date of construction, which is carved into the cornerstone: "Anno Domini MCMXIV."

It was odd, both startling and comforting, to see those ancient num-bers, just upon leaving the scene inside. I wondered if the men who had built this building back in 1914 had any inkling, when they carved the stone, what would be going on here in 1981. They couldn't have, not when they were living in an age that still reached back to Rome and Latin lettering as a way to validate the moment. I started thinking about that, about languages, and the ways they slide and change and overlap and replace one another, and about the things we hold on to. On the outside of the building, "Anno Domini." On the inside, analogs and binary programs, the lingo of the eighties.

It brought to mind a man I had seen in the lobby when I first walked in. Past the door a glossy ASC II word processor had been set up, with a little sign inviting you to try it. The demonstration keyboard was smooth and flat and seamless, its letters and numbers embedded in vinyl or Plexiglas. A dozen people stood gazing at this machine with a kind of blank wonder, looking like a group of Arkansas farmers might have looked on the day the first horseless carriage chugged into town. They too had just walked in off the street, and this was the first thing they encountered. At last a slender fellow in a windbreaker stepped forward, as if fate had chosen him to be the one who risks his hands and fingers. His face empty of emotion, he pecked out *How now brown cow.* The script popped onto the screen, beneath another line, still flickering there from another time zone, earlier that morning perhaps, or yesterday, when someone else had typed, *Now is the time for all good men . . .*

It was just a small moment in the hurtling rush of technological advance. But it struck me as a kind of emblematic touch point—the touching of that man's fingers to the keyboard. Steve Jobs and Steve Wozniak had seized the day, leaped into an opening, and thereby joined the ranks of those who are changing our lives, the ways we organize our time and work, our storage space and our memories. And now, this weekend, in the basement underneath the Civic Center, one of the world's newest industries was making its next incremental leap into the marketplace, giving large numbers of the general public close-in looks at all this scaled-down electronic wizardry. Meanwhile, the man on the street, this fellow in the windbreaker who has just wandered in to see what is happening at the Sixth Annual West Coast Computer Faire, he cannot make the leap all at once, or he chooses to make it tentatively, makes his cautious reach for the vinyl keyboard. Holding a few moments longer to what he knows, he tries to tame the unknown with some last little shred of the tested and familiar, *Now is the time* PRESS ENTER PRESS ENTER *Now is the time for all good men to come to the aid of the quick brown fox jumps over the fence how now* PRESS ENTER *How now brown cow* PRESS ENTER TO CONTINUE.

The Cupertino Psychic

Back in the late 1940s, when my family moved south from San Francisco into Santa Clara Valley, the town of Cupertino consisted of a service station, a grammar school and a feed company. This was some ten years before the valley began to expand and explode. Cupertino was still what it had been for over fifty years, a rural intersection surrounded by thousands of fruit trees. The intersection is still there, four lanes wider in all directions, connected to the past by the feed company storage silos, which somehow have survived. Houses became so much more valuable than trees that nowadays the orchards have all but disappeared, replaced by curving avenues and spreading subdivisions. They spread on one side toward the mountains to the west, and on the other side toward San Jose, which has moved out to meet its proliferating neighbor.

There is not now, nor has there ever been, any direct connection between the community of Cupertino and its name, such as you find in the names of nearby towns like Mountain View and Los Gatos (The Cats), where lions and wild cats once roamed the hills. The name was taken from a creek first crossed by the De Anza expedition in March 1776. Its name is now Stevens Creek. But the earlier name was El Arroyo San Joseph Cupertino, because St. Joseph happened to be the patron saint of De Anza's chaplain and diarist, Fray Pedro Font. The Spaniards stopped overnight, named the creek, then pushed on northward to secure San Francisco Bay for Spain, and the creek just flowed along for the next hundred years, until the first wave of settlers and ranchers had their houses built and their claims staked out and felt the need to identify and christen their scattered community.

Most California place names that survive from the earliest explorations are Spanish. This one happens to be Italian. Cupertino is a small town in southern Italy where Joseph Desa was born in 1603. He joined the Franciscans in 1625 and soon became famous for his powers of levitation. He could actually fly through the air. It is said that he could fly from the door of the church all the way to the altar, over the heads of the worshippers. He once flew into an olive tree and remained kneeling on a branch for half an hour. There seems to be a great deal of testimony to verify that he did such things. Hundreds of people witnessed his miraculous feats. According to *Butler's Lives of the Saints*, Joseph's career "was one long succession of ecstasies, miracles of healing, and supernatural happenings on a scale not paralleled in the reasonably authenticated biography of any other saint."[17]

He died in 1663. A hundred and four years later he was canonized, but only after these events had been "reasonably authenticated"—an intriguing term, considering the extent to which religion relies on faith to explain so many mysteries. Acts such as Joseph's seem to defy reason. Yet if enough people witnessed the padre flying through his chapel, if enough accounts accumulate, then reason somehow is satisfied, the seemingly improbable joins the realm of fact, and Joseph joins the panoply of saints.

What does this have to do with the cluster of suburbs that have mushroomed in the northwest corner of Santa Clara Valley? Well, it is the oblique prologue to a trip I made a while back, to call on a woman who has come to be known as The Cupertino Psychic. Her name is Kathlyn Rhea. In no way is she descended from Joseph Desa. She just happens to live in a town which, by a few quirks of local history, bears the name of an Italian town he once lived in. If there is any connection at all, it lies in the fact that she too is capable of certain feats that sometimes seem miraculous (though she herself would be the first to resist that word), yet have now been "reasonably authenticated." Her visions, the elusive programs she claims to see or hear or sense, cannot yet be measured by instruments but they have produced some astonishing results.

By reading auras, the various colors psychics say we emanate, she can diagnose imbalances in the personality. By projecting into someone else's body she can "feel" what is wrong, sometimes see the ailment and diagnose a physical illness. She can look at a name and assess the reliability of a possible business partner, look at another name and get a mental picture of a criminal or a missing body.

Early in 1979 her inner screen provided facts that led a sheriff and his deputies to the body of a man who had been missing for five months. He was Russell Drummond, seventy-eight years old, from Stockton, California. He had been camping with his family near the New Hogan Reservoir in the Sierra foothills, just about due east of San Francisco, when he wandered off through the scrub oak around the campground and disappeared. A hundred-man search team combed the area for four days with no success. His family later continued the search till winter weather set in. A daughter-in-law finally called Rhea, on the recommendation of a psychologist familiar with her work. After hearing the story and asking some questions, she sat at her Cupertino desk, zeroed in on the old man's program, and taped her perceptions, which the daughter-in-law then delivered to the sheriff of Calaveras County.

The old man had died, Rhea said, and the remains would be found on a hillside three-quarters of a mile due east of the campsite, under vines, near an area that had been cleared. Rhea pictured the site and also the old man's state of mind before he died. "The gentleman was confused. He was tired and he went to sleep. It wasn't a painful feeling for him at all."

When the sheriff and his deputies listened to this tape, they heard enough to convince them it would be worth checking. They decided to reconnoiter the area described, then get an early start the next morning for a thorough search. They didn't have to make two trips. They drove out there, took a look around and walked straight to the body.

Sheriff Claud Ballard said the information provided by Rhea, who had never visited Calaveras County, was amazingly accurate. The dense thicket of chaparral covering the hillside has the look of vines. Some clearing had been done nearby, and clearing for a new road had been started at the bottom of the hill. By the time they found it, the body was too far gone to determine the exact cause of death. But from the bones they could tell there had been no fractures. He had not been hit, and he didn't fall. The old man had a history of brain-damaging strokes. Ballard concluded, "It looks like nature took its toll."

Rhea herself does not release information like this to the press. The story broke from Calaveras County. It made the wire services, and immediately she was flooded with calls for similar kinds of help. As a result, within just a few days another body turned up, near Fresno, owing to extraordinarily precise data she provided in another case. There were more headlines, and a burst of sudden fame. She woke one morning to find two television crews on her front lawn waiting for interviews. Overnight she had become the psychic who locates missing bodies.

The publicity didn't hurt, but she was troubled by the morbid tastes of the media. "I was still doing what I'd been doing all along, for the past thirteen years"—by which she means applying her skills to search out not only missing bodies, but also missing airplanes, missing guns, missing horses, missing health, missing emotions and missing relationships. She has counseled thousands of people, from FBI detectives to hyperkinetic children, on matters ranging from unexplainable aches and pains to speculation in gold and securities ("Should I buy now? Should I sell now? Should I wait a week, or a month, or a year?"). Her accuracy rate is reliable enough that physicians regularly call for her services, corporate executives seek her out, and California police departments hire her to give seminars on how the people in the squad cars can amplify their own untapped potential for extrasensory perception.

She lives on the outskirts, just where the valley's broad basin begins to rise toward the nearest ridges of the Coast Range, giving her a splendid view across the basin, toward Mount Hamilton and the eastern foothills. This recently built, two-story home is her headquarters. Jerda, her assistant, meets me at the door. Jerda has been working here about a year and could be a receptionist or administrative assistant almost anywhere. She is young, attractive and smartly dressed, and the small downstairs office she commands could be almost any kind of office. There are leafy plants, new filing cabinets, stacks of phone books. Jerda comes from Los Angeles. She herself is not psychic. "I didn't know anything about this stuff before I went to work for Kay," she says. She qualifies because she is good at what she does: she takes care of a wide correspondence, takes all incoming calls, juggles the writers and reporters, and schedules consultations for Rhea's many clients.

There are no signs, indoors or out. Down along El Camino Real, the gaudy commercial boulevard that stitches together the many towns along the peninsula between San Jose and San Francisco, you will still see signs from time to time that say "Palm Reader" or "Fortunes Told." That is a different league, a different world, from Rhea's. She does not need to advertise. If anything, she needs this full-time assistant to help her fend off the cranks and the crazies, the curiosity seekers and the hypochondriacs looking for a miracle cure, so she can keep her attention on her work.

Jerda opens one of the file drawers and begins to pull photocopies of press clippings from neatly labeled folders. She hands me a sheaf, with instructions about which to read first, then disappears up the stairway to announce my arrival.

I glance at the clippings. I'm more interested in the office. I don't know what I expected, coming to call on a professional psychic—maybe something Egyptian, or Rosicrucian. There is nothing occult floating in this atmosphere, not even any incense. No god's eyes in the corner, no mandalas or totems, no pyramid boxes. This could be the reception room for a tax consultant or a dentist. I have actually seen more mysterious fixtures in the offices of certain Berkeley dentists who work overtime to look as hip as their customers.

It makes perfect sense. If you are a professional psychic, running a business, you do things in a businesslike way. But this throws me, catches me by surprise, starts me thinking about others I have run into over the years, people who professed various powers, who had followers, or "practices." They have long abounded in this part of the world. According to the editors of *The Psychic Yellow Pages* (Out of the Sky Press, Saratoga, California), one of the nation's largest concentrations of such people—i.e., clairvoyants, astrologers, Tarot readers, graphologists, numerologists, astral travelers, healers, trance mediums—can be found within easy driving range of this office, roughly within a triangle that includes Monterey Bay, Mendocino and greater Sacramento.

I think of Mother Jenny, frail and ancient white-haired medium who held a diploma from The Church of Scientific Natural Laws. At weekly meetings she would fall into a trance, lift a bony hand, and let the voices speak through her. She was such a gentle, ethereal soul you could easily believe that if anyone on earth had touched the other side, it was she.

I think of Frank, the retired merchant seaman who ushered me into his shadowy basement den one damp afternoon in San Francisco and insisted I tell him nothing about myself, not even my name, until his reading was finished. We had never met. He wanted no data that might compromise the flow of his intuitions about my character. I closed my eyes while he felt the knobs on my forehead and the sutures across my skull. His first remark amazed me. "Don't ever take a job where you have to sit down. You won't last. You're a person who has to be on his feet a lot." Frank didn't know I was a writer, nor did he know that a dozen years earlier I had built a chest-high writing table so I could work standing up. How could he have hit upon this, just by feeling around my head? From that point forward he had my undivided attention.

Earthquake Lady was a different matter. I heard her lecture one night in San Jose. It cost me $2.50, which I gladly paid because I was in a mood to believe her. She had predicted a couple of important earthquakes right to the day. I think everyone in the hall wanted to believe. Her picture had appeared once or twice in the *National Enquirer*. She said she could see under the surface of the earth and into its depths. I could go along with that, but I began to backslide when she described what she saw beneath the surface of the ocean. She saw old buildings rising to the surface near Big Sur, evidence of the return of the lost continent of Lemuria. I lost faith entirely when she prophesied that by the year 2025 we would be able to drive on dry land from California to Hawaii.

I am just starting to look through the clippings—

CUPERTINO PSYCHIC
CREDITED IN DISCOVERY OF MAN'S BODY

. . .

PSYCHIC SHOCKS DEFENSE LAWYERS

—when she appears at the door, shocking me with the startling clarity of her gaze. Her hair is red. Her eyes are large and green, with hints of copper ringing the pupils, and they seem to emit light. They carry such a penetrating luster they are almost separate entities. If, as it is said, psychics see things the rest of us don't, these would be the eyes for that kind of seeing, though I soon learn other organs are more important than the eyes. The solar plexus, she will tell me, is where the invisible programs register first; hence the phrase "gut feeling" to describe so many of our precognitions, premonitions and hunches.

We leave Jerda to take an incoming call, and I follow Kay across carpets, up the curving and carpeted stairway to the second-floor living room where there are more carpets and Persian rugs and elegantly padded furniture. The style is slightly oriental, since she spent a couple of years in Japan while a former husband was stationed there. She commissioned a Japanese craftsman to build her a long wooden coffee table that now faces the fireplace. Beyond the table hangs a lacquered, three-paneled Japanese screen. Everything is tasteful and expensive, but not in the way that prevents you from relaxing. Clearly someone lives here, spends time here enjoying the furniture and the view. She is wearing a velour lounging suit and slippers. It is mid-afternoon; her working day is over. She is in her late forties and very much at ease in this domain, in command of things. Kelly, her sleek and curious Doberman, comes sniffing up to me. Kay calls him into the next room where she herself is headed, toward the impressively stocked bar, to pour some drinks, Chivas Regal for her, a taste of chardonnay for me.

I am looking out the panorama window, skimming ten miles of house and treetops. From here you can begin to see how many trees still grow in the valley, in spite of galloping development. In the yards, along the avenues, there are probably still as many trees as people. I am thinking of the trees and also of the fortune tellers and card readers somewhere out there on the distant boulevards, and of other stock images associated with the psychic zone: the witches, who have made a comeback in recent years; the figure in the Gypsy shawl who summons spirits from the past.

Next to the fireplace a long lounge chair is positioned to catch the view. She stretches out on this, kicks off her slippers. I decide to mention the Gypsies, the séance, the apocryphal table that unaccountably rises from the floor.

"Well, I'll tell you," she says. "I don't see anything occult about this. I just don't have visitations from spirit guides. There is nothing religious about it either, as far as I'm concerned. God has never spoken to me. All the mystical trappings and supernatural wrappings a lot of people associate with this, it doesn't interest me one bit. What interests me is how can we use these abilities, how can we apply them in everyday life."

This is what fascinates me about her work, I tell her, the ways she has applied it, for therapy, for crime detection, for medical diagnosis. "But still," I say, "in order to call forth these powers . . ."

"*Abilities,*" she says, correcting me with a stern laugh. "*Powers* is a no-no. Much too mystical. These are abilities everyone has, to some degree or another, and can develop."

"Okay. Abilities. In order to call them forth, something still has to change. I mean, you're not there all the time, are you?"

I am thinking at the moment of Edgar Cayce, the legendary trance medium from Kentucky, who would go into a waking sleep and speak the visions that appeared to him. "Do you go into a trance?" I ask. "Anything like that?"

"What people call a trance, I interpret as nothing more than a self-hypnotic state of relaxation. It can be a key. Whatever you learn as a key and do repeatedly can be a thing that will help you get into the state. If you happen to start with cards, then that is the key that says, Hey, get into that relaxed state. It's the same with the crystal ball, the pendulums, the Ouija board—they are triggers, ways to help you get into that state. I have used them all. One of my early teachers used a crystal ball. She was a little retired schoolteacher down in Florida. She read crystal balls. She read palms and cards. She was like somebody out of *Arsenic and Old Lace,* bright blue eyes, white hair, cute little figure. I spent a lot of time with her, and one of the things I learned right away was that after a while you're not really looking at the ball or the cards. You don't really need anything but yourself, to relax and get into it. Now I can shift so quickly, I might look out at the clouds while we're sitting here and transfer over to this other state of mind. Although just recently I discovered a little crutch I have been using, which I wasn't even aware of. For years I have been using a tape recorder in my sessions. I fell into the habit of waiting for that 'on' key. Those two buttons would go down to start the machine, and *I* would start."

She laughs at herself and sips her Scotch and calls to the Doberman who is barking down at a jogger in the street below the window. I am still wondering how this process works. What is it that *starts?* If it isn't a trance, if there is no spirit guide, if the cards don't really matter, or the Ouija board or the tea leaves—then what is it?

"What you do," she says, "you start perceiving another person instead of yourself. Normally we are tuned in to our own programs, where we're coming from, how we're feeling, who talked to us last, who got mad at us. If I am sitting here, I'm aware of whether I'm thirsty or hungry or have a problem. That is my normal condition. As soon as I go to work with a client, I become as totally aware of that person as I was a moment ago of me, and then I begin to translate what that person is broadcasting."

"But what about the missing body out in the wilderness, or the kidnapper you have never seen?"

"That involves a process I call mind-reaching. Psychically I go to that event and work on it. I reenact it in my mind."

"It's just floating in the atmosphere somewhere."

"Everything exists simultaneously," she says. "Past, present, future. It's a matter of tuning in to the program."

The language of radio and television, I soon learn, is central to her view of psychic perception. Volume, tuning, broadcast, receiver, transmitter, feedback—these are the terms she uses to describe the process she's immersed in. We all broadcast programs, she says, by which she means a signal or vibration each thing in the universe emits—each plant, each animal, each structure, each book, and bracelet and planetary body, each person. As a broadcaster your program contains the total range of your experience. As a receiver your sensitivity will vary, depending on how you are tuned. Some are low receivers, with the dials turned to "off," perhaps because of an overload experience in early childhood that associated certain levels of awareness with too much pain. In the broad middle range there are what she calls medium receivers. We pick up signals from time to time, via hunches or the coincidental caller we can identify the instant the phone begins to ring, but we seldom know what to make of this. High receivers can sometimes pick up thirty or forty programs at once—a liability, to be sure, until you train yourself to single out the program you're trying to hear.

Judging by her track record, Rhea is getting reliable signals from somewhere. As I listen to her describe the workings of the psychic radio, I tell myself this is certainly no more mysterious than the radio itself. Suppose you go into the farthest corner of your house, I think, into the darkest closet. Stand in there, shut the door, and listen. Are you alone? No. Not for a second. There are radio waves all around you. There are famous songs, foreign languages, gospel sermons, car commercials, and talk shows swirling around by the hundreds, unheard. As soon as you switch on the transistor, there they are, jabbering away. If I can accept that remarkable process, is it too great a step to accept the notion that we each broadcast some kind of program on these impalpable wavelengths that a highly tuned person like Kay Rhea has trained herself to "receive"?

I try to put it into other words. "So someone presents you with a name, a picture, a description, and out of this infinite blizzard of imagery and information that is going on around us all the time, you aim your attention toward *that,* and something opens up. You get a detail. Or a scene."

She nods and sips her drink and throws a hand out for emphasis.

"But the most important thing is translation. People get flashes all the time. This is what drives the police crazy. Someone gets a flash about some crime and they call the police. Now, it may be a pertinent flash, but the person who had it doesn't know how to begin to interpret it, and the police shake their heads and say, 'Lord preserve from the kooks and the crazies.' A while back I got called in on a case by a family who had already called in seven or eight psychics before they got to me. Their little girl had disappeared. When I got off the plane the mother and the FBI agent were waiting. Later the agent told me that on the way to the airport he had said to the mother, 'What kind of nut do you have coming in this time?' He and I were good friends by then, and he told me, 'I had had it up to my ears with wackos.' This family had called in one gal who had to have a can of spray paint before she could start to work. She had to spray a cross on the wall. This was her trigger, you see. Well, on the day I landed I told the agent I did not want to talk to the parents until I had worked with him for a while. I didn't want to be confused by their programs. After four hours of talking to me, he told the family that if they didn't want to pay me to stay on the case, he would pay me. I had convinced him I knew what I was doing. But I had also told the family that the little girl was dead, and this was too much for the father, who wasn't ready to accept that. You see, if I get called in, I take things very methodically, step by step. I do not come from the bolt-out-of-the-blue school. I want to make sure the programs I am getting really relate to the case."

When she is talking about cases her voice speeds up, as if trying to keep pace with a leaping mind. One case reminds her of another. Her hands and arms start to dance. I would like to hear more about the family, but she rushes on, free-associating.

"Not long ago a woman came in and told me her horse had disappeared. So I went through it step by step. Where was the horse? In a field, one of these grassy fields where a lot of owners keep horses, surrounded by fence. I tried her horse going over the fence. But no, I didn't see it going over the fence. I checked out each of the other owners. Did anyone leave the gate open? I put myself in each situation, you see—a little theater in my mind—but no, no one had left the gate open. 'Okay,' I said to her, 'how many horses were in that field? Give me their names. Your horse,' I said, 'is the only expensive-looking animal in the crowd.' 'Yes,' she said, 'the others were really just ponies.' I said, 'There are two gates, aren't there?' She said, 'Oh no, you just go through the one gate.' 'I get the feeling,' I said, 'that I can open two gates on this property.' 'There's just the one we go through,' she said, 'and we have a padlock on it that no one touched, and well, oh yes, there is one fence-gate farther down the road, a piece of fencing that can be opened, but it's hardly ever used, no one knows about it, and you can't even see it from the road, because of the brush.' 'Well,' I said, 'the second gate is the key to this. If it's near the road and someone is looking for a way to get a horse out of there and the main gate is padlocked, they're going to find a way.' It was interesting, you see. I had just worked with a fellow up around Redding who had lost a very expensive horse. It had been rustled. I felt his horse had been taken east and north. I described some canyons where I felt it had been taken, and the fellow said, yeah he knew the place, it was outside Redding, a kind of badlands up that way. Even the police didn't go out there. So when this gal came in with her missing horse and it looked like it too had been rustled, I thought, I'll try the same track, see if they took it out into some woods around here or up into the mountains. But what I got were tumbleweeds and desert country. The woman said, 'There are places not too far from here with tumbleweed.' And I said, 'No, that's not what it means to me.' I saw that the horse had been taken south, and they had changed trailers somewhere. Then I got a sixty with it. So we pulled out the California map, and I started at the top working down, still thinking they just might have gone north. But you know where Highway Sixty starts? It starts in Los Angeles and goes across to Phoenix, then up into New Mexico and ends in Amarillo, Texas. But I didn't feel Amarillo. I felt more tumbleweed and box canyon, such as you'd find in Arizona and New Mexico. And I felt that the horse would eventually be seen in a magazine with a slick finish, some kind of cattleman's publication, with a man riding it, carrying a flag, doing something official."

"Did she ever find the horse?"

"I don't know. I just gave you that as one example of how it works. Sometimes I get immediate feedback, sometimes it takes months or years. Sometimes I never find out. One thing I had to learn is not to get bogged down in whether or not someone goes and follows through on what I give them. I give you information that applies to your area, then it's up to you to use it, figure out how it fits. You still have to go out and find the suspect, or chase down the rustler, or make some personal change in your life—whatever it takes. I am only a tool. Like any other instrument people use, I only do part of the job."

She has been a practicing psychic since the late 1960s, when she made the conscious decision to train and open this part of herself. But experiences leading toward that decision began in early childhood. She was born in the Sacramento Valley. She spent her school years in Eureka, a lumber town on the north coast. Around the age of nine she had a moment of out-of-body awareness she still remembers vividly.

"Sitting in the sunlight out on the front porch one morning I suddenly saw that the little piece of me that was talking and thinking wasn't all of me. I was outside looking at this thing that was me and yet looked so foreign, such a strange part of me, and I knew then that the main part of me wasn't that at all. I remember it was like discovering a new world, the excitement of that, and the fear of it too."

Growing up, she had many such moments, sometimes exciting, sometimes fearful. She speaks of nighttime terrors when she was very young, of inexplicable voices muttering in her darkened room. When she was an adolescent, the dating game lost some of its savor because she always "knew" if a boyfriend was going to show up on time or be late, and why. She felt that, for whatever reasons, she was more perceptive than others, but this was not something she understood, and she didn't talk about it. If she had, her mother would probably have discouraged the subject. The mother, who came from Arkansas, once told Kay that when she herself was a young woman she could walk into a room and project the fragrance of flowers so strongly, other people would smell them. But relatives warned her not to do this because it was "evil." As far as Kay knows, this was the only family precedent for paranormal abilities, and the mother had kept it to herself until just a few years before she passed away.

A future father-in-law was the first person she met who had direct experience with psychic phenomena and would talk to her freely about it. He was a physician in Wisconsin, a hospital chief-of-staff, who often used ESP for diagnosing illness. In Wisconsin in the 1950s this practice was not something he could discuss openly with many of his patients or share with the world at large, but he found a kindred spirit in Kay. "He got me interested in the fact that it was part of the human potential, and not just something to frighten me. He was my first real teacher on the subject, though I only listened and made no attempt then to act on the knowledge."

It was 1965 when she decided to do something about this curious awareness she had been carrying around all her life. She was a naval officer's wife at the time, living in Florida. She had four children. She had been a model, and then had run modeling schools. She had been featured on her own TV program, and she had produced beauty pageants. "And I was bored," she says. "I was so bored with all of that, I would organize a fashion show and turn it into an enormous production, just for my own amusement. I would stage scenes, bring in choral groups, rock-and-roll bands. Meanwhile, in my off-time I was going out to investigate this thing, to see if I could make it work."

Where she lived, there was much to investigate and plenty of support for that kind of searching. Certain features of Florida and California are similar in their abundance: sunshine, citrus trees, retirement communities, motorcycles, long beaches, and people professing assorted psychic abilities. Rhea recalls one lakeside town "that is nothing but spiritualists. They own all the land, they have homes, and you can walk up and down the streets for hours getting readings."

In Florida, and later in and around Virginia Beach, headquarters for Edgar Cayce followers, she visited dozens of them—spiritualists, psychic counselors, crystal ball gazers, Cherokee healers, and Gypsy card readers—researching this patchwork sub-world as systematically as she had searched for an organized religion some fifteen years earlier, when she made a list of all the Christian denominations within driving distance and visited the priests and ministers one by one. In 1965 she was watching, and listening, sorting it out. She found some teachers, and she found some charlatans.

"When I first started this, I insisted that I find out how things were connected. I was not interested in mumbo jumbo or a trip to the stars. I wanted to know how it worked, and how I could make it work for me. Believe me, I went and checked out a lot of them. I went to one church where they would turn the lights down and from outer space would come these stones and pebbles, being thrown by your guides and loved ones. Well, outer space happened to be a cardboard box in the back room, where the message reader stored all this cosmic fallout."

At home she devised exercises for testing herself, on the theory that psychic ability is like a muscle: the more you actively use it, the more efficient it can become. She practiced first on small daily events, forecasting the immediate future: At the meeting this afternoon, who will be there, male or female, married or divorced, what clothes will they wear, what colors, and what will be the mood? She practiced on the dog races, until she could pick eight out of ten winners in a day at the tracks. She began to go inward, meditating in darkened rooms, looking for ways to get in closer touch with her subconscious and with the elusive channels of perception.

After several months of this, something opened. She began, she says, to see. "At first I was startled. Yet it was familiar. At last I was reclaiming what I had lost as a child."

From that point onward, while she continued to study and explore, she was gathering clients of her own. By the early 1970s she was back in California, living in Cupertino. Word of her skills spread quietly. Soon Peninsula physicians were bringing her in on difficult cases. Sheriffs were learning to trust her mental images. When the Drummond case broke in early 1979, with the media attention that followed, her career took a quantum leap. The day I first called, she had just spent two hours with a man running for state senate, seeking her advice on ways to approach the campaign. A few days hence she would help a local attorney select the jury in a suit against a large manufacturer. She was also tooling up for a seminar sponsored by the Sonoma County Sheriff's Department. When she invited me to come along, I asked her what it was all about. Since the Drummond case, she said, more and more of her time was going into crime detection. She showed me a mailer sent out from Santa Rosa to counties all over northern California:

THE OBJECTIVE OF THE SEMINAR IS TO AID THE LAW ENFORCE-MENT OFFICER/INVESTIGATOR IN RECOGNIZING AND ENHANC-ING HIS OWN ABILITY TO FORM A STRONG LINK BETWEEN HUNCHES AND SUCCESS IN THIS PROFESSION. THERE WILL ALSO BE DISCUSSION OF THE USE OF PSYCHICS AS A LAW ENFORCE-MENT INVESTIGATIVE TOOL.

She has offered several of these around the state, acting on her belief that all of us have latent abilities tucked away somewhere, with the dials turned usually to off, or low, or medium. I was eager to make this trip, though I wasn't sure why. To meet the detectives, I told myself. To see

Kay in action. I didn't realize until we got there that, despite my readiness to believe what she says, I was embarked on a little detective work of my own.

The all-day meeting begins with a continental breakfast, in the banquet room of a restaurant on the south edge of Santa Rosa. Some sixty men and half-a-dozen women have shown up. Two dozen more were turned away for lack of space. The county sheriff is here, with most of his department. I see FBI detectives, National Park Police from Yosemite, officers from San Francisco and Sacramento, from San Mateo County a hundred miles south, Mendocino County to the north, Calaveras County across the central valley to the east. A few have come under protest, I learn later, ordered to attend by their departments. But most are here by choice. Some have worked with Kay, others want to know more about what she does, and how. Several have taken hypnosis courses, such as those offered for the past ten years by Martin Reiser via the Los Angeles Police Department. For them, ESP is a logical next step. Early in the meeting she asks how many have called psychics in on a case, and at least ten hands go up.

Assisting her is Tom Macris, a police artist from San Jose. Macris is in his thirties, husky as a ranch hand, in his suede jacket, his thick mustache. In college he studied art. After thirteen years of working his way through department ranks he became the man who tries to visualize and draw composite sketches of suspects. In recent years he and Kay have worked together on numerous cases. Macris describes one that would have been a double homicide, had not an elderly woman survived to tell the tale. Her account of the assailant was the only lead police had left, and that had been muddled by fear and shock and old age. The police put her under hypnosis and began to ask for details, while Rhea used her psychic skills to picture what the woman had seen. Macris then made sketches, feature by feature, until the four of them working together—the hypnotist, the victim, the psychic, and the artist —produced a face that investigators could work with.

This is the process that sets Rhea apart from most other psychics who offer crime information. She seems to have endless patience and a willingness to spend hours exploring her visions. During the meeting I talk to Detective Sergeant Rick Oliver, the fellow who organized it. He first heard her speak at a seminar like this in Santa Barbara in 1978. A few weeks afterward he found himself driving down 101 from Santa Rosa to Cupertino to seek her counsel.

"The first thing I had to learn," he says, "was how to work with her information. If you give her a problem and just turn her loose, she will ramble on and on. What you have to do is ask her pointed questions. If she sees a car, ask her what kind, what color, what year, what speed, and in which direction, and so forth. That way, you get this dialogue back and forth, between what she is seeing and what is relevant to the case."

Oliver wears a dark pin-striped suit with vest, giving him the look from across the room of a very stylish stockbroker. He is tall and trim, with sharp, striking features, thick black hair, black mustache, blue eyes as specific as bullets. I have noticed that most of the men sport mustaches. It reminds me of something Kay said earlier. She feels comfortable at these gatherings because the detectives are like the navy pilots she knew during the years she was married to one. "They laugh hard, and they drink hard. For some reason they like to stay close to the edge, in that constant state of risk." She might have added that they generally sport mustaches and have very steady eyes. Oliver could be a fighter pilot. A faint scar across the top of his nose says he once took a serious blow right there. I get the feeling he has absorbed and survived a good many. On his card it says "Robbery/Homicide Investigations." Kay's effect on his work has been twofold: He has called her in on some tough cases. And he has learned to rely more and more on his own intuitive abilities. "After that seminar in Santa Barbara," he says, "I became aware of things I had been seeing, noting all along, but paying no attention to. It's like I had been living in the dark and suddenly the light went on."

When the session started, I found myself sitting next to John Barnes, a probation officer who looks to be in his sixties. He does not pursue suspects. He deals with people after they have been convicted. He tells me he is looking for ways to find "the person" inside certain cases assigned to him, the human being so often screened off by defenses and double-talk. "They tell one thing to the court," he says. "Then they turn around and tell something else to the P.O. Half the time they don't know who they are, and I don't, and yet that is the key to helping them change their patterns." He is sitting in today because he's open to any tool that might provide some insights.

The reasons they are here divide up about fifty-fifty: Kay's inner screen as a crime-solving aid; and some large or small curiosity about the uncharted workings of the mind. Rick Oliver wants more of both. A polygraphist with the sheriff's office wants to tune in more effectively on suspects hooked up to his lie detector. John Barnes wants to penetrate the walls of identity.

And what about me, I am wondering. What am I doing at the Semi-

nar on ESP and Law Enforcement on a Friday morning in this restaurant banquet room in Santa Rosa looking out this floor-to-ceiling window at yet another ridge in the long Coast Range? I discover that I am
simply waiting patiently, like the sleuth with plenty of time on his
hands, hoping a certain piece of evidence will reveal itself, drop into
place. It is not that I doubt psychic phenomena. I believed Mother
Jenny. I believed Frank the merchant seaman. I believe Kay Rhea. But
in an age controlled by semiconductors and data banks and the movements of petroleum from Point A to Point B, this kind of belief can
always use some confirmation. We take the miracles of technology for
granted. Psychic matters move in and out of shadow, always elusive, still
unmeasurable. What I am looking for is an eyeball example of that other
kind of movement, the wireless, nonelectronic, and invisible movement of information from Point A to Point B—one that has not yet been
reported in the papers and one that cannot be explained away. It
wouldn't have to be much, just something to corroborate all the talk.

Rhea is good in a situation like this. She is at ease in public. She demys-
tifies herself and the process as quickly as possible. She knows how to
tell jokes. She speaks with authority, yet she doesn't lecture. She spends
the morning describing sample cases, to illustrate her concept of the
psychic radio. The afternoon is given over to exercises for testing the
extrasensory. The first are quite simple. She holds up oversized playing
cards.

"Can you feel the difference between black and red?" she asks.
"Colors emit different vibrations, which with practice we can learn to
read. Can you feel the difference between hearts and diamonds?"

These soon give way to photographs of criminals, the idea being to
see what you can "get" from the photo, see if you can guess what the
crime was, the motive, the m.o.

She holds up a photo of a desperate-looking fellow with short hair,
a bad complexion and dark shades. It's the blow-up of a mug shot.

Someone calls out, "That's my brother."

As the quick burst of laughter subsides, someone else says, "What did
he do this time?"

A more serious voice attempts a serious reaction. "Kidnap/rape."

"I think he robbed a bank."

"He looks like a killer to me."

"No. I think he robbed a bank."

"Why do you say that?" someone calls out.

"I can tell by the glasses. Bank robbers will wear dark glasses."

"That's not ESP."

"He could be a movie producer."

"He could be a TV writer. I think he writes for 'The Waltons.' "

Tom Macris, the police artist, is at the podium with Kay. He has chosen the photos, from cases he knows, so he fields the comments. "Who said this guy robbed a bank?"

An officer in a sport shirt raises his hand.

"Well, that's what he did," Macris says. "Do you mind going a little further with this?"

The man stands up. Macris says, "What else did he do?"

"He was solo."

"Okay. What else? How was he traveling?"

"No vehicle."

"Sometimes it helps," Macris says, "to try to envision the situation, create a mock-up in your mind of what could have happened. Put a vehicle into the picture and see if the guy gets into it or walks away. Does he drive away, or does he sit there? If he walks away, in your mind, it could mean he wasn't using a vehicle."

In his sketches Macris himself has been learning how to make use of Rhea's step-by-step visualization technique. But it doesn't quite work for the officer who is trying it here for the first time. He ponders a moment and says, "I see a Plymouth from the early sixties, like a Valiant. Beige."

"He did have a vehicle," Macris says. "But it was a red El Camino."

The man sits down, a bit disappointed, it seems, that he couldn't psych the color of the car, but still curious, leaning forward toward the next photo. I have been aware of him since mid-morning when he raised an essential question: "Isn't it possible that what you're calling intuition or ESP is really just a combination of basic intelligence plus years and years of experience?" Kay's ready answer was that sometimes all three are working together and it's hard to separate them; yet at other times certain insights come that cannot be explained by any combination of intellect or training or experience. A female officer, sitting next to the man who asked the question, is about to demonstrate this difference.

Rhea holds up another photo, of a man wearing a watch cap. His eyes are heavily lidded. His skin shines, and his head tilts, as if his whole body stands in a slouch.

Someone says, "This guy is definitely a killer."

"He's a burglar," says another.

"No. It doesn't fit," says someone else. "Burglary and this guy, they just don't fit together."

The woman speaks up, for the first time. "There was a victim involved."

Macris says, "That's good. What else do you get?"

"There is an arrogance about him. No. More than that. He doesn't see other people. He dehumanizes them, depersonalizes them."

Someone says, "I know he was out in the street somewhere."

Another voice says, "He was in a car. Either that, or he had one."

The woman is gazing hard at the photo. She is slim, in her thirties, wearing a long-sleeved blue sweater, short hair—a jogger, perhaps, or a racquetball player. She has that kind of assertive slimness. She says, "He did something with his hands. He pushed down with his hands."

She raises her arms with elbows squared and the hands spread wide, and she pushes them down toward the table. She seems to have more to say, but other theories crowd the room.

"I still think he's a burglar."

"Yeah, I'll go along with that."

"He's a dealer."

"There's a car in it somewhere."

"He deals in heavy drugs."

Eventually Macris reveals that this fellow's crime was combined burglary and violent rape. He had entered an apartment intending to rob the place, had discovered a woman in bed, and before assaulting her had covered her face with a pillow. In describing this act, Macris makes the same arm gesture the female officer made, whereupon she calls out, "That's what I felt! That made her less than human. By covering her face he depersonalized her completely."

Color rushes to her cheeks. She seems indignant, outraged by the scene she witnessed, and also surprised that she has witnessed it. I too am surprised, amazed. Here it is, a small, distinct case of some signal passing from that photo into her brain. She does not know Macris or the fellow in the photo. She comes from another department, in another county. The man next to her, in all likelihood, made an educated guess that the gent in dark glasses robbed the bank and did so alone. The woman's perception—of the arm movement and the deeper motive— is of a different order. It is too precise to be coincidental. Rhea would say it was something picked up from the program being broadcast by the picture. She would also call it an example of the extrasensory perceptions that can be augmented and channeled and trained.

It is strangely reassuring to observe this little exchange. If one such frequency on the psychic radio band is open, so are a multitude of others. I only regret that the signals passing back and forth in this particular room have to do with such a grim and gruesome subject. When it comes to surprising movements from one place to other, I would rather be witnessing the cures of a Paiute medicine man or the leap of Saint Joseph of Cupertino from the church door to the altar, over the heads of the worshippers. But in the 1980s it is appropriate, perhaps inevitable, that paranormal abilities are being explored as new weapons in the crime detector's arsenal. In an eerie way it connects to something Kay said a week later, the third time we met. She suspects that the runaway crime rate was prophesied many years ago by Edgar Cayce, whom so many have looked to when the future of the West Coast is discussed.

We were back in her living room, and the subject was earthquakes.

"I get calls all the time," she said, "from people wanting to know what I think about earthquakes and Cayce's predictions. I know he was accurate a lot of the time. But he was also interpreted by words. His transcribers only wrote down what he said. They did not see what he saw. This is one of the reasons I love working with a good artist. Tom and I get very closely tuned. Through his sketches I can actually show someone else what I see. If you turn off the TV picture and only hear the voices, you're not going to get half of what's going on. Very often I'll start describing something and then realize my words aren't telling enough. I'll go back over it, and more thoroughly, trying to get the picture right. I'm not sure Cayce knew that about what he saw. If you are looking at California, the country of earthquakes, and you see something shaking up out there, just to the point of being flooded or dropping off into the sea—think of all the things that keep happening—why wouldn't he have sensed the feeling of one wave after another until he actually felt that California was going to be devastated? This may be the way to translate the severe quakes and floods he predicted which have not materialized in a geological way."

"The social fracturing," I said, "rather than something right down there in the earth."

We were interrupted by Kelly the Doberman growling at the window. A car had pulled up outside. Moments later a young man appeared at the top of the stairs with Kay's cats, who were home from the vet, where they had been neutered, two Abyssinians seven weeks old, lean and aristocratic in spite of the indignities just suffered. Kay talked to them a while, then turned them loose. I was in the middle of asking, "How do they get along with Kelly?" when the dog, who had been waiting for this moment, leaped across the Persian rug with a terrible bark and sent the Abyssinians, stitches and all, running for their lives toward the back of the house, in a scene from a dog-and-cat cartoon.

"Kelly likes to wind 'em up from time to time," she said, on her way out of the room, "just to see what they can do."

She returned with one of the cats in her arms. "Where were we?"

"The fracturing," I said.

"Oh, I see some quakes coming, no question about it, some big ones. I don't go around predicting things like that, but you know, every time there's a shaker I get a rush of people coming in for counseling." She laughed lightly, the way veteran Californians often do when discussing the apocalypse. Beyond alarm. "Shall I sell my property, they want to know? Shall I sell my company? Shall I move away? And I tell them, 'You just keep in touch with me. When I move, you move.'"

Hearing this, I recalled that as I approached her front door this time, I did not have the impression she would be moving for a while yet. New lawn had just started to sprout. New plants of some ground-covering vine had been recently set out, to preserve the steep slope at the front of her property. As I arrived, she was finishing a meeting with a regular client, a man who operates a small chain of popular health-food restaurants. She had spent two hours helping him think about where to build the next one, and when, and who might manage it, and generally forecasting business trends for the years ahead.

Dobashi's Market
and Other Forms of Kinship

The people who shop here call it J Town, J for Jackson Street and J for Japanese, though nowadays Koreans and Samoans shop here too, and Chinese restaurants named Twin Dragons and Mandarin can be seen and smelled from the doorways of The Ginza and Minato. There is a Buddhist temple in the neighborhood, an aikido school, a tofu factory selling soybean curd wholesale and retail, down the street from the Mai Lai Beauty Shop, the Manila Barbershop, and the headquarters for the Filipino Community of Santa Clara County, Inc.

Inside Dobashi's Market, past the Winstons and the Diet Pepsi and the racks of Laura Scudder's Mini-Tacos near the counter, you come upon the boiled eel, the quail's eggs, the dried seaweed, and the squid-like root called *gobo*, as well as the crinkly cabbage Japanese call *napa*, and Korean pickled radishes packed in Hawaii, and small cans of shrimp paste imported from Luzon. Rice, both brown and white, is sold at Dobashi's in fifty- and one-hundred-pound sacks.

I have been told by Christopher Yip, an architectural historian in Berkeley, that the "oriental" look of San Francisco's Chinatown was actually a Caucasian invention, conceived by designers brought in to restore the district after the original buildings—which were made of wood and resembled many other buildings in early San Francisco—burned down in the 1906 fire and earthquake. Nothing like this has ever happened on Jackson Street. It has never been decorated or developed. The only Asian features visible from the street are incidental—ideograms underneath the wording of a neon sign, the writhing dragons in a restaurant window, the roof line of the Buddhist church, which can't really be seen until you pass Dobashi's and take a left. Here in the shopping district, which covers five or six blocks, the buildings are close to the ground, two stories usually, going back forty or fifty years to the days when San Jose was a middle-size West Coast farm and orchard town instead of what its current promoters sometimes refer to as "America's fastest growing city." To turn off First Street and onto Jackson Street is to move instantly from America's fastest-growing city onto the main street of some small town which is both American and Asian and which has miraculously been preserved: it is neither shopping mall nor tourist attraction. The people who use these stores and restaurants live nearby, or they drive in from other parts of Santa Clara Valley. There is nothing for the visitor to do, unless he is ready for lunch, but prowl around Dobashi's or look at the airline posters in the window of Phil-Am Travel, or stroll along the street, as I happen to be doing, in the company of a remarkable woman.

Her name is Kathy Akao. We are passing through J Town on our way to the offices of the Asian Law Alliance, and we are talking about immigrants, the successive waves of immigrants, from all four directions, who have been settling and resettling California at irregular intervals since the first great wave that followed the discovery of gold in 1848, bringing Yankees from the east, Southerners from Dixie, and Chinese from the coastal counties near Hong Kong. We mention the wave that carried her grandfather here, the long wave sent eastward by events before and after the Russo-Japanese War. We mention the wave sent northward by the Mexican Revolution of 1910–17, and the massive exodus out of the South and Southwest during the Great Depression of the 1930s, and a later exodus, more diverse and less publicized, that followed the severe Eastern winters of the late 1970s, which sent new thousands West in search of milder weather during the same period that another wave of settlers from Asia was approaching from the opposite direction.

Kathy is explaining how a little neighborhood such as J Town, as nucleus and sometime shopping center for the large and scattered countywide assemblage of people with Asian backgrounds (first-, second-, third-, and fourth-generation Californians) helps to account for why so many in the latest wave have settled in and around this valley since the mid-1970's, and all up and down this particular coast.

Kathy herself is *sansei*, third generation. Her features are classic Japanese, such as you see in the prints of Hokusai or Hiroshige: graceful neck, oval face, brown eyes made darker by the pearl-like vitality of her skin. Kathy's ambition is classic 1980s American. At thirty-one, married, with a four-year-old son at home, she has gone back to school to study law. She has another year-and-a-half of course work to complete at the University of Santa Clara, where she is president of the Asian Law Students Association. In her spare time she works with the ALA, a legal assistance group who find themselves more and more involved these days with the recent arrivals from Indochina.

"They like it here," she says. "And I think food has something to do with it, maybe a lot to do with it, just knowing you can get certain kinds of food, and the whole feeling of kinship that goes along with these preexisting Asian communities. Did you know that within an hour of where we stand, you can get just about any kind of food imaginable?"

Her eyes go bright at this thought, a rise of the appetites mixing with her empathy.

"It creates a more familiar situation. Certain kinds of flavors. And having other Asian faces around, even if they don't speak your language, you don't feel so out of place. I have a friend, she is not a refugee, she grew up in Southern California just like I did. She went into physical therapy and got her first job in a town back East where she was the only Asian American for miles around. She said people would actually find an excuse to come into the hospital and stand outside the door where she was working, to look at her. They weren't hostile or malicious or looking for trouble. They were just curious. But it makes you feel odd. I can understand why a person from one of the Southeast Asian countries, whose life is already in pieces, would want to be around people who look familiar. They say half the refugees end up in California sooner or later. No matter where they're sent they land on this coast first, at some base like Hamilton, and the Indochinese working there start telling them about the climate. From the moment they land they are hearing that California is the place to be. It isn't like Vietnam, but it's going to be more comfortable than Michigan or the Rockies. And there are job opportunities. This is what they hear. They call it the Second Migration, Indochinese heading back after they have lived awhile in some other state."

"Tell me more about the kinship," I say. "People with legal problems are drawn to this office because they feel . . ."

"I think there is some kind of bond, a feeling of trust. It works both ways, you see. When my grandfather came over here from Japan, he was in exactly the same spot. For years he worked for room and board, as a houseboy and cook for some politician he had met in Hawaii. In one way it was a break for him to have a place to come to in America. At the same time, it was a demeaning position he had to endure because he didn't know the language or the laws or much about how the system worked. This month one of my cases involves a Vietnamese family who have had a bad time with a landlord. This is typical of what can happen. When he rented them the house, he demanded a last-month's rent of four hundred and forty dollars. Then, after they had done a lot of work fixing up the place, he gave them thirty days' notice, forcing them out, and he won't give them back the four-forty they put down as a deposit."

"What do you do?" I ask. "Where do you start?"

We have reached the offices. In the reception room she hands me a pamphlet called *Landlord and Tenant: Rights and Obligations.* It is printed in Vietnamese. She has taken it from a long rack where other pamphlets—on aliens' rights, naturalization, auto repair—are printed in English as well as five more languages: Chinese, Japanese, Samoan, Korean, and Tagalog.

"We have all this literature," she says. "Sometimes all they need are the simple facts, spelled out in their own language. In the case of that landlord, we are now taking him into small-claims court. But we don't always get that far. Often the refugee family will say they don't want to press charges. Some of them are afraid to come looking for help, or ashamed to. They will just move out and take the loss, afraid if they make any waves something worse might happen. A landlord ripping them off this way makes me angry and I want to nail him, and it makes me very sad because I know someone in my own family has gone through something just like this. My parents told me what it was like at the beginning of World War Two when all the Japanese Americans were rounded up, here in California, and what it was like after the camps closed in 1945. When the war started, my grandfather was picked up by the FBI because he was an alien. He was an alien because it was against the law for him to become a citizen. He had been living in this country for over thirty years, but there was still a law on the books that prevented Japanese from naturalizing. People can get caught in situations like that, and sometimes it seems like there is no way out."

The Asian Law Alliance rents a refurbished, one-story Victorian with three-lap siding, porch pillars, and Grecian filigree across the eaves. Sitting at the corner where Jackson meets First, it is conveniently, you might even say symbolically, located, with a view out one window toward J Town and a view out another toward the gleaming, glass-walled futuristic city and county public buildings that rise between downtown San Jose and the freeway.

In the conference room, where leather-bound law books line the shelves—California Law, Immigration Law—I meet Glenn Sugihara, one of the founding members. A *sansei* like Kathy, Glenn is an attorney now working full-time for the ALA. Back in the mid-1970s, during his student days, he joined a loose coalition of Asian American law students at the University of Santa Clara who were discovering, or rediscovering, their own ethnic origins and felt a common need to connect this with their legal training. They reached first toward the elderly in nearby communities, particularly the *issei*, first-generation immigrants from Japan, many of whom still live in and around J Town, some without families, some with only a halting knowledge of English, or no English at all.

"They have all the problems of senior citizens anywhere," Glenn says, "income inadequacy, political impotence, with the added problem of language. So it was a natural place for us as Asian American law students to offer some service."

He is about six feet tall, with thick black hair, a thick Zapata mustache and ready laugh. At age twenty-eight he is a big, solidly built man with a quiet, forceful strength of character, the kind of fellow who works doubly hard for whatever he is called to do. When he talks about his work, there is the lawyer's thoughtful delivery, together with an urgent idealism and a feeling that things are still being discovered, that in some way new ground is being broken each day. This sense of origins, of his own Asian-ness, is still unfolding.

"In high school," he says, "I ran around with whites. Before that it was Chicanos. I was born in East L.A., right there on Brooklyn Avenue, where the junior college is. So I started out in the barrio. When I was seven, my folks moved over to Orange County into a mainly white neighborhood. Then when I came up here I met these people at Santa Clara, who were just starting to form this Asian Law Students Association, and it was a different kind of thing. Suddenly there was a way I could meaningfully use what I was learning, a basic social end I had always thought was important. When I was an undergraduate, it took me a while to figure out what my politics were. But I knew I wanted to do something positive, to help people. This law group gave me a vehicle; it felt most comfortable because this was the population I came from. I'd like to help low-income and oppressed people generally, but the population we have best access to is the Asian one. I also think this is a population that is under-represented."

Their first support came from a local branch of the Japanese American Citizens League, who offered some money and a small office a few blocks east of their present location, nearer the middle of J Town. Meanwhile their work with the *issei* opened the door to a whole sub-world of legal need that was as unfamiliar to the young law students as it was to the foundations and government agencies they soon went looking to for funding. Here was a *nisei* (second generation) widow with an eighty-nine-year-old father-in-law dying of cancer but disqualified from MediCal because of a discrepancy in his one asset, a $2,000 burial policy. Here was a young Japanese wife abandoned by her American husband, an ex-Marine, with two kids and a mortgage payment. They found a small Samoan colony afflicted with a 70 percent unemployment rate. They discovered a Korean contingent that had swelled from a few hundred in 1975 to over six thousand, five years later. And they began meeting the new immigrants from Indochina—a family facing unfair eviction; another family split three ways, the children in Belgium, the wife in Saigon, and the father here in San Jose bewildered by anxiety and immigration policy; a third family on contract to a Salinas Valley grower who seemed to see them as reincarnated Louisiana sharecroppers out of the 1920s.

Unwilling to walk away from all this, the Law Alliance felt compelled to expand. They went looking for more support and eventually got it, from the city and the county, United Way, and some private foundations. But at the outset they ran into a curious and ironic obstacle: the reputation Asians have for succeeding in American society, for assimilating quickly and taking care of themselves so effectively that there are no longer any problems that might require outside funding.

"A lot of people," Sugihara says, "when they think of the Asian population, envision the so-called Model Minority. The most difficult thing to bring to the attention of government and foundation people, in trying to get money for legal aid for this new wave of immigration, was the dramatic change the multifaceted Asian-Pacific population has undergone in recent years."

I asked him if other groups like theirs existed.

"Up in Oakland there is the Asian Law Caucus. They were established four years before we were. Their focus is Chinatown, with all the problems you can think of in a ghetto. Originally some of us conceived of ourselves as being like the Caucus. Then we realized that this community is really a lot different. It is more like Southern California, and in that sense maybe a more typically California setup. The Asian communities are not located in one condensed district like Chinatown. You have a sprawled-out city with all its divisions and subdivisions, and underneath the top layer of what appears to be typical suburban America are these various ethnic groups sprinkled all over the place with all their hidden problems and treasures."

He comes back to the Model Minority, a concept that is a source of both pride and frustration.

"I think America is an adversary society. Our culture, Asian culture, a lot of the time is not oriented toward that. The part of our culture that is commendable, that does not want to complain or raise the gripes, which has a lot to do with the image that has been created of the Model Minority, can work against you too. Because it is real. It is not only a stereotype. Because of that, generations have been pushed around. It is nice now, that we can take a role, perform a function in this adversary system, on the part of our own people."

This reluctance to complain goes hand in hand with a willingness to carry one's load, and with the stoic acceptance that allowed a generation of Japanese Americans to be interned in camps here in California and other Western states between 1942 and 1945. *Shi kata ganai* was a phrase the elders would repeat. "It cannot be helped, it must be endured." It reminds me of what Kathy said about the renters who prefer not to raise formal complaints against their landlord for fear of something worse. They too had spent time in camps—a different kind to be sure—refugee camps in Southeast Asia. But there is a connection. Certain Americans from the West Coast, like Glenn's parents, and Kathy's parents, along with their alien grandparents, were interned here in their home country during the war because their ancestry was Asian, and America was at war with Japan. These Indo-Chinese pouring into California have spent time in camps set up to cope with the multitudes fleeing the aftermath of another war in Asia, one that America's military forces helped to escalate. It intensifies the ethnic bond, the sense of kinship. Glenn himself was not interned; he was born a few years after the camps closed. But, like Kathy, he has heard the stories. The family memory is always close to the surface. When he says, "Generations have been pushed around," this is what he means, though when I ask him which camp his parents spent time in during World War II he shrugs it off, he laughs. He prefers to treat it lightly.

"Oh, it's a very romantic story. Mom and Dad met each other in camp. They were both at Heart Mountain, up in Wyoming. My father was ice-skating outside the camp hospital and my mother was working inside. He claims he didn't know she was in there, but he was skating around and around on a patch of ice about as big as this chair. That's how they met. Then the next thing he knew he was on a boat sailing for Japan, and writing love letters back to her. He had volunteered for the draft, I guess, and they put him in army intelligence."

Glenn's mood has shifted. He is uneasy talking about Heart Mountain. I try to change the subject. "Did your father have family overseas?"

"He got sent to Hiroshima right after the war. That's where his family had come from. But there weren't many left. Most of them were wiped out by the bomb."

This little bomb of information is allowed to hang in the air only for a moment. Then it is quickly defused. You do not want to be heard complaining about what went on thirty-five years ago inside the camps —the barbed wire fencing, the wind pushing desert sand up through the floorboards—and you do not want to be seen dwelling on what happened to the relatives in Hiroshima.

With a grin Glenn says, "They tell me that nowadays it looks a lot like Los Angeles."

I say, "I guess that's right. It was rebuilt during the same period L.A. was growing the most. They're both postwar cities."

During the five years when the ALA was evolving from a loosely knit student group into a funded legal aid center, the number of Indo-Chinese in California increased from several thousand to well over a hundred thousand. Minh Quang Dovan was among the few living here before 1975. When he completes his law degree at the University of Southern California he will be in an extraordinary position, one he has been growing accustomed to as a volunteer with the ALA and during his four years with the County Department of Social Welfare. Born in North Vietnam, he has spent most of his life in California. He is fluent in English and Vietnamese and has a working knowledge of the legalities in both countries. He also knows from firsthand experience what the refugees are going through, since, as he puts it, "We ourselves were refugees twice."

His family had survived the French war in Indochina. He was three in 1954, when the French pulled out and the Geneva Accords divided Vietnam north and south at the seventeenth parallel. He remembers the hasty, chaotic exodus.

"We left under quite a lot of pressure and left everything behind. We had been what you might call well-to-do. When the Communist regime took over we were basically ostracized. They did not care much for people who had a little bit of wealth. We had to start from scratch. We stayed in camps in the south, and we felt a lot of discrimination there. The distinction between North and South Vietnam is a bit like the distance between Boston and Alabama. It's geographical. It's cultural. They speak the language differently. Luckily my father had an educational background. If he'd had no schooling, we might have starved to death."

In Saigon, Minh's father found work translating from Vietnamese into French for an American scholar on a Ford Foundation grant to Southeast Asia. In time this led to a job in the United States. Minh was ten when the family moved to Monterey.

"We were luckier than many of the others," he says. "When we first came, there were not many Indo-Chinese around and not much strong feeling toward Vietnamese. We are actually kind of intriguing people. Each time I met someone they would think I was either Japanese, Chinese, or Korean. When they ran out of ideas, they would ask where I came from. I would tell them, and they would say, 'Where's that?'"

Like Glenn, he grew up mostly with Anglo kids. He did his undergraduate work at the University of California, Santa Barbara, where he was chairman of the small contingent of Vietnamese students there in the early 1970s. In 1973 he felt the urge to return to his homeland, now devastated by the years of unrelieved conflict. He spent four months in South Vietnam working at a village for children orphaned by the war.

"It was a dangerous time to be there," he says. "When I decided to return to the U.S. they did not want to let me leave. They wanted to draft me into the Vietnamese army. I had dual citizenship, you see. I was a naturalized American. But in Vietnam, unless you renounce your citizenship, you are always considered a citizen. To them I was born in that country, I have Vietnamese parents. To get out I would have to petition to renounce my citizenship, and that can only be approved if the president of the country signs it. Eventually some relatives intervened on my behalf, I wrote out the petition and it reached the hands of the president."

It was one of those wretched twists of political fate—drawn back to the war-ravaged land of his birth by some ethnic and cultural yearning, he had to renounce his citizenship in order to escape.

"You must still have the dual affection," I say.

His face doesn't register much, but the pain of choice, the profound loss, is carried in the way he says, "Yes. It is something intangible."

Minh is twenty-nine, compactly built, with a tennis player's lithe muscularity. Before I leave I will hear him planning a tennis match with one of the lawyers. I notice his covered racquet leaning next to the door. In that moment he is totally American, totally Californian—in the midst of an intense, demanding and seemingly all-consuming workday, programming his leisure time. And yet when he talks about his birthplace and the refugees he counsels, something else takes over. His face does not move much. The eyes don't seem to blink. The skin has that porcelain texture, very smooth, light in color, almost polished. It is not what you call a mobile face, no enormous smiles, no wrinkling of the forehead to convey concern; and yet the very way he contains himself conveys the pent-up urgency that at times seems ready to break right through the smooth surface. I feel he carries a pent-up fury over what he has to witness and a smoldering frustration over how little he is able to do in the face of what he sees. He talks about the pirates on the open sea who attack the boatloads of refugees trying to reach Thailand or Singapore.

"They build these junks and pack people in there, two or three hundred side by side, where they have to sit together for four or five days on the open sea. Everyone I talk to tells me the same story. I have had over twenty relatives of my own killed on the open sea, attacked by the Thai pirates."

The pirates attack and steal and rape the women, and rape them again. Those who survive reach a camp as tightly packed as the boats were, and after months or years of this they get processed and arrive in America, where they find themselves in a HUD housing project on the east side of some city like San Jose, in a state of shock, physical, psychological, spiritual shock so severe they are not only displaced persons in an alien land, some of them are emotional zombies.

"They come in stunned," Minh says. "And there are no resources for them, mentally, or emotionally."

Suddenly he laughs. He recalls a grotesque example of how far apart the cultures are, and this draws a grim laugh. "So I take them to a psychiatrist. They are depressed, and the psychiatrist, he is trying to identify something about their inner world. He says to the person from Vietnam, 'What kind of animal do you want to be?' Then the person from Vietnam looks at me and says, 'Hey, who is crazy here, me or him?' The psychiatrist tries to apply Anglo/Freudian gestalt therapy techniques to someone from a totally Asian culture and it blows everybody's mind."

Those who have the hardest time coping, he says, are the elderly. They arrive here and find that they have merely exchanged one kind of hell for another.

"They sit there in the housing project with a view out over the freeway and they always use the same statements whenever I see them. They say, 'I have a mouth but I cannot speak. I have ears but I cannot hear. I have eyes but I cannot see. I cannot speak English and I cannot hear English. I speak Vietnamese but no one understands me.' They tell me this and I feel terrible and I do not know what to tell them. They came here voluntarily, you see, and when they get here they say, 'I wish I was back there and buried in the land where I was born.' "

Minh is quick to point out that the instinct to survive is as strong as the impact of displacement and culture shock. "It may sound ethnocentric if I say this, but the Vietnamese are very mobile, very industrious, they adapt very quickly. They have gone through so much before they get here, just having to find a job or get the training to take a job as some kind of technician, this is not difficult at all. I have had clients who were attorneys or professional people, pharmacists, university professors. Very often they cannot use their skills in the U.S. because of the language, or licensing. They have to learn a new trade. The majority of my male clients, and some of the female, are electronics technicians, computer programmers. They go to nine-month programs at technical schools and become employable. They are off aid the minute they finish that training. A lot of the people who look in at this refugee situation, they do not see far enough to realize that these Indo-Chinese are only on temporary assistance until they can become self-supporting."

Clearly Minh takes pride in this capacity to survive adversity and prosper. But there is another kind of survival that moves him in a deeper way. He is about to tell a story. He pauses and looks at me awhile, as if deciding whether or not to tell it. I realize later that he is remembering and reexperiencing a moment that was for him an illumination, a flash of insight into who his people are and thus who he himself is and where he has come from.

"I once had a case involving two elderly Vietnamese, husband and wife, both on welfare, and their grandson had broken a car window. They wanted to make good on the damage. They went to the owner of the car, who had already taken care of it through his insurance company. They offered to pay him for the damage, but he said he didn't want the money. It was a small claim, he said, the company would take care of it, and the damage was already repaired. That's when they came to us for legal advice. They wanted to pay someone for their grandson's damage. We called the company, and the agent said they didn't want the money either. To cancel the paperwork already in motion would create more paperwork than it was worth, and they would rather go ahead and process the claim. I tried to explain this to the old man from Vietnam, but he kept saying, 'No, no, I have to pay, I have to pay.' Finally, so much time had gone by with him sitting there, it looked like we would never get him out of the office if we didn't tell him something. So I said, 'We will see what we can do about it. We won't take the money now, but we will try to call the insurance agent again and persuade him to accept some money from you.' The old man said, 'Okay, but you take this money.' And I said, 'No, we don't want it. You keep it until we talk to the agent.' But he kept insisting, so finally I said, 'Okay, we'll take it, and if we can't give it to him, we'll return it to you.' I started to write out a receipt for him, and he said, 'No, we don't need a receipt. We trust you. We trust you with the money. You keep it.' And right there, it hit me. He was giving us all he had left, but it wasn't the money. Here were these two old people with nothing, no resources, no family, no homeland, and no income. They had nothing left to offer but their honor and their trust. I said, 'Okay, we'll hold the money for you and see what we can do.' "

Kathy and I are walking along Jackson Street again, past Kogura Appliance, a restaurant called Ken Ying Low, the meeting hall of the Gran Oriente Filipino Masonic Order. Looking elegant in her lightweight tweed jacket and designer jeans, she is leading the way toward a place where they serve San Miguel Dark, that thick beer imported from Manila, with the texture of port, the malty flavor, the label that looks like a splash of Spanish tile. We are talking again about her grandfather, who was born in Japan in the 1880s. As eldest son he should have had promising opportunities there, but by the time he was seventeen his parents were both dead, and the family's holdings had crumbled. Japan's early efforts to industrialize, to move from a feudal to a modern society in one generation, had depressed the rural economy of his home region. He joined the multitudes leaving for America in the first years of this century. Since the West Coast was where he landed, America for him was California, where he found work and settled. He was a fisherman, a farmer, a strawberry rancher, a man of the sea, and a man of the earth. He raised ten children, who in turn raised more than thirty grandchildren. When Kathy was born it was still against the law for her grandfather to become a citizen of the United States, though the huge clan he spawned were all citizens by birth. This law was finally rescinded in 1952, which in the history of laws is not that long ago.

"It is so easy to forget," she says, "how long it has taken, how late in the day it has been before certain basic rights have been recognized."

Now Kathy is raising a son of the fourth generation, a *yonsei*, finishing up her law degree at Santa Clara, and volunteering legal help for the most recent wave of immigrants. At the ALA they are all young Asian Americans, with the vigor of their youth and the empathies of kinship, raised in places like San Francisco, Monterey, Oxnard and Orange County, looking into the eyes of men and women from Laos, Phnom Penh and Saigon and seeing their own parents or the grandparents who made a similar journey across the Pacific toward this same coastline hoping for the second chance.

Six Reasons
Why I Love Los Angeles

Approaching from the north I begin to feel it when I am still a hundred miles away. I feel it as soon as I squeeze through the rocky gap at Gaviota Pass and swing out onto the coast road below the Santa Ynez Mountains. There is something else in the air, a shift in the landscape, another quality of light. The slopes behind me resemble slopes in Mexico. Where stone shows through the brushy cover, it has the color of bright sand. The air is softer now, and the ocean tropical. Passing through this arm of the Transverse Range I have crossed some elusive border, and already I hear it coming toward me, the highest octave of a distant early warning system. I feel the outer edges of its irresistible magnetic field.

I have entered the Southern California continuum, which can be seen in the pervading tropical style, and in the film on the atmosphere which thins or thickens, depending on what has recently rippled outward from L.A., and in the affection for the L.A. *Times*. In Santa Barbara you will find the *Times* in thousands of early morning driveways, while a bit farther north and on the other side of the Santa Ynez Mountains the *Times* starts competing with the San Francisco *Chronicle,* whose sphere of influence reaches that far down the coast and as far north as Grant's Pass, Oregon. Some say Portland.

Southern California, I have heard it argued, actually begins at San Luis Obispo, or on the final climb outside San Luis where the black oak appears for the final time, or for the first time, depending on your direction. Others will say Santa Barbara is the point of entry. My friend

Noel Young, who lives up the hill from the Santa Barbara Mission, says the line is not a matter of foliage or climate but of dialect. Somewhere between San Luis Obispo and Santa Barbara, he claims, there is a point where people stop saying *rodeo* with an accent on the first syllable, as it is pronounced around Salinas and in the central valley, in Oregon, Nevada and Wyoming, and they start saying *ro-DAY-o,* with the accent where Spanish speakers put it. I would add that in the transition zone, in these borderlands between San Luis and Santa Barbara, one more feature of the bio/social environment begins its subtle shift, defining the passage from one part of the world to another. I am talking about the traffic. The precise point on the roadway will vary from day to day, from hour to hour. But somewhere along here—in my experience, usually south of Gaviota Pass, soon after the coastline makes its dramatic bend inward, eastward from Point Conception—there is a moment when the traffic leaps to its next increment, and something affects the look of the vehicles themselves, the ways they are decorated, the profiles and steering wheel attitudes of the drivers. It is not like traffic farther north, and this is not at all like approaching San Francisco, which comes upon you suddenly and can take you completely by surprise. The very look of this traffic, together with the Mexico coloring of sea and mountain, and the denseness of atmosphere, both thicker and softer, embraces and surrounds you and warns you and announces that, whether or not L.A. is your destination, it is looming and you are almost there.

This is the first reason I love Los Angeles: the mounting anticipation of the approach, arriving from the north, as the traffic accelerates, especially at twilight, when desert hues tint the sky. Then everything ahead of you seems tender and expectant and exquisitely perilous.

Today I happen to be making a late-morning approach. In June this is a serious mistake, but here I am speeding along the Ventura Freeway, bumper to bumper at seventy miles per hour, my eyes afire, and remembering a simpler and purer time, another approach, by air, into L.A. International, some two months ago, looking down upon the cottony lake that I am now plunging into head-on. The peaks of the San Gabriels rose out of it into a perfect sky, sharp and clean against the blue, creating the look of an island seen from afar, with rain-heavy clouds gathered around some old volcano. I thought of Carey McWilliams's book about Southern California, called *An Island on the Land.* The book came out in 1946, before this lake existed. But the lake fits what he was talking about: a realm apart, with its own legends, its own perimeters, its own zany architecture, and nowadays its own self-generated atmosphere, this blanket of cotton camouflage that makes the city invisible from above.

Arriving by plane you drop down into it, becoming then invisible to other planes and passengers as you sink to the bottom of the lake made of smoke and fumes and haze, and after a while, if the city is going your way, as it was for me that day, you simply stop seeing it. It's there, but it isn't there, just as the roar of jet engines goes unheard by people working at the airport.

From the Pacific Southwest depot I went straight to Hertz where a car had been reserved. A terrific smile from the handsome Chicana there, as she handed me the folder with the typed-up forms. I stepped outside to the traffic island, just as the Hertz shuttle pulled up and the doors whooshed open. Climbing aboard, I handed my folder to the driver, who was in command, an airport veteran who knew exactly what to do. There were plenty of seats, plush and roomy. At the lot my keys waited on a little outside table under a canopy, in full view of the rows of gleaming cars. The noise of takeoffs and rev-ups and landings was so thunderous I could not hear what the woman was saying, but it didn't matter. I didn't need words. I needed the car, which she pointed out with a smile, still talking.

It started right up. The windows were clean, the tank full. In seconds I was heading down Century toward the San Diego Freeway, which took me north toward the city. It was miraculous the way lanes opened up in front of this car, as if the path were cleared by unseen cordons of escort police. When the L.A. freeway system is on your side, there is absolutely nothing like it anywhere else in the world. I have also been picked up at this airport by a chauffeur, in a long dark Cadillac, an English chauffeur who wore one of those hats and called me "sir," and that was, for me, a moment to remember. But the fact is, I prefer to do my own driving. It is part of the thrill. In L.A. the freeway is a form of entertainment, a form of action, a form of commitment, a form of engaging the environment on its own terms, and, if you survive, a source of infinite satisfaction. Survival, in this case, means arriving on time, which I did, intoxicated with my own prowess.

I was headed for a studio, where a studio executive was going to talk about a script. There was a place to park near the door of the building. Inside the cool and air-conditioned lobby the instant I pressed a button, the elevator doors slid open. One thing that keeps L.A. charged up is the outside chance that at any moment you can run into a celebrity, and this is what happened on the way to the meeting, during the perhaps thirty seconds I was riding in the elevator. A man was standing there, watching the floor numbers blink. I recognized him, though in the first seconds I did not know why. I tried to place his merry and wasted eyes. As we reached the fourth floor, which was my destination, it came to me. I was electrified. "You're Jack Nicholson!" I proclaimed. The doors slid open. I had to step out. He smiled and said, "That's right." The doors closed and he ascended.

I walked to the reception desk, made of polished mahogany or teak. Square golden columns rose out of sight on either side of the desk. Everything glistened, expensive and new, and she was glad to see me, an alluring woman with her face made up in the highest fashion, her cheekbones brushed with deep color, her eyes dark, feline and attentive, her blouse white, seeming to glow with white. I had a feeling about this receptionist, a feeling that may not be fair to project upon her, since we only exchanged a few words and glances, but she seemed to me in that fleeting exchange to embody, to make palpable, why I love this particular city when it is on my side, rolling in my direction. All this high-speed equipment is located in the subtropical setting, so that all movements fast or slow seem sultrier, more languid and exotic, and also more precarious, because at any moment you could be swept into something indescribably corrupt and ruinous.

She pressed a buzzer and murmured my name, and in the distance a door opened. The executive was coming out to greet me, a young fellow wearing the kind of khaki-colored military shirt a recruit might have worn during World War I right after boot camp but just before going overseas. As I stepped into his office I said something about the weather, just in passing, and he said, "Oh? What's it like out there today? I haven't looked."

It was then 11:45 A.M. The office was cool and appeared to be fully lit by daylight pouring in from somewhere—an effect of the pure white walls, the white furniture, a few shrewdly placed lamps. He pulled back the floor-to-ceiling curtains revealing a gaseous cloud of mangy white pressing right up to his window.

"Hmmmm," he said, squinting into it. "You see that revolving sign over there? It's nearly half a mile away. Some days, when it's really bad, I can't see that sign at all."

Well, I was thinking, if it isn't one thing, it's going to be another. Every place people live has its price. Minnesota has its blizzards, Galveston has its hurricanes, Kauai has its tidal waves, and the Sacramento Delta has its floods. That day I was willing to forgive L.A. everything, because everything I had touched was functioning the way it had been designed to function. The city worked. When L.A. works it is wonderful.

But that was then, as Governor Jerry Brown has said, and this is now, and days like today put your affection to the true test. Racing along the bottom of this lake at seventy, I am still miles from town, when the red lights start popping in front of me, and the traffic slows to a creep, then a crawl. Later on I learn that somewhere far ahead, on other freeways, in other parts of the system, various disasters have conspired to bring us all to a gradual halt. An oil truck has overturned and exploded, setting other vehicles on fire, spilling hundreds of gallons across four lanes, which will be closed off for hours. On another freeway, some distraught mother has thrown her two-year-old from an overpass, horrifying the drivers who must hit the brakes, swerve and spin to avoid the little body on the roadbed. Police have closed that route too. But I don't know this yet. All I know is, here we sit, while somewhere up above, the sky is blue, tinted and murky, but blue, and the sun too, the daily sun, though blurred, is shining through, hot, hot, hot, and today the city is not working very well at all—one of those times you reach out for meaning, and find it, whether or not it's really there, because you need it so desperately.

I reach over and switch on the radio:

Mostly sunny today and tomorrow, with late night and morning low clouds. Highs today on the coast near eighty-three, expect high nineties in the valley areas. The lows tonight near seventy. Condition of the air is unhealthful.

As usual with newscasters, nothing in the tone suggests that unhealthful air is anything to raise your voice about. It is just one more fact in a universe of facts and gets equal billing with the clouds and the temperature. With nothing to read in the tone of voice, I try to read the sequence: pay attention to what comes next. A woman is singing the end of a Cole Porter tune, with a jazzy orchestra behind her, and it seems to be a comment on the weather report:

> *It was great fun*
> *but it was just one*
> *of those things.*

This song also introduces a talk-show host, a psychiatrist, who now begins to talk. She is taking answers to today's questions: "If you were reincarnated, what *thing* could you like to come back as?"

A woman caller is on the line. Her name is Ruth.

"I'd like to come back as a mountain," Ruth says.

There is a long pause. Finally the psychiatrist says, "Have you thought about why you would like to come back as a mountain?"

"Yes."

Another pause.

"Would you like to tell us why?"

"I'd be strong, and solid, and could also give people pleasure. That is, I am thinking of a mountain that is out in the wilderness somewhere, so that wildflowers can grow on it, and wild animals can run free, and people who come there to the mountain can gain inspiration. They could hike up and down and be exposed to the wonders of nature and come away refreshed."

I am touched by this, on the verge of tears. At least, my eyes have started to water. Being from a coastal town much farther north, I don't have an air conditioner, don't ordinarily need one. In this kind of heat I have to keep a window open. Perhaps the ozone and oxides are wetting my eyes. But I think it is this woman's testimony. I see her sitting by the phone somewhere in Glendale, or perhaps standing in a booth in Torrance, staying indoors until the smog lifts, and thinking about what she might become in her next life.

Though I cannot yet see the city, I hear this and I know I am getting close. The naked honesty of her confession. Over the radio. I may be too susceptible, stuck here in my car, reaching out for anything. I may identify too much with her, because she and I, we are both marooned. In this moment I see clearly that here is the third thing I love about Los Angeles. Everything is out in the open, even when everything seems to be closing in. What many observers have labeled as deception and delusion is really an elaborate form of honesty. Nothing is hidden. If you think it, say it. If you like it, wear it. If you need it, let us know. When it comes to exposure, L.A. sets the pace.

Rampant excess has a lot to do with this. Excess and exposure cannot be disentangled here. Every feature of life is so excessive, everything is exposed. A while back an old buddy of mine arrived in Santa Cruz from Los Angeles in a 1972 Cadillac sedan, very long and elegant and looking almost new. It was the spring of 1981, a season of unparalleled energy consciousness. People everywhere were joining car pools, dusting off the ten-speeds, and lobbying for more public transit. Anyone getting less than twenty-eight miles to the gallon was considered part of the problem, not part of the solution, and here came Q cruising up the coast in his Caddy.

It was a great-looking car, inside and out. A fingertip could lower the windows. The seats could swallow you. I asked him what kind of mileage he was getting.

"Oh. Eight in the city. Maybe eleven or twelve on the road."

I did some quick calculating.

"You have just burned up thirty gallons between here and L.A."

He raised his eyebrows in mild surprise. "I guess that's one way of looking at it."

"I didn't think people were buying Caddies these days. Around here they are saying the Honda, the Chevette is the car of the future."

"You're exactly right. That's why I picked this baby up for a grand. It's a buyer's market. There was no way I could get into a Datsun or a Honda for less than seven, so I figure I got five or six thousand extra to blow on gasoline in the next few years, and meanwhile this boat rides like a dream."

L.A., I thought, as he purred down the driveway, heading north. Hard-core and flagrant.

It is common, where I live, to hear people bad-mouthing L.A. for its excesses, and for situations like the one I am still stuck in, trapped on the Ventura Freeway by nameless forces somewhere ahead, perhaps permanently scarring my lungs, with nothing to see but murky subdivisions, the once glorious perimeter of mountain peaks invisible and irretrievable, nothing to hear but lonesome previews from the next life.

"I just don't go in there," one woman told me recently, making it sound like a free-fire zone, or a deep cave full of bats. "Some friends of ours, we've known them for years and the daughter was getting married, and they wanted us to come down for the wedding, but I said no, I was really sorry, but if we had to go into L.A. it just wasn't worth it."

This is what you hear every day from people in the north, gazing south in awe and consternation. At parties they tell jokes:

How many southern Californians does it take to make a cup of instant coffee?

I give up.

Two. One to add the protein-enriched, simulated dairy supplement, made of soybean concentrate, acidophilus culture and brewer's yeast. And one to steal the water.

They talk about secession. "I think it's a good idea," a fellow told me recently, a young attorney who had grown up down there, come north for law school, and never returned. "Just cut those suckers off. What do you think?"

"Well," I said. "I kind of like L.A., you know, from a distance. I wouldn't want to break off relations completely."

"Why the hell not? They have already paved over everything worth looking at. The saddest part of my life was to watch my hometown turn to concrete."

"Where was that?"

"Pico Rivera."

"Did you think of that as Los Angeles?"

"I do now. It's all L.A., man, from Pomona to Santa Monica, from San Fernando to Huntington Beach. When I was a kid, there were fruit trees out there, farms, neighborhoods, rivers ran through town that looked like rivers are supposed to look. You could see the San Gabriels then, so close and so soft you could almost touch them. Then they tore out the trees and paved over the neighborhoods, and the mountains disappeared. Finally they lined the rivers with concrete. That was the final blow. I don't go down there any more. I can't bear to look at it."

The L.A. refugees. They are fanned out through all parts of the West. Their curse is remembering how something used to be, how some piece of California looked before it became a commodity on the world investment market. They move to other towns and join the uphill fight to save them from similar fates. They can be twenty-five or seventy. They can be found in Santa Cruz or Santa Fe, in Mendocino, Denver, Eugene, Spokane, Prince Rupert, Juneau, Banff and Nome. They look back toward where they came from, melancholy over some lost vista or demolished neighborhood, yet giving thanks that they escaped—escaped the place, the condition, the state of mind, what you might even call the organism perceived as L.A. This is the way the refugees, the former citizens, as well as numerous other Californians north of Tehachapi, regard it, as an organism, a kind of tumor attached to a rather small percentage of the physical map, which someday, some way or another, ought to be excised.

From the north, L.A. is seen as many people in other parts of America see California. The fact is, the observers nationwide who scoff and ridicule what appears to be going on in California are usually scoffing at and ridiculing L.A. When Nathanael West wrote about "the people who come to California to die," in *The Day of the Locust*, a jewel of a novel (which some regard as the most telling account of coastal foolishness), he was writing about L.A. In March of 1979, when Mary McGrory wrote in the Washington *Star*, "The nation's most populous state is another country, where there is no slush, no February and no struggle," she had just returned from L.A. In 1940, when Edmund Wilson, in his superb and still-quoted essay "The Boys in the Back Room," tried to describe what troubled him most about California and its writers, he described "the hypnotic rhythms of day and night that revolve with unblurred uniformity, and the surf that rolls up the beach with a beat that seems expressionless and purposeless after the moody assaults of the Atlantic."[18] In no way could such a passage apply to Sonora or Eureka or Salinas or Cloverdale or Susanville or San Francisco. Wilson was referring to things he had seen in L.A., which for decades now has taken 90 percent of the load when it comes to complaints and outbursts about whatever is going on out here—out there—on the coast. This the fourth reason I love the place. For the rest of California, it is out in front, taking the body blows, a kind of cultural punching bag. Luckily L.A. is big enough to roll with these punches. L.A. for that matter hardly notices them at all.

L.A. is so huge I get giddy thinking about it, stupefied. There is nothing else like it for thousands of miles in any direction. When you are inside, driving through, or walking around expecting sooner or later to see some glimpse of a horizon or a demarcation line, there appears to be no end, no middle, no beginning. You see signs here and there, noting where certain limits used to be, county lines, city limits: Alhambra, Inglewood, Culver City, Beverly Hills. Elderly Chicanos can sometimes point out the boundary lines of the original ranchos, a plane of order, a grid one layer beneath the city and the county lines, which are now one layer beneath the numberless boulevards, intersections, unfolding tracts and condo parks that spread ever outward. This is the fifth reason I love Los Angeles. It is now so huge and ungainly and by its very size so vulnerable, it is like the whale in the Yurok legend from northern California. She was a female whale, who found herself marooned, landlocked in a tiny lake after the ocean's waters, which had flowed in to fill riverbeds and canyons, began to recede and flow back into the Pacific, leaving this shallow pond for the whale to float around in. She could flap her tail and stay alive, but the support system required to maintain such a vast and wonderful and misplaced creature was gradually draining away.[19]

By the time the traffic loosens, I am late for all the things I had planned to do in town. The hell with it, I say, and head for the coast. It is fifteen degrees cooler out there, according to the radio, and my friend D who lives north of Malibu has access to the water, to relief. It is mid-afternoon when I finally pull up in front of his house. Within minutes I have changed into my swimming trunks and we are stepping down the bluff, across the sand, sliding into water so much warmer than the waters of Monterey Bay, where I usually swim, I feel like we are in Hawaii. I submerge and scoot along the sandy bottom, cooling off, calming down, taking cool brine against the eyelids. We swim out a hundred yards, slow and easy, to a broad stand of undulating kelp. The slick brown leaves and pods make a blanket across the water. We flop back on this bed of kelp, which does not quite support the body but makes floating nearly effortless—under the sun, in Hawaiian water, gazing back at the cliffs that rise above the beach road. From this far offshore they could almost be the cliffs behind Makaha on the lee shore of Oahu, where the mountains are also very dry.

After we have frolicked awhile, spewing little fountains into the air and submerging under the kelp, D describes how the flames looked coming up over those peaks during the big fire of 1978. He saw them first as they flashed like coronas from the far side of the range, then as they leaped down through brush toward the lower bluffs where the houses stand. For two days he became a firefighter and saved his own house, though several others nearby were lost. From here we can see the empty space where one burned to the ground. Others are raggedy hulks.

It is an awesome memory, flames vaulting the mountains to burn holes into this most westerly outpost of L.A., this shore-hugging string of beach houses. It has happened before, D says, and will no doubt happen again. You wonder how many houses it is wise to build at the base of these dry and fire-prone mountains. But you don't ask. New and expensive houses are already rising from the ruins and right next to the ruins. It is like asking about the smog. It is like asking about the water, those three slender threads that snake toward L.A. from the three nearest sources, which are not that near. The question belongs in a science fiction story or a disaster novel: Suppose ten million people were living in a semidesert where there was not one adequate source of water closer than two hundred miles? L.A. is now so abundantly incongruous in this habitat, the Yurok legend of the inland whale could be its premonition, perhaps a prophecy.

It is the legend of a boy named Toan and his wisdom figure, Ninawa. The boy never actually sees the whale, that is, he never *knows* he sees her. When he is very young his mother takes him into the mountains near their village. They come to a lake which is almost filled by this creature. But the whale lies so still the young boy thinks it is a log. Using the log he crosses the lake from one side to the other. Years later, near manhood, Toan is drawn back to this lake at a time of loss, of grieving over the death of his grandfather. The whale is gone, carried off by "the Inland Spirits." But the whale speaks to the boy in a dream, explains his origins and foretells his future.

This is the sixth reason I love Los Angeles. She speaks to me in dreams—vivid, instructive dreams about the past and the future, sometimes fearful visions of being embalmed for years in dense traffic, with only a radio for comfort, bizarre nightmares easy to shrug off and laugh about here in the kelp beds a hundred yards from shore.

She was a bastard, according to the legend, a young bastard female whale possessing uncanny power.

13

Beachtown Renegades

In Malibu you go barefoot a lot. You wear jeans or shorts, shirt or no-shirt, depending less on the weather than on your mood. The houses are strung, like close-packed beads, for miles along a narrow strip of beach, mostly on the ocean side of Highway 1, where the traffic is fast and constant. If you are arriving from the south, with the beach and the houses on your left, the prospect of that simple left turn can start your adrenaline pumping.

They don't keep front yards here. The fences, garage doors, retaining walls are pushed up right to the edge of the outside lane. Cars hurtle past within a few feet of the houses, and the sound is like the rumbling thunder of an impending storm. Yet once you park and step through one of the picket gates or barricades of fencing and walk down the path and into one of the houses, that sound disappears. It is almost miraculous. You don't have to go inside a house to experience this. You can remain standing on the deck. The steady rush of surf in front of you will drown the roar from the highway behind and above. It is very reassuring to know that in this little shoreside struggle for control of the sound waves, the ocean can still make more noise than the traffic.

The sun is setting when I arrive at the beach house of my friend V, who has been here in Malibu for many years. He works in the film industry and makes a comfortable living by putting in long hours and by being perpetually on or near the scene. V is a workaholic, but of the West Coast variety, which is to say, he is also a playaholic. That is why he likes it here and why, though he mumbles from time to time about "getting out," he stays right where he is. The location allows him to be both intently professional and intently physical. Early evenings you will find him jogging along the sand, or out there catching a couple of waves with one of his kids, or swimming with his wife, M, who is an excellent swimmer and who also values the indoor/outdoor life.

Surfboards lean against the side entrance to her kitchen. Swim fins are stacked behind a lounging chair, its blue pad faded nearly white. There are scuba-diving face plates on the deck, beach towels drying, shells and chunks of driftwood thrown around in a semidecorative way. Jute matting covers the walkway up from the beach, and the matting guides you past a nozzle where you hose off sand before stepping onto the deck. Sliding glass doors are open most of the time, so that the balmy air and the salty smell and the sounds of the sea float in and out. Even when you're inside and the doors are closed, the outside remains immediate.

V and M have raised three children here, put them through the local schools, fed them nutritiously and kept them out of serious trouble. It seems incongruous in Malibu, which has come to hold such a lurid place in the collective imagination, but these two have actually stayed together, raised a family and, against rather formidable odds, managed to impart to their children some crucial skills. In addition to all the rules of road and water safety, their children have learned—or, perhaps more to the point, have not forgotten—what many consider the most basic human instinct: survival. It is a strange and ironic feature of these California beach towns, but climate itself turns out to be the gravest hazard of coastal life. I should say, climate accompanied by a certain level of income. When the sun is warm too many months in a row, when bodily needs can be too easily satisfied, the survival instincts can go untested for years and years and years. They can actually begin to atrophy. Sometimes they disappear completely, or turn inside out. In such a climate a careful parent has to work overtime just to stay even with the rest of the human race.

This was made poignantly clear to me in a little after-dinner conversation, when one of their sons came home and joined us on the deck.

Dinner had consisted of a slab of London broil, which V cooked on the outdoor grill, along with foil-wrapped ears of bright yellow corn. M tossed a salad and warmed up a loaf of her homemade zucchini bread. It was one of those nights when you could sit outside as late as you wanted, with a breeze off the water but no chill in the air. We were picking the corn out of our teeth, sipping an excellent zinfandel, and watching the last blush of twilight when the son came striding down from the highway in his beach shorts and his T-shirt.

They had already told me he was working two jobs this summer, graphic design during the week, moonlight construction on Saturdays and Sundays. The construction work shows in his forearms and in the sun-tinted hair. He is sturdy, healthy and handsome, very sure of himself, and yet at this moment slightly shell-shocked. He has just left a hospital where he was visiting a young woman emerging from a two-week coma.

His good looks are not like those perfectly sculptured faces you see in the ads for certain Beverly Hills fashion shops that feature glossy backdrops and zippered leather—faces that frighten you, they are so devoid of feeling or of any potential for feeling. This fellow has just been through something, and his face shows the impact. Whatever he's seen has hit him like a two-by-four to the head. Perhaps it was the look of the woman in the hospital, or more likely—as I suspect from the line of his remarks—what her look says about the milieu that put her there.

V says to his son, "Did she recognize you?"

"Yeah, she knew me. I could tell by her eyes. She just can't talk yet. There was definite brain damage."

"What happened?" I ask.

"Overdose."

"What was she taking?"

"It's kind of embarrassing," he says, with a glance around at our three faces, and then a smile that wants to apologize for his friend's excesses.

We wait, while a slap of shore break sends some white water slithering across the beach.

"Alcohol first," he says.

"And then?"

"Quaaludes. She passed out. Somebody at the party saw her on the floor and gave her a shot of morphine. I wasn't there, but people told me later she looked dead. Or dying. So they called an ambulance, then everybody split because they were all so wasted on coke they didn't want to be found there themselves. I think she probably *was* dead for a few minutes, before the ambulance showed up. You know. The brain gets starved for oxygen. All the vital signs went out. She lost some brain cells in the deal. You can recover from that, I've heard, but it takes a long time. It could take years. You have to relearn things. This was two weeks ago, when it happened. When I heard her eyes were open, I stopped by the hospital to be with her awhile. She's lucky to be alive."

"Have you known her long?" I ask.

"Since she first came out here. I guess a couple of years. She's from Delaware, came out to the coast to go to college."

"Were you . . . are you very close?"

"We're friends. But . . . close? I don't know. I'm not sure she's that close to anybody, which could be part of the problem."

I look at V and M, but they have already heard this story. They are looking at me, listening to how I read it.

"Tell me something," I say to the son. "Do you think this happens more to people who come out to the coast like that from somewhere else—people, say, who maybe lose their bearings when they find themselves in such a wide-open situation?"

He immediately shakes his head, then smiles again with that apology for the excess over which he has no control.

"Four or five people I grew up with, right here, and went to high school with, have already died, just like she almost did."

"Overdoses?"

"Total burnouts, man. You know what they say? They say, 'What else are you going to do?' They say, 'What else *is* there to do?' I am kind of lucky in that respect. Trying to be a healthy and productive person is a radical stance to take around here, among people my age."

"How old are you now?"

"Nineteen. I'm not a saint, you understand. I have my little vices too. But I can have a terrific identity, be a real renegade and defier of conformity by choosing not to self-destruct—just by trying to behave myself and live a more or less decent, normal life."

He glances again at his father and mother, and I get the impression he has never before voiced this in their presence. They all seem a little surprised, and pleased, that something they all agree on has suddenly been said out loud. Parents can wait a lifetime for one of these confirming moments, and I know that V is moved. But he is not going to make much of it. He looks at me, father to father, and a smile flickers across his face. Then he reaches for the nearly empty bottle and pours out the last of the zinfandel. The twilight is long gone now, just the near-dark overhead, the soothing Southern California nighttime sky. A while later father and son start clearing the dinner table. M and I move the deck chairs inside to preserve them from tomorrow's morning dew.

Meeting Tom Bradley

Seen from the air, Los Angeles City Hall can get lost among the downtown highrises. If the smog is not too bad, and the sun has half a chance, the light flashing off those glassy towers can blind you and completely obscure the city hall. But from street level, if you are approaching by car, its tower is still higher than all the nearest buildings, a thick white obelisk that must have been truly stunning when it was dedicated in 1928, when the skies around it were always blue.

I am on my way to meet Tom Bradley, who two days from now will be out on the steps for his third inauguration ceremony. Later on, after the interview, as I search for connections and continuities—which are few and far between in this city—it will occur to me that maybe the mayor and this building he inhabits have some things in common. For one, it was built to last. For another, it is not high-tech or avant garde like the futuristic showplaces a few blocks away, the new Bonaventure Hotel, the Security Pacific headquarters. But neither is it archaic and out of date. In a city obsessed, or you might say assaulted, with novelty, where new is best and fad is king, it is comforting to see a building that has been in one place for over fifty years—not long in most parts of the world, but that qualifies as an island of stability in L.A.

There are several thresholds, little borders to be crossed, between me and Mayor Bradley. The first is the armed guard at the door of the Main Street parking tunnel. He stamps a ticket and flags me through, and I wind around to the visitors zone, where a uniformed attendant checks my ticket, takes my keys, gives me a second ticket and points me toward a red carpet that leads to the elevators. The city hall is built on a hillside, putting this parking tunnel two floors below Spring Street, where the palatial entry steps spread out.

Beneath a high arch that says "Office of the Mayor" there is another guard wearing a pistol, perched at a low desk logging people in and out. He notes my arrival time, then guides me through a door at the far end of the corridor, where a receptionist bids me sit while she makes a call. Soon the assistant to the press secretary steps through another door and ushers me into another corridor, lined with many doors, one of which is the press room, where I sit again, to wait awhile, because the mayor is running behind schedule. This week the city council is electing a new president—no small matter, since the council presides over a population now larger than that of twenty-three of the fifty states. Pre-vote intrigue is filling these halls like a vapor. The revised city budget is also being drafted this week, as well as the speech for his inauguration. Film crews planning to cover that event are already checking in. A man and a woman from Argentina pass me in the corridor, with cameras and a tripod. Tom Sullivan, the mayor's press secretary, tells me they are expecting crews from Germany, Mexico and Japan.

Behind Sullivan's desk four TV monitors are mounted on a high table. They look out of place, a little too technological in this room which harks back to the thirties. The entry door features one of those long panels of mottled and translucent glass, the kind detectives' offices had in pre-World War II films, so that you see vague shadows passing along the hallway. At any moment Philip Marlowe could walk through that door, or Raymond Chandler, or maybe old man Harry Chandler, publisher of the L.A. *Times* in 1935 when the paper first moved into the Times-Mirror Building right across the street.

Framed photos of the mayor hang along two walls—Bradley in track shorts, winning the 440 at U.C.L.A.; Bradley in police hat, grinning the day he made lieutenant; Bradley reaching into a sea of hands on election night, 1973; Bradley being sworn in by former Chief Justice Earl Warren; Bradley with Muhammad Ali.

He takes a good photo. In each of these shots he has a presence, a commanding presence. If Bradley is in the picture or in the room, no one is going to miss him or ignore him. And yet, as I look around at this album spread across the walls of the press room, I am thinking that, in a world where politicians increasingly must compete with talk-show hosts and quarterbacks for our short-lived attention spans, Bradley has had astonishing success without ever becoming a media personality. He is not flashy. He does not drive fast cars. He is not eager for interviews, nor does he take outspoken stands. His opponents, in fact, say this is his gravest shortcoming: he is so firmly positioned in the middle, they say, he never takes a stand on *any*thing. But so far the middle route has worked. In this state known for its frivolity and filigree and high-handed politics, the polls tell us that Bradley, as of his third inauguration day, is California's most favorably regarded politician. In this city known around the world as the gateway to Disneyland, he was recently re-elected to an unprecedented third term by "running on his record," without once so much as raising his voice. He is the antithesis of what the world has come to expect from this town and this state, which is to say, Bradley is not an entertainer.

I ask Sullivan if this is a calculated stance.

"Does he deliberately play against the rising tide of political show business?"

Sullivan grins and shakes his head. "Nope. That is really the mayor's authentic style of doing things."

I have one more stop, on the sofa in the outer sanctum of the inner sanctum, while his appointments secretary hurries past me twice, saying nothing, flipping pages in her datebook. Then, suddenly, the final door opens and she says, with a hurried but generous smile, "The mayor will see you now."

The door closes behind her, closing off all the corridors of noise and busyness, and we are shaking hands.

He is tall, six foot three, and the long lean lines of the track star still show underneath the cloth of the suit, the way the leg bends, the loose hang of the arm. His hair is thinning on top, almost gone. Except for that, it is hard to believe he is sixty-three. His face is unlined, seemingly unmarked by tension. The brow is smooth, the cheeks are smooth. The brown eyes are clear and steady. While we talk he does not blink or turn away or glance toward the window, yet neither does he challenge with the eyes, as I have seen Jerry Brown do at a first meeting. Brown the aggressive Irishman looks at you and his eyes say, "Tell me the most important thing you know." Bradley looks at you and his eyes say, "I will listen to what is on your mind."

He gestures toward a sofa, inviting me to sit. It is square ended, with matching chairs positioned at a long glass table. He sits back in one of the chairs, and we talk first about California, a place, I remark, where things are said to happen like they do not happen in other places.

He chuckles, a low-octave chuckle that makes his shoulders lift. His voice stays in that low range between baritone and bass. "If they're going to happen at all," he says, "they happen here first."

I know he arrived in Los Angeles at the age of seven, after a long trip from Calvert, Texas, where he was born. His father was a sharecropper who packed his wife and five kids and all they owned into a rattletrap Model T in the early 1920s and started west. Crossing New Mexico and Arizona, their car broke down more than once. They ran out of money and stopped for a while outside Yuma to pick cotton. I ask him what his parents had in mind when they pulled up stakes.

"Did they see California as their specific destination?"

"Yes, they did," says Bradley. "We had to stop in Arizona briefly, while my father came on to take a job in order to prepare the way for bringing us out."

"Was it a job he knew would be waiting for him once he got here?"

"Oh no."

"California was just the place he wanted to reach."

"That's right."

"Why did he think of California instead of, say, heading north, or into the Midwest?"

"People who lived in Mississippi or other places closer to the Midwest seemed to move in that direction. But at that time I think people who lived in Texas thought more of moving to the West than they did moving up to Chicago. As far as they were concerned, California was the land of opportunity. My father thought that would be the place to strike gold for his family, and he decided to move."

"But that is not what he found when he got here," I say.

Bradley's sense of irony—the contrast between what his parents dreamed of and what they got—pulls another low chuckle from the baritone chest.

"That's right. I would say bitter disappointment, because it was a tough struggle to get a job. Life was not that good or that easy for blacks and other minorities. But he had made his choice, so he brought the rest of the family out, and struggled to make a go of it. He moved from job to job, from handyman to Pullman porter to working as a waiter on a boat that sailed up and down the Pacific Coast."

Money was always short. The hope of striking gold out West quickly turned to dust. Soon after they reached L.A. the marriage broke up, and in the years that followed, Bradley's mother, Crenner, a devout Baptist and unswerving moral force, began to raise the five children on her own. They all found jobs where they could. Bradley himself recalls gardening, working as a swamper in a produce market, delivering papers for the old L.A. *Daily News*. His bittersweet memory of those times comes through when we talk about the district they lived in, near Temple and Alvarado streets. Back then it was called West Temple.

"It's not very far from where we're sitting," I say.

"That's true. It's just over the hill a couple of miles."

"And is that district still intact?"

"Yes."

"It hasn't been redeveloped?"

"It is still very much the same, except for the freeway having gone through there. That actually wiped out the site where I lived, the last house I lived in before moving from there to southeast Los Angeles."

"That's a real California story," I say. "Your house getting knocked over by the freeway."

His laugh this time is deep and hearty. His whole body moves with the laughter.

"I have often driven by there," he says. "And I'd point and I'd say, 'Now see that corner of the freeway? Right there is where we'd slide down the hill on a sled.' Grass at the end of the summer would dry out, and we could glide down over it on a homemade sled. You could get up pretty good momentum. By the time you got to the end of the cliff, there wasn't anything to stop you, so it was an exciting and scary thing to tumble off the side of that hill. I don't know, it probably wasn't more than ten feet, but when you're a kid it seems like a mile."

A door opens without a sound and an aide walks in, a small *nisei* woman bearing a note. He glances at it and says softly, "Excuse me just a moment."

There is a call he has to take. He strides to the far end of the room, tipping his upper body forward slightly, as very tall men will do in the presence of someone much smaller, such as this aide who precedes him. He opens another door, into what I later learn is his "real" office. Before it closes I catch a glimpse of the bright overhead light beaming down onto a desk heaped with folders and reports, layer upon layer of paperwork. Bradley, they say, is very thorough, reads everything set before him. In this brief glimpse I can see where he must put in a good part of the fifteen hours a day he spends at this job.

While he's gone I have a chance to look around his "official" office, this ceremonial room where visitors are received and proclamations are delivered, where he stands and sits for photographs. Things in here are remarkably subdued, it seems to me. I cannot help thinking of the rest of Los Angeles, of the imagery we connect to it, those of us who live in other parts of the state and the world, cannot help continually trying to locate Bradley in that context. If you were going to list two hundred words to describe this town, *subdued* would not even get an honorable mention. But in this room, the light is unlike the light I saw in that paper-filled office beyond the door. Here it is filtered through drawn blinds. The air somehow is fresh and comfortable, though I hear no sound, have no sense of a conditioner at work. Carpets keep everything quiet. Overhead the ceiling beams are exposed, with painted scrollwork that echoes California mission design and, like the vaulted corridors outside, echoes further back, toward Arabia, where the Spanish style gets so much of its flavoring.

Wooden paneling covers the walls. The furnishings—this sofa, for instance, covered with a sumptuous, tawny velour—are elegant but not obtrusive. In the middle of the low glass table there stands an exquisite floral arrangement, a gift brought in by someone from the Japanese American community, centered three blocks away in Little Tokyo. The arrangement changes from week to week. Today a salmon-colored and perfect antherium is flanked by two long sprigs of dollar eucalyptus. On the far wall, as if a backdrop for the flower, hangs a four-paneled Japanese painting, full of open space, full of sky. On another wall, between the two doors, hangs a large oil, a landscape of the L.A. region before the roads went in and the buildings began to rise. The sky in this painting is moody and panoramic. Open country. The good old days.

At the opposite end of this long room, and behind his "official" desk —which is highly polished and free of all administrative clutter—there hangs an oil painting of his wife, Ethel. The painting is lit. In mid-afternoon it is the only electric light in use. She wears a pink formal dress, and the light gives her dress its full luster, so that one's eyes are continually pulled in that direction.

I have read that she was his boyhood sweetheart, that they met in a Baptist church here in Los Angeles, went to the same school, belonged to the same clubs. But, Bradley has said, it was his success as an athlete that first attracted her serious attention. At Polytechnic High he was a sprinter and an All-City tackle, talents that won Ethel and also won him a scholarship to U.C.L.A. They were married in 1941, a year after he joined the Los Angeles Police Department. She was a beautician then. Nowadays they live in a mansion donated to the city by the Getty Oil Company—three stories in the Tudor style, fourteen rooms with an acre of grounds, one block north of Wilshire. The Bradleys are the first of L.A.'s first families to occupy what has been, since 1977, the mayor's official residence. But for a quarter of a century they lived in the two-bedroom frame house Bradley bought in Leimert Park in 1951, a house they had to buy through a white intermediary because they knew no one in that district, in those days, would sell directly to blacks. Until 1948, when the U.S. Supreme Court outlawed restrictive covenants, blacks in Los Angeles had been confined to two residential districts. The day the Bradleys arrived in Leimert Park with their two young daughters, ready to move in, they heard kids on the street call out, "The niggers are coming! The niggers are coming!"

Bradley said nothing at the time. Pushing at that color line was like pushing at the sound barrier. He knew there was going to be intense pressure from all sides. He expected it. He tried to ignore the taunts. Whatever he may have been feeling was not allowed to show. Displays of rage and indignation have never been his style, a trait that sometimes mystifies and frustrates the more militant of his black constituents. In 1978, upon the occasion of his sixty-first birthday, he told an L.A. *Times* reporter, "I think you can burn up your energies. You can get angry with people or with society to the point where that becomes your mission in life, just to have a seething rage all the time; or you can continue on your way. I often describe it as moving like a Sherman tank over those obstacles and on to your destination."[20]

For twenty-one years Bradley worked in the segregated L.A.P.D. (Black officers and white officers did not work together until 1964.) It took him eighteen of those years to make lieutenant, while he watched less qualified men moving past him. The only thing that stood in the way of further promotion was race. Charlie Lloyd, who later became his law partner, once said, "If Tom had made captain, he would still be on the force."

But in those days no black officer had ever moved higher than lieutenant. So in 1961 Bradley retired. By that time, working nights and weekends, he had a law degree from Southwestern University, in downtown L.A. He had passed the California bar exam. He also belonged to sixty-two community organizations. After two years in private practice he won a seat on the L.A. City Council. In 1969 he ran for mayor against incumbent Sam Yorty and narrowly lost. In 1973, backed by a growing coalition of blacks and west-side liberals, he ran against Yorty again and won.

In his own resolute and steadfast way—the Sherman Tank approach—Bradley had rolled over barrier after barrier. Long before he challenged the housing code, he was among the first black athletes to compete for U.C.L.A., on the same track team with Jackie Robinson, who later made history by breaking through the color line that had kept blacks out of major league baseball. Bradley was the first black elected to the City Council. He was the first black elected mayor here, and at the time he was the third black ever to be elected mayor of a major U.S. city. Once he had reached that point of high prominence, the next challenge seemed to be identity itself.

In 1979 a high school student visiting City Hall on youth-in-government day said to him that the city had ended up with "a black Gerald Ford rather than a black John Kennedy." Bradley objected, less to the political implication than to the color coding.

"I am not a black this or a black that," he said. "I'm just Tom Bradley."

He has said it in other ways time and time again: he does not want to be thought of as the black mayor of Los Angeles, or as the mayor of black Los Angeles, but as Tom Bradley, the mayor of all Los Angeles. Critics have accused him of denying his color. That is not what he is denying. When he says, "I am just Tom Bradley," he is taking a stand against that final barrier, which lives in the mind and can turn any kind of "difference" into a screen that prevents us from seeing the person. In a region this racially mixed and volatile, it has not been an easy stance to maintain. But it is an attitude about himself and about the city he governs that has generally gained him wide respect.

As mayor, they say his greatest virtue has been his ability to bring people together, to share ideas, or to resolve whatever the dispute may be, to seek solutions. He is a suave negotiator and a diplomat, more interested in results than in making the grandstand play. Bradley's first order of business has been the city's economic health. If life in the city is to be improved, he says, that is where it must begin. That is what produces jobs and the support system for civic and social programs.

Though numerous activists are still unhappy with the trickle of funds toward their neighborhoods, and though housing has reached the crisis stage, and though the legendary L.A. smog still hangs over the city like a shroud, no one can deny that during his first two terms, while certain other U.S. cities have staggered in and out of bankruptcy, L.A. held on to its triple-A bond rating. All the city's budgets were balanced. Federal grants increased from $80 million to over $800 million. International trade through the L.A. Customs District increased from around $5 billion per year to around $35 billion, a process that was certainly nudged along by Bradley's official visits to Japan, China, Hong Kong, Taiwan, the Soviet Union, Korea, and New Zealand—cities and countries that encircle this great marketplace they call the Pacific Rim.

The relationship between city government and L.A.'s business community has never been tighter. Soon after he took office, Bradley borrowed Fred Schnell from Prudential Insurance, where he was a senior vice president, to develop stronger links between city hall and downtown executives. Schnell organized the Mayor's Economic Advisory Council, which has brought corporate leaders right into the policy-making arena. Since that time new towers have been sprouting like trees downtown, while some of the older classics have been revitalized, and the city, they are saying, "is on the move."

As a matter of fact, Angelenos have been celebrating their birth and rebirth all year long. El Pueblo de La Reina de Los Angeles was founded four blocks from here in 1781. Today, outside the city hall, a Bicentennial banner hangs above the traffic, slung from light poles on either side of Spring Street. It says,

L.A.'S THE PLACE

Having just arrived from a town 400 miles north, I find it slightly surreal to be exposed to this kind of civic enthusiasm. From the north, L.A. is often viewed as a blight upon the face of the earth. From the East, it is often regarded as something both threatening and comical, like a cartoon of the Loch Ness monster. But when you are here inside the city it is not at all uncommon to hear people talk the way Bradley does, people who believe in L.A.—senior vice presidents, editors at the L.A. *Times,* architects who call it the City of the Future.

When he returns from the phone call and is seated again, he tells me they foresee another million people in the coming years.

"According to our zoning pattern we technically could grow to a city of ten million. But that is unthinkable. So we decided—I introduced a motion when I was still on the Council, so that's over nine years ago—it was adopted by the council, after some study. Four-point-one million was determined to be the maximum number of people this city could accommodate."

A quick mental calculation tells me that would be an increase of 33 percent in a city that already seems painfully overextended. Another way to read it, of course, is continued and steady growth. This is what the big planners envision—more people, more towers, a world center for travel and commerce, in the cosmopolitan vanguard, with multicultural vitality and multinational support. And somewhere along the way they want the city's image to improve. They would like more respect.

All of this was on Bradley's mind, a few years ago, when he started working to locate the 1984 Olympics in Los Angeles.

"I thought it would be good for the city," he says, "and good for the young people of the city."

It became his personal crusade. When the International Olympic Committee finally said okay, and the City Council finally said okay, it was a personal victory.

The biggest obstacle had been financing. After the 1976 Olympics, the city of Montreal went a billion dollars into the hole—a terrifying thought for taxpayers, especially during the spring of 1978. That spring happened to be the time when the Olympics dialogue in L.A. was the loudest, and also the season when Proposition 13 was being debated up and down the state, the property-tax initiative that had everyone, on both sides of the issue, fearing for the financial future of everything. To guarantee that L.A. would not be held responsible for any losses incurred in 1984, a law was added to the city charter. Meanwhile, city attorneys were asking for more control over funding than the International Olympic Committee, at first, was willing to grant. In the midst of all this there came a moment when an exasperated Bradley, playing his hole card, recommended to the City Council that L.A. withdraw its Olympic bid completely. It must have led to a tense discussion at IOC headquarters in Lausanne. Among other things, L.A. was the only city bidding. Twenty minutes later Bradley had a cable from the IOC president saying, in effect, "Why don't we talk this over?" That was the turning point in what he now calls "the toughest, longest-running political battle of my career."

Since those days the local organizing committee, keeping that promise built into the charter, has been finding sizable chunks of money in the private sector. It is just the kind of partnership Bradley's administration has supported from the start. In addition to the $225 million ABC is paying for television rights, more millions will be coming from ARCO, Coca-Cola, American Express, 7-11 Stores, Anheuser-Busch and McDonald's.

"The idea of having private sector make contributions to fund the games, to build facilities is a new concept," he tells me. "Our actions, which I think will result in a substantial profit, will be the thing that saves the Olympic movement. Had there been another city with a major deficit, I think the whole movement would be in danger. Already Nagoya, which is bidding and is a primary candidate for the 1988 games, has been over to see us twice to determine how we organized and planned that."

Immediately a question springs to mind. Isn't there a danger here? Doesn't corporate sponsorship lead to corporate meddling? If McDonald's is brought in to build the swimming pool—since that is what their contribution will consist of—isn't it only a matter of time before gold-medalists will be backstroking through golden arches to reach the finish line? Could the strategy for saving the Olympics, I almost ask, actually destroy them?

I hold my tongue. Anyone can be the gadfly. When you are not in charge, when you are from out of town and merely passing through, it is easy to find holes in the plan. The person in charge has to do what he can with whatever is available. If civic funds are shrinking in the wake of inflation and Proposition 13, if state funds are shrinking, and all federal budgets, save one, are shrinking, and you still want to host the

Olympic Games, where else do you turn? It's either McDonald's—which is, in its way, local, having started in San Bernardino, less than sixty miles due east of here—or the Defense Department.

As Bradley talks about this juggling act, I have the feeling he long ago weighed all such risks. Moreover, as I think of him juggling these particular ingredients within the context—again—of greater L.A., of all it has come to mean, and as I think of the millions who will pass through town while the Olympics are going on, and of the crowd milling through right now, today, heading north or south or east or out to sea or nowhere fast, and the multitudes each new year brings, along with the dreams that propel them toward this rather narrow bowl between the mountains and the beach—the prospect of governing or even appearing to govern such a tumbling swarm is overwhelming.

This city hall is made of granite and old sturdy timbers, and it is soundly anchored here on the slope between Main Street and Spring. You could say the whole city is anchored that way, streets and buildings attached to earth. But, more so than any other part of California, Los Angeles is a region of the mind, still fed by all the legends we know so well, by all the movies still filmed here, and the countless novels set here —Hollywood novels, detective and police novels, decadence and drug novels, Malibu novels, family sagas—and by all the songs. It lives in the minds of all those people who at this very moment are getting ready to make the trip, just as Bradley's father made the trip in 1922. They dream of work and money. They dream of cars, or a warmer winter, the sexier lover, the sudden deal. California is the destination, but when they say California, as often as not they are thinking of L.A.

How do you administer such a place? How do you govern a land of dreams? Do you have to be nuts to attempt it? Insanely ambitious? Hopelessly corrupt and greedy? Or some kind of dreamer yourself? Some kind of visionary? Truly, a person of high vision? Where do you find a solid place to stand?

I have been looking at Bradley, while we talk, trying to see behind the words. There is something very substantial about him, and an uncanny peacefulness. Here he is, not only in the midst of this careening mega-city, but also in the midst of a mayor's busiest week, and he seems at peace. His face shows no signs of stress. It makes him look more youthful than his years, and suggests to me that somewhere along the line he has cultivated the inner resources we call spiritual. I have been wanting to ask him about this dimension of his life. Politicians in California are seldom given the chance to comment on matters of the spirit. From most of what you hear and read, it would be easy to get the idea that they have no inner life at all. When I finally raise the question, toward the end of the conversation, Bradley is not only willing to talk about it, he pays immediate tribute to his first and most influential teacher.

"It really started," he says, "with the guidance and direction my mother gave me from a very early state. I have always been pleased and happy about that. It has made the difference in my life. I was asked the other day, how do you handle tension? Well, I don't have it. I don't experience it. I think it's partly a matter of self-confidence, a matter of control, and of being at peace with myself. It permits me to be at ease. And I trace it back to my mother."

"In nineteen seventy-seven you wrote an article for *Guideposts* magazine in which you talk about faith in God."

"Yes."

"In the Christian sense."

"Yes."

"And I suppose that article would still voice your . . ."

"I have been active in the church since I was seven or eight years old, and I am still very strongly active."

"Baptist?"

"I started as a Baptist. I switched denominations, must have been about nineteen sixty-one or 'two. I now belong to the First African Methodist Episcopal Church."

Guideposts is a magazine of spiritual uplift, published out of Carmel, New York. In the article he describes a stop his family made in Summerton, Arizona, when he was six years old. They were stalled, car broken down, and out of money. Young Tom wanted to try his hand at picking cotton. He had seen the grown-ups do it. He wanted to see how much he could pick. It seemed easy, at first, because he didn't have to bend over all the time like his mother. But as the bag grew heavier and the sun rose in the sky, the prickly bolls began to hurt his fingers. By the end of the day he was worn out and he had not come close to his goal of fifty pounds. "That was the first day in my life," he says, "that I understood the meaning of ambition."[21]

At age six he decided the fields were not for him. That night, while his mother soothed the red-raw hands, he told her, "I am going to be somebody."

"Son," she said, "the only way you can be somebody is if you *are* somebody."

He didn't understand what she meant. "But how do you know if you are somebody?" he asked.

"You know it," his mother said, "when you stand up before God and say, 'Lord, you gave me life. You gave me this body and this brain. Now, Lord, how'm I doing with these things?'"

As she spoke these words, he could picture God standing there, approving or disapproving. "If you were living your life this way," he wrote, fifty-four years later, "then, to Crenner Bradley, you *were* somebody. . . . My mother's God was a real God, and from the time we were tiny children she strove to make him just as real to us."

The door opens again. This time it's the appointments secretary, her poise and calm stretched to the limit. The outer office, which was empty when I walked in, is now filled with waiting people. The mayor is two meetings behind. "We have a traffic jam," she says. Pressing my luck, I ask for one last question. He nods and says, "Sure."

"Do you have any personal philosophy or guideline for governing a city as complex and unpredictable as Los Angeles?"

I am thinking of something akin to what former Governor Pat Brown once said about the state: "Managing California is a little like tuning a car going sixty-five miles an hour. It isn't just a problem of taking care of the engine. It's the running alongside while you do it." I am thinking of what William Mulholland said when he was asked to run for mayor of L.A. in 1913. "Gentlemen, I would rather give birth to a porcupine backwards."

This is what a California political figure is expected to say. It doesn't have to make perfect sense, so long as it is upbeat and quotable. And this is precisely what Bradley does not say.

He thinks about it for a moment and says, in his careful and deliberate way, "I do the best job I can with the problems and challenges and opportunities that face me every day. At night when I go to bed I am at peace with myself, content that I have done the best I could that day. And I don't let anything worry me. Next morning I'm up taking on some new ones."

How is it possible—I am thinking as I push through the crowd in the outer office, as I say good-bye to Tom Sullivan who is simultaneously welcoming another film crew and huddling with one of the mayor's aides, as I head on down the corridor past a display of posters honoring the Bicentennial and the display of opulent gifts from every port around the Pacific Rim—how is it possible, in this city of one-liners, right here in this gambler's den and World-Wide Headquarters of Hype, that a man so straightforward and unflamboyant should be at the political helm?

Is it the surprise factor itself? Or could it be that I am asking the wrong question? Perhaps Bradley's presence seems incongruous because I myself have been observing L.A. from the outside, and from too far away. Thinking back over what we talked about, I realize that here is a man who has seen everything and survived just about everything the world can throw at you—from the hand-to-mouth poverty of a migrant family, to vice squad duty in the roughest streets of a city that has always been known for its violence, through ten years of in-fighting on the city council, to this ongoing dialogue at the high levels of corporate investment. That is what you see in his eyes—the total range of this life, or several lives. After fifty-six years in these many districts of the past and present, Bradley knows the layers of Los Angeles as few people have ever known them. He knows exactly where the pain is, and he knows exactly where the power is. I am thankful now that I did not bother to mention the possible dangers that come along with money from ARCO, or Coca-Cola. There cannot be a danger in this city he is not familiar with. I doubt that anything you could possibly say or imagine would surprise him.

The Wide Open Spaces

Heading east along the Pasadena Freeway I begin to think of the movie *Kramer vs. Kramer.* In the opening scenes, Meryl Streep has reached her limit. She walks out on her ad-man husband, Dustin Hoffman, and their six-year-old son, leaving them to fend for themselves in New York City. When she returns, sometime later, she is different. Though she doesn't want Dustin anymore, she wants her son. She wants to start again. As a person, as a woman, as a mother, she understands herself in a new way.

How has this happened? All we are told is that she has been to California. We do not find out whom she talked to, where she lived, what books she has read, what methods she may have tried—whether it was The Intensive Journal, Rolfing, Feldenkrais, acupuncture, Rebirthing, EST, Subud, Primal Scream, aura balancing, or gestalt therapy with a purification diet. For the purposes of the film it is enough to say that she has been to California. The audience will know what this means. She is going to be on some level transformed. No one gets out of Hawaii without a suntan, and no one gets out of California unchanged. So goes the legend.

Speeding past Dodger Stadium, across the Los Angeles River, I am reminded again, by the urgent traffic, that these days when most things are changing whether we want them to or not, they change here at a faster clip. Why? This reputation itself has a lot to do with it. After a hundred and fifty years California is still seen as a place you can travel to in order to change your luck or your life. Obviously the human quest

for transformation and renewal goes back a lot further than that. It is
as old as history. But has there been another place on earth more closely
linked to this particular urge? I can't think of one. Unless it be America
itself. Or Jerusalem. Or Lourdes.

Taking a left off the freeway, into a neighborhood of cottages and
bungalows, I hear again the voice of a woman I met not long ago, a
woman of perhaps thirty, and married, who recently moved West from
Atlanta, Georgia.

"When it looked like I was really going to get up and go," she said,
"some of my friends became very concerned and worried. 'What if you
change?' they said. 'Aren't you afraid to get out there and just . . .
change?' 'Why, that's exactly the reason I want to go,' I told them. I
want to change. But that worried them a whole lot, you see. The last
thing any of them wanted was something that would disturb their lives.
They didn't want to do anything but stay put."

As I listened to this story my own sentiments were equally divided.
For that woman, eager to start anew, staying put was a kind of curse.
But staying put is by far the more common tendency. Change is fearful,
especially sudden change. We may crave it, yet we will cling to stability.
There is something in us that will stay put until the last second, holding
to what is known, whether it be the place we inhabit or whatever we
think we know about ourselves.

Here in California you can look almost anywhere and see these
tendencies grappling. No matter what brings you West—you may have
been drawn toward the promise of anarchy itself—sooner or later there
comes a time when you begin to yearn for stability. You want your
personal change to occur, and then you want the general situation to
stabilize so you can settle in and live your life. You want to get a spot
staked out, your couple of acres, say, right up next to a watershed that
is protected by the state, and then you start lobbying like mad for
legislation to halt further change in your part of the county. Then you
are in for a full-time, perhaps a lifetime, battle, because one feature that
gives this region so much of its character—or shortage of character; let's
say, its predominant characteristic—is this reputation for change itself,
which keeps the air alive with a reaching for new possibilities.

I am climbing now, up out of the lowlands. The road is narrow,
bordered with retaining walls and banks of trees. Suddenly the freeway
is gone, the traffic is gone. I am alone and winding upward. I could be
somewhere on the seacoast of Italy. It is hot, muggy. Steep, brush-
covered slopes fall away to the south. I am up here looking for a woman
named Marilyn Ferguson. In 1980 she published a book called *The
Aquarian Conspiracy.* An amazing book. Full of light, and full of hope.

At the time I was reading it, America seemed ready to go to war with Iran. Inflation was out of control as were the brushfires raging over thousands of acres just a few miles from this hillside. As usual, if you were following the papers, the world seemed to be on a collision course. And here came this book from a woman somewhere in L.A., about large numbers of people, in all their various walks of life, participating in a "conspiracy." Conspire, she says, actually means to breathe together, or to share a common spirit. The common concern of these people she writes about, the thread stitching together the many subjects she touches on—from psychology, religion, and American history to physics, chemistry, and preventive medicine—is the evolution of consciousness. If there are solutions to the crises of contemporary life, they will come via new levels of awareness, new modes of perception.[22]

About halfway through this book she devotes a chapter to the state of California. She calls it "A Laboratory for Transformation." I think I know what this means. But I have been wanting to meet her and talk some more about it.

Her house is set among trees, tall and square, with flat planes of siding, a wall of glass. Landscapers are working around the outside when I arrive, trimming hedges and old limbs, hauling things away.

She ushers me into a huge living room, huge in volume, since the ceiling is two stories overhead. The inside paneling is also redwood. The feeling is fresh and gracious. The asparagus ferns and small palms are very green and shimmer with life. There are many cushions, a thick carpet, a floor-level sofa where I sit looking first at Marilyn, then at the soaring paneled wall behind her, then at the bright pane of glass high up this wall, glass stained blue, yellow, red, purple, white. A sunburst of gulls fly through the light, as if flying right through the window.

Marilyn, curled up in a chair beneath this pane of color, makes me think of a bird. She is small-boned, and her hands float like wings when she talks. Her voice is bright and fast. She is remembering her first impressions of L.A., back in 1968.

"After we'd been here for a few months we bought a house, on another hill facing the mountains, a few hills over from here. Our neighbors across the street were Free Methodists, very conservative fundamentalists. In the next house down was a jazz group. A number of gay people lived on the hill. Our next-door neighbor was building a boat that he planned to sail to Hong Kong. His wife wrote poetry. Next door to them lived an elderly couple from Minnesota. Our neighbors on the other side owned a travel agency. It was his fourth marriage, she was Danish and he was Swiss. They were both amusing and eccentric, and I remember thinking that this was just a wonderful variety. All these options and choices. People could just be whoever they wanted to be."

As she says this, the burglar alarm goes off, with a howl that fills the house for thirty seconds. When it stops she does not apologize for the noise, she merely explains what it's doing here. Today is not an ordinary day, she says. The landscapers picked today to trim the trees, and a plumber picked today to fix a leak in the hot water heater. Last week, when the carpet crew was here, someone drove a staple through a wire, shorting out the alarm system. Today, it too is being repaired, and this was a test. Hearing the noise—a sound you might hear if a flight of pterodactyls were at war with a helicopter, a prolonged clatter that would scare away all but the most delirious PCP addict—I am reminded again that the permissive society has its many prices. The view up here is spectacular, but so is the burglary rate in greater L.A. It is part of the trade-off, the great flea market and gumbo mix, the free-form system that allows the free flow of everything including new options, new relationships, new ideas.

"There is an immigrant consciousness here," she says. "People move from other places and they see that 'This is my place. This is where they will permit me to be anything I want to be.' So you have a climate that is hospitable, that allows for the linkage of minds that are comfortable at the edge. Sometimes that manifests itself as the flaky fringe, and sometimes it is the scientific avant garde."

She pauses, then says, "What about you? Where were you from originally?"

When I tell her I grew up in San Francisco she says, "As a native it must be a little hard sometimes to get a fix on what other people see here."

"That's part of my mission," I say, "trying to find what holds Californians together. Most places you can at least start with common ancestry, the blood kinships, or some common birthplace. But that is not the common ground. . . ."

"Let me tell you what I think it is," says Marilyn, as she settles back into her chair and somehow, in the same movement, sits up straighter.

She is one of those people who get excited by ideas. Not just interested, or curious, but stirred and excited. It is kinetic. Her hands dance and her sharp eyes shine as she describes an idea recently brought to her attention by Warren Bennis, former president of the University of Cincinnati, and now a business professor at the University of Southern California.

"For several years off and on he has been working on a book about power. One thing he kept wondering was, What is personal power?

When we say someone has personal power, what do we mean? Warren had long suspected that whether it's a singer or a politician or whatever, there is some common trait. Suddenly he saw that what we mean by personal power is the ability to create a new context for other people to play in."

Her voice leaps, and she almost rises from her seat, as she says, "Now *that* idea itself is really powerful!"

As she says this, my mind is leaping toward examples. All sorts cross my scanner. I think of the potter Marguerite Wildenhain, who is one of the most powerful people I have met. And yes, it applies to her. She studied at the Bauhaus in Dessau in the early 1920s. For forty years she has occupied a few acres in the hills above the Russian River in northern California, which she has made into a place, a space where ceramics students can spend a summer on centering—centering the clay, centering their lives. I think of a powerful performer like Willie Nelson and his 1978 breakthrough, cross-over album "Stardust." Why was it such a hit? He opened, or reopened, a context, and made it allowable for millions of people to discover, or rediscover, the great American pop standards from the thirties and forties. I think of Marilyn herself, who found a name—the Aquarian Conspiracy—for this emerging network and thereby shaped a new kind of space.

"I must have received twelve hundred letters," she tells me later, "from people all over the country, most of them saying, 'Thank God, I thought I was crazy, or I thought I was all alone.' "

The example Marilyn now offers is California itself, which she sees as a *place* with this power to create a new context for people to move into, expand into. She talks about "a climate for that kind of synergy."

Her phrase calls to mind another book that was hatched in this region. It is called *The Dancing Wu Li Masters*, by Gary Zukav. The subject is quantum mechanics. In the opening chapter he describes how it began, over dinner at Esalen Institute, one night in 1976.

The elements are candlelight, organic food, and a contagious naturalness that is the essence of the Esalen experience. Sarfatti and I joined two men who already were eating. One was David Finkelstein, a physicist from Yeshiva University (in New York) who was attending the conference on physics. The other was Al Chung-liang Huang, a Tai Chi Master who was leading a workshop at Esalen. We could not have chosen better companions.

The conversation soon turned to physics.

"When I studied physics in Taiwan," said Huang, "we called it Wu Li. It means 'Patterns of Organic Energy.' "

Everyone at the table was taken at once by this image. Mental lights flashed on, one by one, as the idea penetrated. "Wu Li" was more than poetic. It was the best definition of physics that the conference would produce. It caught that certain something, that living quality that we were seeking to express in a book, that thing without which physics becomes sterile.[23]

This conversation is the seed for the book that follows, a superb study that makes relativity and quantum physics richly accessible to the nonscientist. It is in fact a very successful translation, from the language of mathematics into English, and done with a true sense of wonder. And the key to the book, the organizing pattern, comes out of this first conversation with David Finkelstein and Al Huang, who explained not only the Chinese approach to physics but the eightfold meaning of the phrase Wu Li.

Now, what struck me about that opening scene is that most of the ingredients arrived at Esalen from somewhere else. The physics theories came from Germany. The multileveled ideograms came from China. David Finkelstein came from Yeshiva University. Al Huang had studied in Taiwan. What Esalen provided, on its cliff right there at the Pacific's edge, was a meeting-ground, a certain kind of space, or as Marilyn called it, a context. This can be a way of looking at the place, the space called California: as a touch point, where lines of force converge. Here, as has often been said, East meets West. Asia meets Europe. Mule skinners meet Zen monks on the hiking trail. Athletes meet molecular biologists on the jogging trail. People infatuated with the body meet people infatuated with the intellect. Sparks fly. Perceptions change.

Since Marilyn herself moved into this arena from somewhere else, I ask if there was any direct connection between that move and her work of the past ten years. Her answer turns out to be a short course in the history of the human potential movement.

She grew up in Colorado. She was married and living in Houston when her husband, an editor with the Houston *Post,* came out to take a new job in Los Angeles. Things began to happen soon after they arrived. "Some of them were simply circumstantial," she says. But taken all together they turned her in a new direction: inward.

First she heard her name being called, just at the time her father passed away in another part of the country. She wanted to understand this experience. She began to ask herself the question she has been asking ever since: How does our mind work? She did not go to a medium seeking the answer. She took a course in parapsychology at U.C.-

L.A., and she began to read everything she could find on the subject.

Then her younger brother, Rick, came back from Vietnam and lived with them while he started college. He discovered Transcendental Meditation, which in 1969 was still a recent import and little known, even in Southern California. It worked for Rick. He urged Marilyn to get initiated. She resisted for a while, "mainly because he was my little brother."

About the time she got her mantra she came across an article in *Look* magazine dealing with a then new process called biofeedback, wherein machines are used to monitor body functions such as brain waves and heart rate, and feed back a tone or light to show change. The article focused on the early researches of Joseph Kamiya and Dr. Barbara Brown, who was at the time Chief of Experiential Psychology at the V.A. Hospital in Sepulveda, some fifteen miles away, in San Fernando Valley. Her lab contained the most sophisticated biofeedback equipment in the country. Eventually Marilyn and Rick volunteered as subjects for experiments in telepathic rapport. But before that happened, Marilyn tried an experiment of her own.

"That article described how your brain goes in and out of this alpha wave pattern from five to thirty times a minute. In my naiveté, which sometimes can be a terrific advantage, I thought, 'Well, if your brain is doing this on a regular basis, maybe you can feel it.' I learned, with no biofeedback device, to pick up that rhythm and sustain it. I found that you get this wonderful feeling across your forehead, kind of a hum going right across here. I could do it any time I wanted. I would just kind of think it, or tune it, and it was just one of those novelties I kept in the back of my mind. Then one day something happened, after I had learned to do that. . . .

"I lay down one afternoon to take a nap and started doing that brain wave trick, because it seemed it would be calming. I fell asleep, and moments later I woke with a start, feeling paralyzed. Lights seemed to be flashing inside my head. It was quite frightening. Half an hour later I was confronted with a situation that was potentially very stressful. Earlier that week a friend had become acutely psychotic and tried to take her own life, then committed herself to a psychiatric hospital. Now she was calling, saying that she had run away. She was asking me and a mutual friend to come after her.

"We did, but getting her back to the hospital and calm was a major effort. Afterward, my companion, who was feeling distraught, took a tranquilizer. She asked if I wanted one, and at that moment I realized I had not felt the stress. There was no sense of alarm or tension in my body, despite the traumatic circumstances. From that day on, when faced with a crisis, I have almost always been able to respond without the usual physical reaction to alarm, the so-called fight-or-flight response—rapid heart rate, heart-in-throat, panic. Something in my nervous system had changed permanently. It now takes something really disastrous to provoke the physical alarm symptom most of us associate with crisis."

At this moment she is living evidence that what she says is true. Considering what's going on right around her, inside and outside the house, she is amazingly focused and unruffled. In addition to the landscapers trudging back and forth outside the big picture window, and the fellow fixing the burglar alarm and the plumber working on the pipes, there is a woman upstairs on the loft above, demonstrating a Vector III word processor Marilyn may soon buy. From time to time the printout chatters down at us, while this woman goes through the procedures with a young fellow who just joined Marilyn's staff as editor of *Leading Edge Bulletin,* one of two bi-monthly newsletters she publishes. Snippets of their electronic dialogue drift over the railing:

"Now how do I get to Memorite Three?"

"From the Directory. And from Memorite Three you can go to Manual . . ."

"And to get from one mode to another?"

"Press ESCAPE."

"Whatever happened that day," Marilyn says, "the tuning in, the flashing lights, the paralysis, that whole kind of experiment—something changed. And all this stuff got me more and more interested in 'What on earth goes on in the brain and in the nervous system? What are the possible limits to what you can do with your consciousness?' "

Along with the meditation, the parapsychology, the biofeedback, the telepathic rapport and the alpha waves, Marilyn was watching her three children grow and learn. Her oldest, then five, had been tested by the state and found to be highly gifted. This put her in touch with the parents of other gifted children, and they would discuss what that label implies.

"Among us we had become convinced that this whole thing is very misleading. It is not so much genetic as it is environmental—stimulation and interaction. I went to a workshop for the parents of gifted children, where they were talking about some research at Berkeley, using animals. Rats who lived with Tinker-toys showed brain change, compared with the unstimulated rats."

Again her body rises, the kinetic response to an idea that ignites her. Her voice slows for a moment, as if she wants to hear each of these words.

"There was brain change associated with stimulation."

The brain, it seemed, was the common denominator linking all these realms and zones that had captured her attention. The result was the book called *The Brain Revolution* published three years later. Subtitled "The Frontiers of Mind Research," it was a 350-page overview, a state-of-the-field report. Out of that, out of the voluminous correspondence with researchers around the land, came *The Brain/Mind Bulletin,* a four-page newsletter she has published for the past six years, a regular update on such topics as the brain's natural opiates, the brain density of schizophrenics, the interplay between the right and left hemispheres.

"We try to take these ideas which in their scholarly presentation are sometimes very esoteric, even to other scientists, and try to be clear enough about it that people can see the relevance, the linkages."

Her next project began as a long look at social alternatives. But the subject kept opening and expanding, as she found more and more interplay between changing institutions and views of ourselves, between our unfolding knowledge of how the brain works and the ways certain avenues of science and certain spiritual traditions have led us to the same place—the mysterious center of human consciousness. Basic to what she came to call the Aquarian Conspiracy is the idea that modes of perception shape reality. The yogi says this world is a product of the mind; the subatomic physicist says his effort to perceive the electron changes what he is trying to perceive. Jesus said faith can heal; medical professionals now chart how feelings and beliefs influence the immune system, making us more or less susceptible to disease. It became a book about people taking responsibility for their bodies, for their lives, for their communities, not within a system that is gradually closing down around us, but within the context of unfolding potential.

The research and writing absorbed her for about three years. It culminated a ten-year inquiry and personal quest. It also brought an end to her marriage. "The book was a strain," she says. "It was really the breaking point."

She talks now about the many partnerships we see dissolving because of changes undergone primarily by one partner. She talks about the new status of the intact family in America, i.e., its minority status, and the widespread search for other forms, other kinships. She quotes a line from Richard Bach's *Illusions:* " 'Rarely do members of the same family grow up under the same roof.' "

She makes a prediction.

"That force, that tearing and rending and tension that goes on within families, and between parents and children very strongly, is going to be with us for a while. But when we come through, I think we'll end up with a variety of forms of people being with one another and caring for one another that in a sense will be new institutions but less sharply defined than what we have now."

The subtitle of the book is "Personal and Social Transformation in the 80s." You could say that she herself is a case in point. Living through the mind-bends and life-turns of the seventies, she has now made a career of transformation itself. She has written these books, she oversees these newsletters, she lectures and travels, while a staff of ten people stay busy in the office/headquarters, a converted Spanish-style house down in the canyon—editors, clerks, typists, a business manager. I stuck my head in the door, before starting the climb, and two phones were ringing, the typewriters were clicking, a stack of mailers was on its way to somewhere, and a new edition of *The Brain/Mind Bulletin* was nearly on its way to the printer.

Up here in her high-ceilinged living room with the three-hundred-and-sixty-degree view, we are sipping coffee and she is saying, "Uncertainty is the way of things. There isn't going to be any final truth. The path is trackless. That is why in the book I seldom use the word transformation by itself. I talk about the transformative process. There is the illusion of an end point. But you don't get *there*. What finally happens is you accept that you are on a different journey."

As she speaks, Glen the plumber calls through a doorway to say that the water heater is working again. "I sealed up all those pipes," he says. "They oughta hold for you now."

He is interrupted by the burglar alarm, filling the house again with its relentless howl. Glen is standing in the doorway with his wrench, in mid-sentence, waiting for the test to end. Above us the printout starts to chatter. Beyond the picture window the landscaper's pickup is backing slowly down the driveway, loaded with limbs and shrubbery.

Still thinking of transformation—or rather, the transformative process, which never ends—I look at Marilyn, who is smiling over the coffee cup. She is enjoying it all.

"Please don't think this is an ordinary day," she says. "It isn't always like this. Just twenty-five percent of the time."

How Various Legends, Large and Small, Move Around the State of California

Culver City still calls itself "The Heart of Screenland." That phrase is written across the city's crest—a knightly shield divided into quadrants in the classic manner. If you look closely you will see in one quadrant a rising California sun, in another the Golden Bear, in another a camera dolly with visored cameraman. The crest and motto hark back to the days before World War II when over half the films made in the United States originated here.

When Samuel Goldwyn leased the old Triangle Studios in 1918, they were surrounded by open country, and a long way by electric train from downtown Los Angeles. I happened to be approaching from the east and passed a city-limits sign just where Culver Boulevard and Washington Boulevard intersect. Without that sign there would have been no way to know I had left one city and entered another. The streets, the rows of houses, the traffic, all of it is continuous. On the map you will see Culver City as an island of pale green inside a great lagoon of urban yellow (a.k.a. L.A.).

I was approaching a low fortress, which stands in the middle of that pale green island, enclosed by a wall that looks vaguely ancient, Greek or Roman. That wall, or what remains of it, borders the MGM lot, or what is left of it. Temple columns are spaced along the wall, and portico entrances. If they were doing a remake of *Quo Vadis*, Roman legions could lean in its narrow shade, at the end of a long hot march. Inside the wall, palm trees stood motionless under a smog-blurred sun. Rows of expensive cars were parked nearby, and beyond the cars I could see

236

the Irving Thalberg Building, an art deco classic from 1938, now studio headquarters. The effect of all this, upon arrival, was perfect, exactly the look one hoped a film studio would have. There was no line between the real and the imaginary. History swam in false history. Or rather, they swam together.

Across the street from the studio entrance I stopped at a mini-market where they sold wrapped sandwiches, beer and wine, soft drinks, sundries. Since I was in screenland, *Variety* had replaced the *National Enquirer* at the point of purchase. Next to the cash register, photos of stars were spread out under a glass counter top—glossy eight-by-ten's of Debbie Reynolds, Bo Derek, Larry Hagman in cowboy hat. A crate of ripe avocados was set in front of the counter, and a Pakistani family was standing there, feeling the avocados, deciding which to buy, and how many. The wife, in floral-patterned trousers, held one up to the light, while her mustachioed husband said something, evidently disagreeing with her opinion of the avocado. The wife's eyes flashed, her tongue was sharp. The husband reached in and found one more to his liking, and handed this to the youngest child. Three swarthy children all held avocadoes in each hand. Finally the parents were satisfied and ordered the children to place them on the counter. One rolled over the eyes and nose of Debbie Reynolds, another covered Hagman's hat.

The Editing Room

I was on my way to meet a man who was making a movie. I did not yet know much about it. What attracted me was the book it had been based on, an elusive and mysterious book by a non-mysterious writer, John Steinbeck, about some deathless American dreams as they were once lived somewhere in California.

In front of the Thalberg Building a security guard leaned out of his traffic-island sentry post. He was friendly, almost intimate.

"What can I do for ya?"

"Where is Cannery Row?"

"Ya see that building straight ahead? That's Payroll. Ya see that yellow line along the road? Find a place to park in this lot here, then follow the line around the corner. You'll see the sign."

The yellow line led me to a small sign just inside the doorway. Its words startled me, there in the Payroll Building at MGM. Originally Cannery Row was much farther north, three hundred miles up the coast in Monterey. If I could believe the sign and the arrow, it was now somewhere upstairs.

As things turned out, it was and it wasn't. The production office was upstairs, beyond a door with another sign. David Ward, the man I had come to see, was in there, but not for long. He had written the script. A few months earlier he had directed the filming. Now it was being edited, and he was in a rush to get back to the editing room. We headed down the stairs, plunged immediately into talk about Steinbeck, his characters, his world.

"For me," Ward said, "the magic of film, when I was growing up, was that it always gave me a sense of potential, of possibility. The people in *Cannery Row* seem to have very little going for them. They don't have families, they don't have money. But what makes them attractive and makes their lives ultimately bearable is their sense of community, and their sense of possibility. They are not people without hope."

Ward, I soon found, is an idealist and something of a romantic and, like me, he is a Steinbeck fan. He had fallen for this particular book fifteen years back and was now vacillating, from moment to moment, between the high excitement of a production nearing completion and the high anxiety of a project that may have taken too long. In his mid-thirties, about six feet tall, he was wearing studious horn-rims and, that day, a short-sleeved shirt because it was warm everywhere and warmer in the editing room, right across the street, where *Cannery Row* was currently being stored in—if you will pardon the expression —rows of cans.

We stepped up to enter its semidark and windowless interior, filled with the whirr of fans and the flap of loose film. Amidst the tiers and shelves of footage, editor Dave Bretherton was leaning over his tiny screen watching a scene roll through. He had won an Oscar for his work on *Cabaret*. He was talking to Michael Phillips, the cool and slender producer *(Taxi Driver, Heart Beeps, Close Encounters of the Third Kind)* who had won an Oscar for co-producing *The Sting*, the Best Picture of 1973. That film was based on David Ward's script, which also won an Oscar. All three of these men had won Oscars for something, and now they were debating whether or not to cut a scene that showed four derelicts hauling a piano up a slope from the beach. The piano was a gift for Doc, the hero of the story. Bretherton wanted to get rid of the scene, but Ward still liked it. He had written it into the script, and writers tend to like all their scenes. It is very easy for a writer to overlook William Faulkner's most painful advice: "Kill all your darlings," by which he meant, don't be afraid to excise your favorite scenes and sentences. A good editor can perform this service for a writer or director, as Bretherton was doing then, the old hand, the studio veteran. He wore a blue polo shirt, a couple of gold chains around his neck, a hammered gold watchband. He glanced down at the viewer, then over the top of his half-glasses with a kindly grin. "It's a lovely scene, but it takes too long, it slows the pace right here, and I don't think we need it."

Ward still wasn't sure. In the book and in the film the California coast is a presence, almost a character, and those four men lugging the piano were silhouetted against a spectacular sunset over the ocean. He kept running it through, while the parallel ribbons of film and sound track billowed out into laundry baskets behind the machines, then fed back through on the re-wind.

Though Phillips tended to agree with Bretherton, he didn't say much, he let them work it out. This was the first picture Ward had directed. Phillips kidded him a little, to soften the atmosphere. "You know, David, you are one of the few directors I have worked with who has really done credit to the writer."

In the end the scene was cut. After Bretherton had been back and forth to the splicing table, to perform the execution, I was invited to peek at some of the opening scenes: Nick Nolte as Doc, the self-employed marine biologist, was waking up in his disheveled beach-house/laboratory on the shore of Monterey Bay, while across the street the bums and drifters of Cannery Row, known generically as Mack and the Boys, were also coming to life. Mack, played by M. Emmett Walsh, was sleeping inside a length of abandoned boiler pipe. He was somewhere between forty and sixty, stretched out in his grubby longjohns, snoring and wheezing. His face was grizzled, yet he seemed content: The Complete and Ultimate and Irredeemable Bum.

It was a strange moment, for me, to be seeing him in there. A déjà-vu experience. I did not know if this was due to some quality of the filming, or simply to the fact that the scene now existed on film. Something in my head started to buzz. When Bretherton stopped the reel to study another detail, I was glad. I did not want to watch any more of it just then. I wanted to dwell on that scene and why it should be working on me. It had triggered a flash, a coastal flashback. One advantage books still have over film, you can stop the frame any time you want, to savor something, to think it through. The editing room is one place you can also do this with a reel of film.

The Book

I was fifteen, or sixteen, reading a novel someone had given me, a teacher perhaps, and I came across a scene about a man and a woman who had moved into an old boiler and set up housekeeping—chairs, tables, mattresses. I was delighted. What a grand and refreshing and original way to live! Captivated, I read on, loving the bums, Mack and The Boys, their unkempt "Palace Flophouse," their carefree life. I gobbled it up. It was the first novel to grab and hold me, to truly work a spell. I read it twice, and had no idea why, nor did I even wonder why at that age.

Years later, I saw that these characters appeal the way Huckleberry Finn appeals. We have always had a soft spot for dropouts with a sense of humor, who refuse to toe the line. The lovable drifters. It is a taste that goes back at least as far as Johnny Appleseed and continues right into the 1980s. Country singer Johnny Paycheck has made a small fortune belting out one potent line, from the David Allan Coe song, "Take this job and shove it."

When a few more years had passed I saw that Doc appeals for similar reasons, but he is actually further along the renegade's path to freedom. Doc has some education behind him, he has a job, and he has found a way to live out one of our dearest dreams. He has learned how to do two things at once: be his own person and pay his own way.

Doc, of course, was patterned closely after Steinbeck's longtime friend and mentor, Ed Ricketts. As the years go by, as the Cannery Row legend proliferates, it becomes harder and harder to separate the two. Ricketts is revered in certain circles now—it would not be exaggerating to say a Ricketts cult has rippled outward from Monterey—because of the life he actually lived, together with the life Steinbeck described in the novel, the free-spirited life of a singular man.

I think of him as the classic case of a certain type of Californian. He came west seeking not worldly riches but a way of living. Born in Illinois, he studied biology at the University of Chicago, then migrated to Monterey where in 1923 he set up the Pacific Biological Laboratory, a free-lance operation for collecting and selling marine specimens, with sufficient time left over to explore the coast, enjoy classical music, womanize, philosophize and spend comradely hours with his multitude of friends. Long before the word "life-style" was coined to denote the aggregate worth of one's work/income/leisure habits/ place of residence, years before that idea was fixed in the national vocabulary, Ricketts had worked out a rare one for himself. Steinbeck memorialized him in the novel—the man, and the spirit of the man. And in some curious alchemy the spirit of the man as captured in the novel has come to be synonymous with the spirit of the place we still call Cannery Row.

The Legend

The book has almost nothing to do with the industry that gave the district its name: catching huge quantities of sardines and putting them into cans. Monterey's first cannery was built in 1902. By the mid-1930s, when Steinbeck and Ricketts were drinking buddies, Monterey had become the world's third largest port for annual fish tonnage. There were thirty canneries and around them had grown a raucous, smelly, wharfside community—"a poem," Steinbeck called it, in the book's first line, "a stink, a grating noise, a quality of light, a habit, a nostalgia, a dream."[24]

"Dream" is the key word there. He was not setting out to describe the rugged lives of the Sicilian fishermen or the daily struggle of the women who rose at dawn to stand at the assembly lines. He had already told the working-class story, told it over and over again, in *Of Mice and Men, In Dubious Battle, The Grapes of Wrath,* and he would come back to it one more time in the screenplay *Viva Zapata.* In those stories all the characters have dreams, but the *places* they inhabit would never have been described as dreams.

He wrote this novel at the very end of World War II, when the world was in shadow, and he was in the mood to explore something other than what he had just witnessed as a war correspondent in Europe. He looked back a decade to a sunnier time, when the world had a shine around it, looking not at the working stiffs but at the "characters" who had gathered along the waterfront. He cast them all in a warm, whimsical and affectionate glow, so that they walk perpetually in filtered light.

Though there are whores along his Row, there is no sex. Though there is mental instability among his bums, there is no violence. Though there is a hero (Doc), he is an unusual bird in popular fiction. He is not a crusader, not a detective, not a spy or a cowboy or a victim or a man on the run. He is mainly a person who savors life to the limit and manages to do so without harming anyone else.

Steinbeck's detractors have called the book sentimental, simple-minded, adolescent and shallow. But none of that has diminished its evocative power or its worldwide popularity. People still fall in love with this book. In turn they fall in love with the place called Cannery Row, or the place that once was, or the place they and Steinbeck wish had been. So compelling is the memory that fans and readers and literary pilgrims seek it out when they come traveling up or down the coast—a habit that goes back to the first months after publication. In

"About Ed Ricketts," his preface to the 1951 reprint of *The Log from the Sea of Cortez*, Steinbeck wrote:

> As the book began to be read, tourists began coming to the laboratory, first a few and then in droves. People stopped their cars and stared at Ed with that glassy look that is used on movie stars. Hundreds of people came into the lab to ask questions and peer around. It became a nuisance to him. But in a way he liked it too. For as he said, "Some of the callers were women and some of the women were very nice looking."[25]

The book appeared in 1945, the year of the Row's biggest catch ever. Some 242,000 tons was processed there, mostly sardines. Six years later the row was dead. For reasons that are still debated, the sardines disappeared completely, never to return. During that time Ricketts too had died, in a freak train accident. A Southern Pacific track runs along the slope uphill from the warehouses. In April of 1948 he left his lab late one afternoon, heading for the meat market. It was a route he traveled almost every day, but it was dusk, and the crossing had no signal, and his car evidently made so much racket he could hear nothing but his own transmission grinding away. He didn't see the train.

Today, as you approach Cannery Row, this length of track where Ricketts met his Maker is actually one of the thresholds, points of entry. If you're coming down Lighthouse Avenue, take a right on Drake, toward the water. The tracks cross Drake where they parallel Wave Street. Bear left at the next corner, and there, where the old purse seiners used to anchor offshore to transfer their catches to the noisy sheds along the beach, you will come upon the Row's modern incarnation as a tourist mecca and shopping mall, a half mile of warehouses and packing sheds reshaped as gift shops, bottle shops, boutiques, delis, seafood restaurants, and chartered vans and Gray Line buses.

In the busiest plaza you come upon a bust, a good likeness of Steinbeck, cast in bronze and set on a four-foot pedestal. The eyeballs are missing—in the manner of old Greek statuary—two round hollows there in the greening bronze. Considering what these eyeballs would have to look at now, I think it is just as well.

Behind the head, where the eyes aren't looking, the view hasn't changed much over the years—intensely blue water, the bay's curving shoreline, and in close the black seaweed draped over water-etched stacks of rock. It is what rises in front of the statue that could make bronze eyes blink and squint. Up the slope the old Edgewater Packing Company has become an arcade with pinball machines, video games, a costume photo booth and an indoor merry-go-round. Painted horses and tiny lights spin all day long. To the right the warehouse of the former Monterey Canning Company is faced with corrugated tin, its fine Victorian roofline trimmed in white. Preserved from the old days an overhead corridor crosses the street to a beachside packing shed that now houses The Historic Wax Museum and a gift shop called "Sweet Thursday," where you can purchase a brass sea lion, a ceramic dolphin, a plastic pelican, a Cannery Row bumper sticker, and pick up a copy of the Monterey Peninsula *Review,* with a full-page ad for the Row's diverse attractions. "Walk," the ad says, "where John Steinbeck walked, a hulking figure in his sheepskin coat."

On this street, half the history of the West is capsulized. How many times have we watched it happen? Somewhere on the horizon a mystique appears. The entrepreneurial spirit chases and ropes it, wrestles it to the ground like a recalcitrant steer, to be labeled and priced and fattened for market. The thing is, you don't often find a novel being given this treatment. From one point of view—in a land where marketing and spending are the ultimate acts of faith—the new shape of Cannery Row might be interpreted as yet another tribute to the appeal and the magic of the book.

But when you open the elaborate packaging, what's inside? Where is the world he wrote about? Do any shreds of that time and that place remain?

At one end of this Row, a venerable storefront claims to be the site of Lee Chong's grocery, where Doc bought his whiskey and his beer in the novel and where Ricketts bought his whiskey and his beer in real life. It is an antiques store now. The woman who owns it takes pride in the fact that she is carrying on "the tradition." When I ask her what this means, she points first to the old walk-in icebox—"the original icebox" —which is still in place, though not in use. She touches the counter we stand next to, a polished oak frame with a slab of beveled glass across the top, installed, she says, in 1918. She then quotes me the first line from Chapter One: "Lee Chong's grocery, while not a model of neatness, was a miracle of supply."

Flinging an arm toward the tables and counters piled with old cannery labels, pottery, postcards, shawls, and hanging necklaces, she laughs a throaty laugh and says, "Nobody would *dare* call this place a model of neatness . . . and we are still a miracle of supply."

If there is a true shrine here, it stands across the street from this store. The model for Doc's lab in the novel, it actually housed Ricketts and his car and his Pacific Biological Laboratory in real life. He moved there in 1936, after his first quarters burned down. One story high, with weathered redwood siding and a low garage door right next to the sidewalk, it is unmarked on the outside and, from what they say, little changed on the inside. It is one of the few buildings along the Row not open to the public. A consortium of local Ricketts buffs who revere the legend own it and have kept it that way.

We are looking at it through her cluttered window, looking, as it were, from fiction to fiction (if it weren't for the novel, both of these buildings would be long gone), and she says, "I knew John. I knew them both. I grew up here, you know. When I was a girl I used to sit at the feet of Doc Ricketts. I thought I was going to be an ichthyologist back then, and I soaked up everything I could."

She says this with such a shy, proud smile, I decide not to press for verification. She wants it to be true. And I want it to be true. I wouldn't mind some flesh-and-blood continuity here.

The Script

When David Ward first saw Monterey, in the late 1960s, the street had not yet taken its present shape. The mystique was roaming freer. He was an undergraduate at Pomona then and had traveled north for a summer job, painting houses. He came across a copy of *Cannery Row* that summer, and the experience of discovering this book in the town where it was set worked a double spell, one of those heady spells that lives on the edge of the mind for years. It might have been a triple spell. Like Ricketts, Ward was born in the Midwest. When he was eight his family moved to St. Louis, Missouri. His fondness for Steinbeck goes back to a sixth-grade class in St. Louis, when the teacher read *The Moon Is Down* out loud. "It took her about a month and a half," he says, "reading a little to us every day, and I never forgot it."

When he first contemplated a film about Doc, he imagined something lyrical and impressionistic, like the book. The slender story line, however, was just too anecdotal to hang a movie on: Mack and the Boys want to do "something nice" for their good pal, Doc; they engineer a manic frog hunt to raise some cash, to throw a wild party which, in turn, brings together all the characters along the Row, and this tribute nearly wrecks the lab. It was when Ward read *Sweet Thursday*, a few years later, that he thought he had found the remedy. Published in 1954, this novel describes life on the Row in the years following World War II. Doc is a little older and feeling the short end of his bargain with life. After many years of independence he is craving some long-term companionship. Into this empty space walks Suzy, the new girl in town. Down on her luck, she takes a job in one of the Row's bordellos, right across the street from Doc's lab. Destiny being what it is, they soon meet, or rather collide.

As is the case with many a sequel, *Sweet Thursday* lacks the magic of the original. But the love story is there. Blending scenes and incidents from both books, Ward came up with his first version of the script in early 1977. By this time he had spent a year in U.S.C.'s film school, then moved on to U.C.L.A. There he had written a graduate thesis called *Steelyard Blues,* which became his first collaboration with Michael Phillips. During the filming of their next project, *The Sting,* he got acquainted with Paul Newman, and it was Newman's opinion of the new script that sent Ward back to the typewriter.

"I had tried to stay as true as I could to the books," Ward said, "to the dialogue, and the flow of the scenes. I showed Paul the script because I was seeing him in the role of Doc." But from an actor's point of view, Newman told him, the Doc of the books was too passive. There was a danger that, on screen, he would be overshadowed by the colorful cast of hookers and pimps and grocers and drifters. Doc could get buried, said Newman, unless you beef up the role somehow.

"It was a frightening thought," said Ward. "Beefing up the role meant sooner or later I would be tampering with Steinbeck's material. I didn't want to violate the spirit of the book or the character. I sure didn't want to bring down the wrath of Steinbeck buffs and literary scholars who might think I had gone too far. At the same time, I knew Paul was right. If a picture was going to be made, *some*thing else had to go into the writing. So the first thing I did, I gave Doc a past."

In the two novels, Doc has no past. It just isn't part of the story. You could call this another classically Californian feature of his character: what counts most is not where you have been but the life you're living now. *Suppressing* one's past, of course, is equally Californian. For the film Ward gives him an earlier career as a baseball player, a pitcher who left the major leagues for reasons no one on Cannery Row has ever bothered to look into. It is Suzy who draws the story out of him, so that his shadowed past soon loops around their budding romance.

The Set

When he described this evolution, we were sitting in his office, with a view out the window, through still-life palms, toward the Thalberg Building. On a wall next to the window hung a glossy blowup of the stars, Nick Nolte and Debra Winger, sitting on a sandy hillock near Monterey. Ruggedly handsome, with his 1940s hair slicked back, he was gazing at her, while she, with his coat around her shoulders, was lovely and radiant, gazing toward the sea.

"Nice shot," I said.

"Yeah," said Ward with a wistful grin, "too bad it isn't in the movie."

Spread across a low coffee table were back issues of the regional monthly, *Monterey Life*. When I remarked that you don't see many copies of this magazine south of Big Sur, he said, "I subscribe. I still love it up that way. One reason I was hoping we could film on location, I wanted to spend some more time there."

The idea of shooting on location had been scrapped when they found out how expensive it would be to restore the current high-rent district to its former low-rent look. The spot they wanted was in the heart of the tourist zone, and some eighty-three clearances were involved, eighty-four if you count the Coastal Commission, which would have had to approve any construction within a thousand yards of the water.

While this complex news was sinking in, British designer Richard MacDonald had begun to envision another location—one that, to his mind, would be truer to the book than anything now standing on or near any West Coast bay or cove or harbor town. MacDonald had first read *Cannery Row* in England, at school, and from that distance he had never seen it as anything but a myth, a fable. It wasn't real, and in his opinion the film should not be realistic, but highly stylized, mythologized, seen through a softened lens. He was thinking of a constructed set, an elaborate stage inside the studio.

Though Ward and Phillips had been reluctant to give up the idea of location filming, MacDonald gradually persuaded them. The economics were good—they would save about $2 million—and the theory was good, since the place Steinbeck evokes is not really going to be found on any map.

Stage 30 at MGM happens to be built over a giant water tank, where Esther Williams filmed some of her aqua-movies thirty years ago. There MacDonald created an indoor ocean and completely stocked a 1940 grocery store and erected a Victorian whorehouse. On the walls of Ward's office I saw some marvelous sketches of that set, in charcoal and wash—the wharves, the dockside warehouses, Doc's lab in the lee of a salt-eaten packing shed. The sketches were all that remained of the set. Like the novel they were nostalgic, sun-lit renderings of something that came and went, rose and fell, a real place that was never really there at all.

The W.O.M.

Before meeting with David I had called my friend V in Malibu, to ask if he had heard anything about this movie.

"My impression," he said, "is that the W.O.M. is very good."

"You mean word of mouth?"

"I have heard nothing but good things about the script. And they say the set was fabulous. I know people who drove all the way over there just to see the set."

"What was the excitement?"

"Everybody is so geared up to go someplace like Portland or Manila to make a movie. Shooting indoors at MGM, it's like filming in black and white. It's like the old days. It's so rare it's a big adventure."

"How about the picture itself?" I asked.

Here his voice dropped. "They say Raquel Welch is suing for two million."

He paused, as if to decide whether I could be trusted with the rest of the information, then went on to explain that Raquel had been the first actress cast to play Suzy, the female lead. Suzy begins adrift, and in the course of the movie she grows and changes, she learns things, and she finds herself. The role had range, and there was a classy, literary aura to the production. Unhappy about being forever viewed as a sex symbol, Raquel saw this film as a way to upgrade her image. She wanted the part so badly she signed on for considerably less than she was used to getting paid, and then, two weeks after filming began, she was released. Debra Winger was called down from her mountaintop in New Mexico. The official word from the studio was breach of contract: Raquel had failed to report for work at such and such a time on such and such a day. The W.O.M. was that someone decided she wasn't right for the part. She was outraged. She called her attorney. She felt misused and betrayed. She claimed she had not been given a chance.

For the next six months if you had asked anyone in Screenland what they knew about *Cannery Row,* chances are they would have replied as V had. "I understand Raquel Welch is suing for two million." Someone who reads the daily trades might have had a more precise figure: "a million eight," or "two million five." A true insider might have murmured, as V had to me before hanging up, "She *wasn't* right for the part, but it was brutal the way the studio handled her. They *deserve* to be sued."

W.O.M.—it is like the Roman wall around the studio lot. Through the years the gathering of all the W.O.M. surrounding all the pictures is the ongoing legend of life as it is lived in Screenland. It may be true.

It may not be true. That is not important. It runs on a separate reel, but it runs simultaneously with the pictures themselves. A split projection. On one side you have the pictures, on the other those legendary dollars and legendary lives.

The Stars

The film premiered in Salinas, which calls itself the capital of Steinbeck country, and rightly so. He was born there. He finished high school there in 1919. The town and the fertile valley keep turning up in his books and stories. It was these very books and stories, of course, that turned the town against him for a few decades. In certain circles he was actually despised for the picture he offered to the world—of working conditions, field life, local politics, the underbelly of corruption. There were also people in Monterey who complained that their town's reputation had been sabotaged by his fiction. But Steinbeck passed away in 1968. By *Cannery Row*'s premiere date, time and the Nobel Prize had healed many wounds. Both towns were laying proud claim to the Steinbeck heritage. When MGM chose Salinas as the site, civic leaders were delighted. Not only would this bring movie people into town—and movie people, wherever they go, seem to spend more money than normal people do—it meant they had won some big points in the ongoing cross-county rivalry. Salinas is tired of always running second to Monterey when it comes to class and prestige: cattle and farming town versus spiffy coastal resort. Being the Salad Bowl of America has never seemed quite as satisfying as being the home of the Crosby Invitational at Pebble Beach.

It was a big week for Salinas, with the testimonial luncheons, a fresh spot light on the Steinbeck Memorial Library, and the renovated family home. And yet Monterey still wound up with a galling slice of the pie. When I called MGM to find out where the film people would be staying, a public relations man said curtly, "The Hyatt."

"Do they have a Hyatt in Salinas?" I asked.

"Do they have *hotels* in Salinas?" he retorted, the way Don Rickles might say, "Do robins have lips?"

After the Friday night screening, a fleet of limos cruised the twenty miles back to Monterey, followed by the bus-loads of reviewers who had been flown in from every part of the U.S., all of whom were up early the next morning for breakfast in the Terrace Room and press interviews with the stars.

The Hyatt Del Monte is a ranch-style deluxe hotel, built around a golf course and spread across a gentle slope. Its numerous two- and three-story buildings cover so many acres that room service delivers meals via jitney trucks. From the lobby you can gaze over Highway 1 toward the bay, with half of Monterey visible on your left, up the side of the hill above the harbor. You can almost see the roofs of the old-time canneries, around that hill's curve a couple of miles away.

The interviews were staged in four conference rooms, each holding fifteen to twenty writers and critics, who sat sipping coffee, fiddling with their tape recorders, and comparing notes, while studio aides maneuvered the performers from group to group. I was in the Windjammer Room when Debra Winger strode through the door, talking as she walked and igniting the place with her husky voice and her infectious laughter. Before sitting down on the low-slung sofa she piled two cushions for some altitude and said, "It's like walking into a psychiatrist's office, and they give you a chair that's half the size. . . ."

"How tall *are* you?" a woman asked.

"Five four," said Debra. "But six three with these suckers on," pointing to her boots, which were gray and high-heeled and reached to her knee, Three Musketeers style.

"Did someone design those suckers for you?" the woman said.

"Design?" said Debra with a shrug. "I don't know. K-Mart, probably."

She was jaunty and refreshing and woke everybody up. When the first laugh settled, a man said, "Had you read much Steinbeck before you made this film?"

"Sure," she said. "I had read the normal amount everybody reads in school. Someone asked me before if I had seen Suzy the way Nick had seen Doc, someone you *wanted* to portray. I don't think I could really read Steinbeck that way, because he sees most women as whores. I never did really pick up a book and say, 'Yeah! I gotta lot to say about life through *this* character!' " (Another laugh from the crowd, which she waits out with professional timing.) "I mean, he is a male-oriented writer, so I didn't have that feeling about him. I had read him the way I had read Hemingway and . . ." (again the timing, a perfect pause) . . . "*Screen* magazine" (more laughter, followed by her own deep laugh). "I mean, the way you read *every*thing is what I'm trying to say.

"It was David's adaptation that blew my mind. Honoring Steinbeck totally, he was able to bring in elements that made it something I wanted to play."

"Can you tell us some more about that?" I said. "Specifically, what attracted you to the script?"

I knew she had been in great demand after filming *Urban Cowboy* with John Travolta. She had read and turned down many scripts before this one came along.

"The first step is, if you read a script and like the story and it captivates you, then you say, 'Okay, what is this character about?' For me, choosing a female character, I use the parallel of, if she were a pioneer and she was coming across in a covered wagon, would she make it? Whatever manifestation that character takes, I can live with, if I know *she'd* live. There has to be somewhat of a pioneer's spirit, no matter how contemporary the role is. There has to be a strength of character."

A woman in the group had some trouble with this imagery. Her voice sounded Eastern. She had probably flown in the previous afternoon from one of the East Coast cities. She wanted to know what was so appealing about the pioneer, and in connection with that, was it true that Debra had a house somewhere in the middle of New Mexico, and if so, did she live alone?

"Yes," said Debra, "I'm alone a lot. And I travel a lot. I was born in Cleveland, and if you're born in Cleveland you immediately think of . . ." (the comedian's pause) "traveling." She let the laughter rise and break, then said, more seriously, "When I was very young we *Grapes-of-Wrath*-ed it out to California looking for bigger and better things. I think it was inherent in my own life. But also, we are in the United States, we're a young country, and the pioneer spirit is something people let go of too easily. People get settled where they are and don't remember there might be new ground to forge—not to ruin—but maybe venture back into situations that aren't so safe. . . ."

Cannery Row was Debra's fourth picture. She had recently finished shooting her fifth, *An Officer and a Soldier.* At twenty-six, she was a rising star. She had a sweet and sudden smile, with a habit of catching the tip of her tongue between her teeth. Her hair was loosely combed, her eyes were clear, her face was alive, and her body was moving all the time—not nervous but active—an arm thrown out, a fist, two hands in prayer, a pointing finger. She sat for a while with her black jeans down into her boots and one boot across her knee, like a polo player sitting on the sidelines, telling us about her life and her work. She was honest and direct and accessible. At the same time she was delivering a captivating performance: the star as direct and accessible person. She was *up,* she was *on,* she made us laugh, and she made us think, and it occurred to me as I watched and listened that Hollywood is a lot like Cannery Row. It used to be a place, but it isn't anymore. If you go to the place on the map called Hollywood, you won't see any film studios and you won't meet any stars. Screenland is wherever you find it. That

morning it was there, in the Windjammer Room of the Hyatt Del
Monte, on the south shore of Monterey Bay, with Debra giving us a
wonderful show, and the press corps scribbling, while the studio aide
paced restlessly outside the sliding glass doors, glancing at his watch.
When thirty minutes had passed he opened the door and said, "Thank
you all, thank you very much," upon which Debra stood up, still talking,
still laughing, and made her exit, and in walked the leading man.

It was 10 A.M., and Nick Nolte moved as if he had been up all night,
or had been in a fight, or both. His boots were scuffed, his jeans were
rumpled, the cuffs of his blue work shirt were unbuttoned and flapping
nine inches past the bunched-up sleeves of his jacket. The reluctant
celebrity, he muttered hello, as he accepted a cigarette from someone,
then dropped himself onto the sofa, looking out at us with his line-
backer's eyes, which are deep blue—not deep in color but deep behind
a layer of protective lidding, ready to squint shut if something comes
at him from the side.

Nolte has spent the last six years being famous *(Rich Man Poor Man,
North Dallas Forty, Heart Beat, Who'll Stop the Rain)*. Every move he
made said that here is a man who has also spent a lifetime being the
alpha male: the rugged jaw, the full neck, the shock of blond hair across
his forehead. He scarcely resembled the trim and chiseled biologist we
had seen him portray on the screen the previous night. Someone asked
him why he had darkened his hair for the picture.

"The dark hair was my choice. I wanted to romanticize Doc as much
as possible."

"Is this a character you had always wanted to play?"

"No. It wasn't the character. I'd always liked the books, plus *Tortilla
Flat* and *To a God Unknown*. But I hadn't really thought of playing
Doc. I had thought more of playing one of the boys."

"What got you interested in the character, then?" a woman asked.

Nolte was not eager to talk. He waited for questions. He took his
time. He thought about this one and said, "I think what turned me
around mostly on it was that Doc was my age. He was dealing with some
problems that come around the age of forty." With a sly grin he added,
"And I'm told not to talk about it."

"Why not?" asked the woman eagerly.

"Well . . . it has to do with menopause."

The half-dozen women there all laughed at once, and one called out,
"That's a socially acceptable subject!"

"Who told you not to talk about it?"

"They don't want anyone to think the film's a downer about a guy
who's going through menopausal loneliness. This made the role more

difficult to play, of course, because I had to play close to my own insecurities."

"What do you mean by that?" another woman asked. "Your own insecurities."

"Doc was really in an area of his life when he was starting to feel something was missing. It's around forty when you begin to realize you missed something. Maybe. I mean, that might not be universal. My mother says the age is seventy."

This drew a laugh from the crowd, and a tired grin from Nolte. To elaborate, he called up an image from the novel.

"Doc is like a tidepool," he said. "When one thing goes wrong in a tidepool, the whole tidepool goes wrong."

It was another one of those moments when the line blurs between history and fiction. Was he talking about Nolte, or Doc, or Ed Ricketts, or all three at once? He said this with such laconic effort, shifting in his seat, he seemed himself to be caught in some tidepool of middle life, grappling with the great squid that lurks just below the surface.

The Reviews

Central to *Cannery Row*, the tidepool was also central to the life of Ed Ricketts, who studied the shorelines from Alaska to La Paz and eventually wrote what is still the authoritative text on the subject, *Between Pacific Tides*. An early ecologist with a sense for whole systems, he showed Steinbeck how each pool was a carefully balanced world unto itself, a microcosm wherein no part could be fully understood except in relation to the whole. Steinbeck tried to build this biological idea into his novel about an inspired biologist, and then he looked very closely at one tiny creature to find a key for how to proceed with the writing itself.

"When you collect marine animals," he noted in the prologue, "there are certain flat worms so delicate they are almost impossible to capture whole, for they break and tatter to the touch. You must let them ooze and crawl of their own will onto a knife blade."

Steinbeck was talking about his book. He could almost have been describing why the film did not hold together—a noble attempt that did not quite work. Though all the ingredients were impressive, taken separately—the script, the shimmering sets, the award-winning editor, the famous cameraman who had worked with Bergman, the John Huston voice-over, the studio commitment—the delicate center broke and scattered.

Reviewers said the film suffered from indecision: a fable one moment, a real-life romance the next; a musical-comedy sunset concocted in Culver City, followed by a day-for-night stroll across real sand next to the real Pacific.

Ironically, the very way the film did *not* work serves to advance the legend. The action wobbles, yet the place survives.

The film begins offshore. A marker buoy is bobbing in dawn waters. Slowly the buoy recedes, the water growing all around it, the buoy growing smaller as the water grows wide, until we are seeing the timbers of the first building and begin to meet the early risers who inhabit the nooks and crannies of Cannery Row. An hour and a half later the film ends with a long hold on these same waterfront buildings—not on a face, or an embrace, or someone strolling along a beach toward the future, but on this tableau of sheds, the wharf, Doc's lab, the salt-cured canneries, their pilings washed by a timeless sea.

That is what the book is about, and what the film set out to explore, a place somewhere on the coastlines of our imagination. If it exists at all, you will find it, most days, floating offshore in the fog, out there just beyond the reach of the camera, or in the softened light as early sun begins to break up the fog—floating above the water in that kind of light. A glorious mirage. An ecosystem of the mind. Like Hollywood. Or like that isle called California the early Spaniards tried to map.

The Heart of Screenland

I was heading south from Castroville, five miles out of Salinas, when I saw three long silver beams wheeling in the night sky. They came from searchlights set up behind Sherwood Auditorium where the world premiere was being staged. From that distance they seemed to be rising from the fields around the town. I was crossing some of the West's most nutritious bottom land. At night, I couldn't see the furrows and the crops, but with the window down I could smell wet earth and manure and the pungent whiff of artichokes and broccoli. At Sherwood the limos were parked in front, outside the lobby a four-piece combo was playing "California, Here I Come," and "Roll Out the Barrel," and upstairs they were already sipping champagne at the $50-a-ticket reception. As I sped through that dark and open country I was thinking that there would be other limos and other combos and other glasses of champagne, but chances were—unless this county were attacked from the air—there would never again be scene like this: the long glamorous beams of silver light seeming to rise from windows in the soil to swing through a black sky above the broccoli fields of the Salinas River delta.

I used them to guide by, then lost my way a few blocks into town, when urban lights obscured the high beams overhead. On Main I pulled into a service station.

I asked the manager, "Where is *Cannery Row?*"

"It's about twenty miles from here," he said. "But you're headed in the wrong direction, Bud. You must've missed your turn at Castroville."

"I mean the movie, the world premiere."

"Oh, that. You're almost there. It's right up ahead. You can't miss it. Just look for all the cars."

III

DANCERS ON THE BRINK
OF THE WORLD

Facing west from California's shores,
Inquiring, tireless, seeking what is yet unfound,
I, a child, very old, over waves, towards the house
   of maternity, the land of migrations, look afar,
Look off the shores of my Western sea, the circle
   almost circled. . . .

WALT WHITMAN
from *Leaves of Grass*
(1860)

The Discovery of San Diego

I enter San Diego as a tourist. I have to. I know absolutely no one in the city. Not a soul. In search of guidance I stop at the Visitor Information Center, just to the right of Highway 5 as you approach town from the north. It is shaped like Darth Vader's helmet and sits on a knoll overlooking Mission Bay.

A small traffic sign says "One Way." A second sign, a wide banner hung across a balustrade you pass on your way to the parking lot, says "YOGURT." Of all the things one might announce to the multitudes arriving in San Diego for the first time and stopping here for information, this seems like an odd beginning. Odd, until you taste the yogurt, which is frozen and very good after a couple of hours on the speedway south through Anaheim, Garden Grove and Santa Ana. To stand at the balustrade with yogurt cone in hand turns out to be a fine way to begin to see the town.

Years ago Mission Bay was a swamp and stinking estuary. Nowadays it is an elegantly maintained recreation zone. I have arrived at 11 A.M. on a Tuesday morning. Within sixty seconds I see four joggers, five cyclists, a man in a headstand, six sailboats skimming across the well-protected inshore waters, a pair of roller skaters arm in arm, and four young men in shorts and Adidas shoes playing a leisurely game of two on two. The water is blue and wrinkled by coastal breezes. The grass glows with health. The air is as balmy as the windward side of Oahu.

Everyone in sight is tan and trim, and it is all instantly familiar, even though, from where I live, this town lies so far south that I have seen it only three or four times in my life, and then I was in a hurry, passing through on my way to Mexico. From my bay to this one it is roughly the distance from Providence, Rhode Island, to Richmond, Virginia. And yet it is almost like home. This too is a harbor city, a one-time Mission town that has become a resort and recreation area. Many pleasure boats are anchored here. Many tennis racquets flash in the constant sun. There are long beaches and an ambitious downtown redevelopment plan, which many taxpayers are resisting, and tremendous pressures on local housing. There is, in short, nothing unusual about how people live in San Diego, as far as this stretch of the world goes. Life here resembles life as it is lived all up and down the coast. What amazes me is the scale and the magnitude of things. Like many places in the state, this county has multiplied drastically in the last ten years. Santa Cruz County has increased by 50 percent, which has meant about fifty thousand new people. I know from personal experience that you feel the accumulation of these numbers—five thousand every year. It builds up around you like water filling a reservoir. San Diego County has increased by half a million. It is as if during the past ten years the entire population of Vermont had been added to this fifty- by seventy-mile southeastern corner of the state and the nation. The space they occupy is actually narrower than that. It is more like fifty by ten, since people here press as close as they can get to the ocean, as close as they can afford to get.

During this same decade San Diego has moved from sun-drenched obscurity to a place on the list of America's ten most populous cities. And every moment its population grows. As I stand here at the balustrade watching the tan bodies exercise at Mission Bay, two more families are moving in somewhere. The city-limits sign I passed, just south of Del Mar, says 754,000. I don't know when it was last amended, but according to the 1980 census, the sign is over a hundred thousand people behind. And five months into 1981, the census count itself is lagging by twenty thousand or so, if you can believe the local growth analysts, who say nine hundred to a thousand new people arrive here every week. People, that is, who are planning to stay. Not the visitors like me.

At the Information Center I learn that seventeen million people a year visit San Diego, to play, to swim, to surf, to bask, to dine, to see the Air and Space Museum (Lindbergh's *Spirit of St. Louis* was designed and tested here), to walk through the world's largest zoo. Around Monterey Bay, they talk about six million visitor-days per year. And you feel that too—more water rising in the reservoir, or tides of water rising and receding around you, and rising again. Because you feel it, you believe the Chamber of Commerce when they announce six million. But it is hard to *imagine* six million of anything. Let alone seventeen million. That is the entire population of Australia passing through town every year.

I try to break this down to some manageable number. It roughs out to fifty thousand people per day. Plus a thousand new residents per week.

How many places in the world can you describe this way? Even in California it is awesome. There is something about the flow of people into and out of San Diego County that stuns the imagination. Hoping to comprehend it I have added myself to the flow, to today's fifty thousand or so, to see the sights, wander here and there and take my chances.

I drive out to the tip of Point Loma, a thumb of land that shapes the harbor, pointing south. I go there first because it is where San Diego begins. It is also where California begins. It is where Juan Rodriguez Cabrillo stopped in 1542 to claim this bay for Spain. A landmark. A moment in world history. A tourist mecca.

Two small dark men from Calcutta join me on the observation deck, then a busload of school kids from somewhere inland, followed by a busload of Japanese tourists bristling with lenses. Three French women commence a loud and friendly argument about where two should stand so the third can snap a picture that will include the ship now sailing into the famous harbor, a guided missile cruiser called the U.S.S. *Horn*, returning to port after eight months in the Pacific.

In computing the flow of people I forgot to count the sailors. The Visitors Bureau doesn't count the sailors, nor do the growth analysts projecting into the 1990s. The eleventh Naval District is headquartered here. Yesterday forty-seven hundred sailors arrived aboard the U.S.S. *Ranger*. Today another shipload arrives aboard the *Horn*. The kids are waving down at them. A few crew members wave back, so small below us their movements are a kind of white flicker against the sleek, gliding gray of the cruiser that follows the same course the old caravels must have followed, past this peninsula, past the little outcropping called Ballast Point where Cabrillo is thought to have touched shore four hundred and forty years ago, on into the harbor and the wives and sweethearts waiting at the pier.

"This explorer will be easy to remember," my fourth grade teacher told us. "California and Cabrillo both start with the same two letters."

Gazing down at the tropical water, then south toward the mountains of Mexico a few miles away, I feel the nostalgia and the yearning for those great days of discovery. I want to be out on the deck with the old navigator when he first spies this perfect and untouched harbor. His mission, according to documents displayed in the little museum here, was to sail from the Mexican port of Navidad, to explore the northern coastline "Until Its End and Secret" were known. Those few beguiling words come from a letter to the emperor of Spain by Pedro de Alvarado, then governor of Guatemala. They had sent Cabrillo looking for the Straits of Annian, the mythical northwest passage, and anything else he could find. He died before the mission was completed. If he learned any secrets they are buried with him, on or near San Miguel Island, in the Santa Barbara Channel.

Its End and Secret . . .

Such a phrase makes you wonder what else Alvarado may have had in mind. What did he imagine lurked in this landscape no European had yet seen? Remote and alluring, it floated in and out of focus for decades and centuries. Here at Point Loma sixty years went by. Then Vizcaíno made a brief stop, sailing into the bay in 1602. Though his voyage is less well known, he is the one who dubbed this harbor with the name that stuck—San Diego de Alcalá, whose feast day it happened to be.

After an overnight stay, Vizcaíno sailed on up the coast, and this time a hundred and sixty-seven years went by. Very quiet years by today's standards. Just the Indians and the antelope and the condors and the abalone. It was 1769 when the first European settlement was planted in San Diego, the first in California, the first on the Pacific Coast, remembered now in a hillside grove called Presidio Park, which is my second stop.

Pines, palms, olive trees and vibrant bougainvillea fill the grounds around the Serra Museum, a white, Spanish-style building designed to resemble the chapel and courtyard of an early mission. On this high bluff Junípero Serra dedicated the first mission in Alta California, the mother of the twenty more that followed. From here Portolá set out northward on the first overland expedition. Spanish soldiers established here the first of their three coastal presidios—a scattering of thatch huts, lean-tos and corrals. From the white parapet you can see why they would choose the spot. The only major source of water through this region, the San Diego River, flows nearby. From this height you could have observed all ships entering and leaving the harbor. And the bluff itself would be hard to attack even today, without helicopters and heavy artillery.

But listen. The old presidio has been surrounded and ambushed in another way. Listen. Standing at the parapet, what do you hear?

The thunder of heavy traffic covers all other sound. Serra's Museum overlooks the busiest intersection in the county, where Interstate 5

connecting L.A. and Tijuana crosses Interstate 8, the main trunk line
to El Centro and the Imperial Valley. Roaring along at the base of this
bluff, 8 follows the river east through what used to be the river's valley
and is now a wide channel filled with condominiums, subdivisions,
highrise motels, and vehicles rushing toward the suburbs of La Mesa,
El Cajon, Santee, Ramona.

If you squint inland, from this parapet you can almost see the bell
tower of Mission San Diego, which was relocated farther upstream a
few years after its original dedication. Many of the old bricks and beams
are still there, as well as Serra's quarters and the tower itself, which
never quite caved in, though the building suffered years of neglect
before it was finally reconsecrated as a shrine and monument. Its five-
bell design is unique among California's missions. If you stand on the
steps in front of that bell tower you can look directly down upon several
acres of roofs tiled like the mission, hundreds of buildings the color of
adobe, with iron grillwork across tiny balconies—all part of Mission
Plaza, Adult Condominiums. Next door there is a large development
called Mission Playmor. Its buildings, two stories high with shake roofs,
seem to fill all the land between the tower and the river.

From the far side of this valley, looking back—if you are, say, driving
east on Interstate 8 and happen to glance toward the five-bell tower—
you can see that new condos also line the bluffs above and on both sides.
If you can locate it at all, you see that the Mother Mission, which not
too long ago commanded a rather prominent place on the side of
its own low hill, is overshadowed, dwarfed, and entirely surrounded,
before and behind, above and below, by condo units, all of them built
since 1975.

In this little tableau you get the full effect of the San Diego double
whammy, a city that is now two things at once. It is the oldest town in
California, and the newest. And it is spreading at such a rate, the unfolding waves make me think of Hawaii, which is the largest Hawaiian
island and the newest, the traditional seat of native culture, yet so new
in geological time it is still being formed. The great flows of lava come
pouring down the sides of Mauna Loa, across the bench lands and into
the sea, covering everything that may have preceded it.

I should make it clear that I have nothing against the city and county
of San Diego. Year after year, millions of people have a grand time
around here. Lava, moreover, is both destructive and creative. In Hawaii, the lava actually adds new chunks of acreage to the surface of the
earth. It is just that something is going on, something fundamentally
Californian, that can be observed here almost in isolation. If you want
to observe the way lava flows, you fly to Hawaii just when Mauna Loa

is erupting. If you want to observe the action of a glacier in its natural habitat, you visit Alaska. If you want to observe the leaps-and-bounds way in which California grows, and observe this under nearly ideal conditions, you won't find a better example than right here at the frontier of Sun Belt expansionism.

In the deserts beyond the town, nothing much has ever flourished. As a result, there is almost nothing in the way. There are no timberlands to be despoiled, no croplands to be displaced, as there have been in Los Angeles and in Santa Clara County. There is an openness, an unused chaparral rawness, to this landscape that heightens the presence of these instant neighborhoods and sudden villages spreading outward from the harbor. It is volcanic, and like a volcano it is mesmerizing. The fact is, it stops me in my tracks.

Instead of proceeding on to *The Star of India* and Balboa Park—the next stops on my visitor's list—I check into one of the high-rise motels down there in what is called "Hotel Row," a tourist ghetto in the lee of the bluff where the Serra Museum takes its precarious stand. In my room I pull the rubberized sound-drapes to muffle the roar of traffic, and I read through all the literature they leave for you on top of the television set. I read *Inn Room Magazine, Today in San Diego, Senior World,* the restaurant guide, and the brochure for The Harbor excursion. I am thinking to myself, this is not it, the real tour of this region is somehow going to involve something else, something more than museums and zoos. When I begin to flip through a monthly listing of services and events, I come across an ad that seems to promise what I may be searching for:

NEW VISTAS
The San Diego Land and Property Tour
Nine Dollars with this Ad
Free Hotel Pickup and Return

I call the number. The next group is leaving in an hour.

Three people are sitting in the Datsun 510 wagon that pulls up outside the lobby. I climb in next to the driver, who tells me they have a bus for the larger groups but on days like this the Datsun is more comfortable. His name is Barry Green. He is in his mid-thirties, wears jeans and a polo shirt. He is one of those lucky salesmen who genuinely love their product—which in his case is not any particular house or apartment he might point out in the course of this tour, but the region itself, with its endless supply of sunshine bathing every piece of property in perpetual warmth.

When I ask him why so many people are pouring into this county, he grins and throws one short-sleeved arm out the window, palm up, as if to grab a handful of the weather, or a falling grapefruit.

"Look around," he says. "You've got the best climate in the United States. You can be a bum in this town without two cents in your pocket, sleeping on the sidewalk summer or winter, and never get cold."

"And it's good dry heat," says a voice from the back seat, the voice of Mrs. Blake, who I now learn is out here with her husband from Sarasota, Florida, looking for a change of humidity.

"Back there," she says wearily, "you just melt away in the summertime."

"You've come to the right place then," Green says. "You have to look real hard in this town to find an air conditioner. People don't use them, don't need them."

To me this is news. We are down here next to Mexico, after all, at the same latitude as Tucson, Marrakech, the upper edge of Saudi Arabia, in a zone where ten inches of rain is a very wet year. I turn to share my surprise with Mr. Blake, whose eyes have gone wide at Green's remark.

"Place where we've been living," Mr. Blake says, "has a seventy-percent vacancy rate in the summer. They just can't take it. Everybody goes back north for the summer. But to do that, you have to keep two houses. That's why we retired. So life would be simpler, not more complicated."

"Back north" means Michigan. A year ago they moved to Sarasota, bought into a condominium community, planning to relax and enjoy the sunset years. Now they are shopping in San Diego.

When Green asks me if there are any particular kinds of properties I'd like to look at, I tell him this is my first day "in the county," and I am mainly interested "in an overview." When I begin to scribble things on the back of the duplicated map he hands me, perhaps he thinks I am jotting down prices and terms. But I know that he knows I am not a likely prospect. At least not today. How does he know this? I can see it in his eyes. This is a tour anyone can sign up for. The numbers vary from day to day, from two to twenty. It is his business to sniff out who is serious and who is just killing time. So as we sprint along the freeways in his Datsun, as we wind in and out of neighborhoods, up and down the hillsides, across the mesas and through the duplex-filled arroyos of San Diego County, the Blakes get most of his attention, and the stops we make are designed for them, since there is no question that they are seriously in the market for a condo like the one they have in Sarasota. You can see it on their faces, especially on the face of Mrs. Blake, as she too makes notes, true shopper's notes on the back of her copy of the real estate map. Behind the rimless glasses her eyes squeeze in concentration, and the lips purse. She is not fooling around. Later I learn that Mr. Blake is also thinking of looking at Seattle, since he worked there as a young man. Mrs. Blake is resisting this idea, and Green is helping her resist.

"Very, very wet up in Seattle," he observes. "Another thing about living here, it may cost you a little more to get into something. But it doesn't cost you nearly as much to live. No air conditioning, for one thing, like I said. No heating either. You hardly ever need heat. You only need one wardrobe. No mittens. No topcoat. And your car is going to last forever, because there isn't that moisture in the air to eat the body up, or salt on the roads in the winter to work at it from underneath."

Cars indeed do well in San Diego, perhaps better than the trees, which are still scarce and might even be outnumbered. Except along the riverbanks, trees only appear after people have settled somewhere. In a couple of the older neighborhoods we cruise through—where the houses go back forty and fifty years—trees and bushes offer shade and fill the spaces. But as we move into the outlying districts where the great condo developments proliferate, the view quite often is unobstructed by anything but the next barren hillside and bulldozed mesa top.

There is one such compound that Barry refers to several times before we actually see it. This is the place he feels will most appeal to the Blakes, and he has orchestrated our tour to make it the climax. It is called Rancho Encantado, and we see it first from half-a-mile away, a fortress of low buildings that cover a long dry ridge, reminding me of villages I have seen in the Pyrenees, from across a canyon, with no visible access road. The roofs are red in the afternoon sun, and if the tiles were not so new and shiny, if the siding were not so startlingly white, it might appear, at this distance, to be just that—a totally self-contained mountain community.

The second time we see it we are approaching from below, and Barry explains that the part we saw and are about to enter is the newest segment of a development that will eventually serve some fifteen thousand people. The units we'll be inspecting start at $137,000. An hour ago that might have sounded high for a six-room apartment with no yard, but we have seen places that range from $65,000 to $265,000. We have seen neighborhoods you wouldn't walk through alone in the daytime, and we have seen neighborhoods so expensively equipped that Barry speeded up because the Datsun itself was an embarrassment. So $137,000 now sounds sensibly moderate, the kind of prudent investment a fixed-income couple should be thinking of.

Four styles are available, all with Mediterranean names—Barcelona, Costa Brava, Ibiza, Aix-en-Provence. We each receive a glossy brochure from the hostess on duty and proceed across the narrow street, empty of traffic, through a low iron gate, down some stairs and into a light-filled apartment that does in fact make you feel as if you have just been transported, if not to the Spanish Riviera or the south of France, then someplace equally exotic. Lots of glass. Lots of mirrors. Total carpeting. Wide straw fans from Manila are pinned to the fabric-covered walls. The dining room table is set, as if the lucky occupants—you and I—are about to sit down to a gourmet meal. Opaque skylights send diffused sunshine throughout the interior, onto the sofa, the color-coded easy chairs. It is built for comfort, and I can imagine that life in such a place would not be bad at all, as long as you did not have to make a mortgage payment—the interest alone could run a thousand a month—or look out the broad picture window at the view.

On an absolutely clear day you might be able to see the ocean. Today, though free of clouds, is not free of what one must charitably call a thickening haze. No California city pushing toward a million can claim to have air that is not thick with something. So what you see, down the slope and across the lowlands, are more condo complexes, spilling, unfolding, marching toward where the sea should be, more family units, townhouses, two-story compounds.

The Blakes like it here. It reminds them of the place they have in Florida.

"It has all the same conveniences," she says. "And we really do love everything about it there except the heat. We actually never even think of it as being attached or connected to anything."

"Boy," says Mr. Blake, "I wish we could pick up our place in Sarasota and move it right up onto this hillside."

"That's what they all say," says Green with a little chuckle, as he leads them upstairs to the master bedroom and the sumptuous bath.

I can hear them prowling around overhead, hear shoes whispering through the deep pile. I stay by the first-floor window, considering the view from here to the water, thinking of some of the things Barry has been telling us. He is not going to take the Blakes all the way to the coast. That would be too demoralizing. The "bargains" there cost half a million. Rather, he uses those prices to further underscore the bargain we're getting this far inland.

For one thing you get the temperature trade-off. For every mile inland from the beach, you can expect one more degree of heat. It can be lived with quite easily, he says, until you pass beyond a range of peaks east of town. The wind comes through those peaks and through Mission Valley and cools everything between here and the sea. But east of those peaks, look out. "You've got desert," says he, "real desert."

Listening to him talk, you begin to get a realtor's view of the county and this part of the world, a view of gradually declining temperatures and increasing prices as you move ever closer to the bodies of water that shape this region—Mission Bay, the harbor, finally the ocean beaches with their access to surf and their views of the Pacific. To hear him talk is to be reminded of the incalculable worth of the coastline itself, which is far and away this state's number one commodity. It shapes the shipping industry. It shapes the tourist industry. It shapes our recreation habits. And it shapes the value of real estate, in some kind of pricing factor that radiates inland, applying upward pressure to the worth of any livable parcel within driving distance of the water.

Barry considers himself fortunate to have bought property in a high-rent beach area soon after he moved here. He took a two-year lease option. By the time the option came due, the property value had doubled. The purchase price was locked into the lease, so he got full financing with nothing down.

He laughs when he talks about how money moves around. He calls it wacko: "California is the original home of wacko financing."

Since he bought the place its value has doubled again, at least twice. "My place would actually be worth more now," he adds, "if I demolished it."

"How is that?"

"For some guy looking to put up a high rise, the lot alone, stripped to the ground, is worth more than the house and the lot together."

I can't help remembering the infantry officer in Vietnam who stood in the smoking rubble of what had once been a village and told reporters, "To save it, we had to destroy it."

Another thing this coastline can shape and sharpen is your sense of destiny. As I think of it, as I stand by the picture window in the living room of this $137,000 condo called Costa Brava on the hillside six miles back from the beaches of San Diego County, I am reminded once again how profoundly this is built right into the psychology of California. Some would say, into the delusion or pathology of California. You may not have earned it or deserved it, but you acquire a sense of destiny, if only through a nearness to the coast. It keeps you on the brink, which is where Californians like to be. For all our love of the great outdoors and growing things, we have never been quite content with daily life in and of itself. You want daily life with an edge on it somewhere—daily life, plus destiny.

Consider these lines by Robinson Jeffers, from his long narrative poem "Thurso's Landing." He is writing about the view from a bluff overlooking the Pacific, above a canyon, along the Big Sur coastline:

> You'd think
> This rocked-in gorge would be the last place in the world
>   to bear the brunt: but it's not so; they told me
> This is the prow and plunging cutwater,
> This rock shore here, bound to strike first, and the world
>   will watch us endure prophetical things
> And learn its fate from our ends.[26]

Jeffers wrote that in 1932, when the state's population was about six million, and when he had the only house on the beach south of Carmel. Out there all by himself, with nobody around for miles, he was brimming and bursting with a sense of destiny. And somehow the coastline itself, "this rock shore here" would be the register.

If you happen to live in Southern California and your sense of destiny is wavering, all you need to think about is the fact that these three coastal counties—Los Angeles, Orange and San Diego—now contain one out of every twenty people in the United States. That does not count visitors, tourists, aliens who have sidestepped the census count, or military personnel on temporary duty. Those are the countable residents. Some people say this is too many for the available space, since these three counties, taken together, are smaller in area than the state of New Hampshire. But it's really too late to worry about that. One out of every twenty live there, and more are on their way. For every family who decides to leave, two more are deciding to arrive. That in itself has to alert you to large and momentous events looming somewhere.

It takes many, many forms, this sense of destiny. Some feel themselves on the brink of apocalypse. These Southern California towns are filled with third- and fourth-generation Anglo burnouts who bludgeon one another to the music of Fear and The Dead Kennedys, seeing themselves on the final brink of existential death.

Meanwhile and simultaneously, just as many feel on the brink of impending opportunity. Take the immigrants. This has always been a land of immigrants and new arrivals, who always bring along some sense of hope, the ambition to be more than they are when they arrive.

Here in San Diego the community leaders prophesy more boom times ahead for a city whose moment has come at last. A 1980 feature piece in *California Business* was titled "The Cinderella City Comes of Age."[27]

But on my way back up the coast I will meet a young fellow in Santa Barbara who grew up in La Jolla and does not share this civic excitement. He will soon graduate from the University of California campus there, with a double major in biology and environmental studies. Slender, blond, well tanned, he is one of those athlete/diplomats who can surf well and also get himself into law school. His college room is filled with surfing trophies, small statues of golden men crouched on the slopes of golden waves, while his bookshelves are crammed with volumes such as *Coastline in Crisis, Protecting the Golden Shore, Citizens Guide to the California Coastal Act of 1976.* In between classes, he has lobbied to preserve the north coast counties from the invasion of Lease Sale no. 53, the federal proposal to reopen five marine basins to offshore drilling. He has lobbied against piping state water through the mountains and into Santa Barbara County because he believes that water is one of the surest limits on environmental overload. As for his hometown, where beachfront property can sell for a million or more, he does not think he will ever be able to live there.

"It has just changed too much. It isn't what it used to be. It's like L.A. In fact, it *is* L.A. That's how I see it now, everything from Ventura to the border, it is all L.A."

"When did this happen?" I ask him. "When did you personally start to feel it?"

"There had always been a two-story building limit along the beaches. After that was lifted, the first thing that went in was a highrise hotel, right where Mission Beach turns into Pacific Beach. There had been highrises downtown, but never anything built right near where I was living. This was just about the time it was in the papers that San Diego was passing San Francisco to become the second-largest city in the state. I was in high school, and I thought it was just great that now we had our own hotel and this meant we were going to be a big city. Actually it was the beginning of the end. Three more have gone in there since then. On weekends the whole area is hopelessly congested. Now I see how my first reaction represents one of the misconceptions we all are raised on—that progress is good, and bigger is better. It makes me think of people I used to know who would rip off their younger brothers and sisters by trading them pennies for dimes. The pennies were bigger, so the young kids automatically figured they were worth more."

"What will you do?" I ask him. "Where do you think you will live?"

"I don't know yet. Maybe I will head for New Zealand. Maybe I will stay here and fight it. Somebody has to fight it."

"Fight what?"

"The total destruction of the state. Somebody has to take a stand against what is going on."

He is not bitter as he says this. He seems very objective, very settled, as if he has already come to terms with the nature of his surroundings. It leads me to suspect that, though he claims to be making up his mind, he has already decided. This year he has interned with the Environmental Defense Center in Santa Barbara. He talks about running for office here in Goleta, the nearest town to the campus, to try for an opening on the water board. This is how we breed environmental activists. You grow up falling in love with some magnificent place on earth that is being systematically assaulted, and this experience can nurture the protective instincts. Runaway growth creates its own adversaries.

Everything depends, of course, on your comparisons. Native Californians compare the state now to what it was like at some halcyon moment in the past—fifty years ago, or twenty-five, or five, or last week. The Blakes, meanwhile, compare it to the dripping summer heat of Sarasota. Others, seeing San Diego or L.A. or Cupertino for the first time, think of dying factory towns in Michigan or Saskatchewan in deep winter, or Saigon under siege.

Green himself remembers New York City.

After we have dropped the Blakes at their hotel, after he has passed them his card, with the prediction that he will see them on their way back from Seattle, I ask him how long he has been in California. The answer comes quickly.

"Nine years."

"How long have you been in the San Diego area?"

"Nine years."

"What brought you West?"

He gets reflective. We are in the parking lot where I left my car. He puts the Datsun in neutral and lets it idle, with his foot resting lightly on the brake pedal.

"I grew up in Chicago," he says. "Nine years ago I was working in Manhattan. Two jobs. One was driving cab. It was December. I was sitting in my cab between Forty-eighth and Forty-ninth streets, trying to get from about here to that exit sign over there. It took me forty-five minutes. It was cold and it was wet and it was getting dark, and I said to myself, 'That is it, THAT IS IT!'"

"And you came straight to San Diego."

"Like a rocket."

"It sounds like you're planning to stay awhile."

"Hey," he says. "I love it here. How can you *beat* this?"

Again—in that expansive gesture that says it all—he throws an arm out the window to embrace the weather and reach for a handful of sunshine, his palm cupped for that succulent grapefruit that just might come falling from the sky.

I Often Think
of My Homeland

Driving north from San Diego, on the last leg of my travels, heading home, I felt again the buzz of discovery. I felt some goofy and romantic kinship with the old-time discoverers, the Drakes and Vizcaínos who first followed this coastline, watching the virgin landscape as they floated past. It is a five-hundred-mile trip. I had plenty of time to think. I thought again of Portolá and that first overland trek, and thought again that maybe this is where I myself should have started. This, after all, is the classic way to explore California. You follow some linear track, usually from south to north, a track that follows the natural flow of the land. Portolá set the pattern in 1769, leading his mules and his fevered soldiers from San Diego to San Francisco Bay, breaking trail for what would become the famous El Camino Real, the King's Highway that linked the chain of missions and linked Alta California to the rest of Mexico.

In the 1830s Richard Henry Dana followed a similar route by ship, working as a common seaman in the hide and tallow trade, adventures he later recounted in *Two Years Before the Mast*. In the 1860s, when the California State Geological Survey set out to map the whole region for the first time and assess its mineral wealth, they started from the village of Los Angeles, heading up the coast to San Francisco, then angling inland toward Sacramento and Mount Shasta.

Such routes are still tempting. They are classic and clean, and they sing in the mind, seem to put you in touch with the flow of the land, which has not changed in all these years, one of the few things that haven't. This is the predicament. The transformations have been such, there is no longer any single route you can follow through this territory. The linear route, the circle route, the oval route, the zigzag route—no one of them quite serves in modern times.

But what about the concentric route? someone might ask. Why not find the center and start from there?

Well, the truth is, before setting out I gave that approach considerable thought too and finally had to accept the fact that in the state of California, there is no center. A journalist with a lot of experience covering regions and subregions of America had the habit of arriving in a city or a state and asking the first people he talked to, "Who is in charge around here?" Within a short time he usually found out, went to that person or committee, and began his inquiries. Upon arriving in California he followed this routine and soon found that no one could answer his question. Why? No one has ever been in charge.

There is no political center. There is no economic center. There is no social center, nor any one social ladder. There is no ethnic or cultural center, no intellectual or spiritual center, nor is there even a very useful history. The *region* has a history, but most of the individuals who inhabit the region now do not sense it much or even hold it in common. Half the people living here have arrived from somewhere else. If California has a working history, it really consists of this intersection of pasts from every direction, from Arkansas and Sonora and Vietnam and Bengal and Armenia and Canada and Italy. That is what California is, an intersection, a world crossroads of extraordinary and sometimes maddening diversity. There is enormous interchange and energy and vitality and motion and flux. It just happens that there is no center, no clear point of departure that, once identified, will give you a place to start.

This does not necessarily mean that the state is falling apart or flying to pieces. Or, if it is falling apart, the lack of center is not the reason, since California does not seem to be disintegrating at a faster rate than many other places in the world. It just means there is no center. Here the laws of centrifugal force do not apply.

Now, an entire planet designed like California *would* fly to pieces. The state's very nature depends upon the fact that something else is out there, something other than itself, and near enough to reach by car or plane. It needs the rest of the world to play against. It is like the wild card that gives the game an edge and an expectation. But the wild card is not a microcosm of the deck. With the wild card alone there would be no game. As Carey McWilliams made clear in his prophetic book of 1946, California is The Great Exception. It is the free-fire zone, the launch pad, the social laboratory.

You live here, watching it, and you keep waiting. You wait for the elements to *fix*. And they won't. They swirl and mix, highly volatile chemicals in solution which never quite crystallize or settle or resolve. You can't fight it, or catch it. You can barely describe it. A book, by its very nature, tries to catch and hold, to take something moving and make it stand still long enough to be contemplated. California has to be listed among the less manageable subjects for a book. By the time you have made your puny effort at catching, it has already shifted. The part you were watching is already gone.

Originally a system of mountains and rivers and river valleys and broad deserts, it is now a political unit with representatives in Washington, D.C., and an economic force with advisers in Toronto, Mexico City, Osaka, Peking and Las Vegas. But beyond all that, or before all that, it is a certain kind of process, like a person's life, or like an electron— which is often depicted in the physics books as a thing, a particle in orbit around the atom's nucleus. It is pictured this way so you can begin to talk about it. In actuality, they say, an electron behaves like a wave— until you try to catch it. At which point it begins to behave like a particle. Then you blink, and it is moving like a wave.

Take Fresno. You hear that the absolute geographical center of California has been located in somebody's backyard on the outskirts of Fresno. What's more, there are now so many millionaires in that county, the Fresno *Bee* has lost track of them all. What is happening in Fresno? You drive over there and you find grapes, grains, cattle and calves, and the largest single cotton-producing county in the United States. Clearly a center for something. But would you call it *the* center?

No.

Try Sacramento then, a hundred and fifty miles up Highway 99. You think the center might be there somewhere, if you knew where to look. Perhaps in the governor's office. Then you learn that the state's annual budget is $26 billion, while the annual gross for the state's number-one corporation, Standard Oil, based in San Francisco, hovers around $42 billion. Bank of America, the world's largest bank, is also based in San Francisco, along with the Southern Pacific Railroad, which is the state's largest private landholder (two million acres).

So you are beginning to think San Francisco might be the center, maybe the bar or the billiards room of the venerable and exclusive Bohemian Club on Taylor Street, when someone points out that the truly big money is in L.A. Arab money, Hong Kong money, cocaine money, the rest of the domestic oil money. And for a while you are thinking L.A. is the center, an opinion that seems confirmed by the downtown mall, where you find a view that is as astonishing, in its way, as Yosemite Falls or the Big Sur coastline looking south from Nepenthe.

The mall is a landscaped and terraced park that climbs the hill northward from Spring Street, bounded on the south by the formidable tower of City Hall. Standing on the City Hall steps, you are one block from the equally formidable offices of the Los Angeles *Times*. Along the sides of this park are stacked two rows of county, state and federal buildings that find their climax at the top of the mall in a glass-walled monolith. This Parthenon of Southern California is the sixteen-story, moat-surrounded headquarters for the L.A. Department of Water and Power, said to be the largest municipal utility in the country, with enough power at its disposal to reshape rivers, turn valleys into desert, and empty lakes five hundred miles away. In the middle of this terraced park, amongst all these influential buildings, a quiet fountain spills water into a reflecting pool, and if there is a place that *might* qualify as the center of California, I would say it hovers right there, somewhere in the air above that pool.

And yet L.A., by reputation and by the very hydra-headed look of things, is such a sprawling, unfocused free-for-all, it is hard to take seriously as an anchor point.

You are wrestling with this incongruity when someone reminds you that in California, population has always been the key, and although L.A. is still expanding, it no longer sets the pace. The fastest growth is farther south, in San Diego County. But has San Diego ever been the center of anything? What do they *do* down there?

A lot of them, many thousands, work for the Navy. We haven't said much about the Navy. We haven't said much at all about Defense. Some believe it is this state's biggest business. They claim 40 percent of the federal budget for military hardware, research and development is spent in California. Could defense be the key? Who gets all that money? Rockwell International gets a pretty good slice. So does Lockheed, and the Rand Corporation in Santa Monica, and Stanford. The University of California gets some, and the Lawrence Livermore weapons lab, and Cal Tech in Pasadena, and numerous Silicon Valley firms. Edwards Air Force Base, where the Columbia Space Shuttle landed, goes through a lot of it. All told, there are ten main air force bases in California. There is the Sixth Army Headquarters in San Francisco, and the seventeen thousand troops at Ford Ord in Monterey. There are the marines at Camp Pendleton, and the big naval yards around San Diego, home for some 30 percent of the U.S. fleet. Statewide the military payroll alone runs into the billions. What's more, the federal government owns forty-five million of the state's one hundred million acres. And of that federal land, over half is part of some military installation.

Defense. It is bigger than tourism. It could be bigger than drugs. But who controls the defense money? Not the governor. Not the chief engineer at L.A. Water and Power. Could the center of California actually lie somewhere outside the state?

I thought of Lew Welch's poem "Geography"—the world as seen from the shores of Marin County:

> The Far East is west of us
> and nearer by far
> than the Near East
> and mysteriouser.
> Is the Middle East
> really the Middle West?[28]

Then I remembered something I had read in *Black Elk Speaks,* the true-life story of the great Sioux holy man. At the age of nine he went into a twelve-day coma, during which he had a vision. It included all his ancestors and was the turning point in his spiritual life. At the end of the vision he was standing upon a mountain surveying the sacred hoop of all being. It was a mountain, he said, which stood "at the center of the world." Many years later his biographer, John Niehardt, upon hearing this story, wanted to know where that mountain was located.

Black Elk told him it had been Harney Peak in the Black Hills, and then added, "But anywhere is the center of the world."[29]

Remembering that, I saw that I had a perfectly suitable *anywhere* right here in Santa Cruz, the town I have lived in for these past twenty years. And this gave shape to the traveling I have done, these short takes outward, to the north and to the south, into the valleys and up the river canyons. It happens that my home county lies about midway between Oregon and Mexico. From here it is seven hours to L.A., five to Lake Tahoe. From my house I can reach the ocean in four minutes or bike into the Coast Range, which rises beyond the town.

Santa Cruz means "Holy Cross," named after the local mission founded by Franciscans in 1791, later famous as the birthplace of both the loganberry and Zasu Pitts. The image of a cross has come in very handy, though not in any sense the padres had in mind. I am thinking again of an intersection, a place where cars and trucks and vans and campers and trail bikes and ten-speeds intersect from four directions, and also, sooner or later, every feature of West Coast life. I don't think it is stretching too far to say that all things Californian cross here eventually. It has been a handy place to set out from and return to, my hub for these radial excursions.

Santa Cruz is a city, and it is a county, and it is a mecca of sorts. There is a university campus here, and one of the state's 107 community colleges, and a branch of Lockheed, where nuclear weapons components are produced. There is a chewing gum factory and a skateboard factory, and every fall an invitational surfing contest is staged out beyond the cliffs near Seal Rock. We have fifteen wineries, three lumber mills, and a fishing fleet. On the foggy and fertile bench lands north of town, 40 percent of the nation's brussels sprouts are grown, while a few miles to the south you can see scarps and outcroppings that mark the path of the ubiquitous San Andreas Fault.

It is said that over fifty nightclubs in the greater Santa Cruz area offer live music at least five nights a week. And it has been said that this county, perhaps due to some magnetic quirk, some still uncharted pattern in the local substrata—the famed "Mystery Spot," where golf balls roll uphill, has never been satisfactorily explained—is a power zone. Revered teachers and spiritual leaders often speak here or are drawn to stay awhile, take up residence, offer seminars, workshops, and retreats.

In the early seventies a series of grotesque killings made it clear that underneath the apparent pastoral surface, minds were going to pieces at a rate no one had expected, let alone dared to admit. Those killings were reported more extensively than anything else that has ever happened in the county. Friends sent me headlines from Europe. For a while it was hoped the notoriety might discourage people from moving into the region—the one possible positive after-effect of those terrible days. If anything, the reverse has been true. According to the 1980 census report, Santa Cruz County all by itself experienced more growth during the seventies than the state of Pennsylvania, which is the fourth-largest state in the union; and by California standards this is not a particularly big county in area or in numbers.

Lunacy still flourishes. So do drugs. The drug trade here is immeasurably lucrative. We were dining out not long ago at a rather spiffy gourmet restaurant and on the wine list I noted bottles selling for $40 and $50, others for $140 and $150, with a few reds going for over $200 a bottle.

I said to the wine steward, "Does anybody buy this stuff?"—by which I meant, this is not Beverly Hills, after all; we are up here on the north coast where the climate, though not harsh, has its biting edge in the fall, where as a community we are at least 50 percent in favor of the idea that small, if not always beautiful, is at least worth talking about, and where, though we hope to enjoy life to the limit, we do not flaunt life the way certain people farther south are known to flaunt it.

The wine steward said, "Oh sure, we sell these bottles all the time." "Who buys them?" I said.

"Dealers, mostly. They come in here with their pockets full of cash they can't deposit. So they blow it on Château Lafitte."

The unofficial economy rides on drugs. The official economy rides on real estate, recreation and tourism. It is still a resort town, as it has been for a hundred years, a place weekenders and vacationers from the Bay Area and Santa Clara Valley like to visit in the spring and summer. They keep cottages at the beach or along the rivers that snake seaward through the nearest mountains. There is a precarious excitement about the mountains beyond the town. You can find hermit people as carefully secluded as moonshiners in the Ozarks. You can get lost out there in minutes, if you don't know where you're going. Ten miles from what some people consider to be the best-kept and most breath-taking old-time roller coaster on the Pacific shore, you can plunge into total wilderness.

Above the town there is a spot where both the wilderness and the roller coaster are visible at a glance. It is a broad meadow ideally perched between the inland forests and the coastal curve. When I get back from San Diego I drive up there, park and hike out to the edge of this meadow, just where it breaks and slopes down toward grazing land, and sit and look out at Monterey Bay.

I have long admired a man who once claimed this slice of landscape for his own. His name was Henry Cowell. Whatever crimes he may have committed against the Indians or the wildlife or the numerous men who worked for him and helped him compile his fortune, he had the eye, the sense of place to stake out for himself one of the coastline's glorious views. It is the kind of view that can still make people fall in love with California. Today, twenty-five miles across the bay, mountains float in and out of the fog like a fabulous island. The bay itself is textured by a light wind, like a blue-gray carpet beneath the very blue sky. The coastal tribes used to call this shoreline the brink of the world. According to Alfred Kroeber, who compiled his exhaustive studies in the *Handbook of the Indians of California,* the Costanoans would dance on the shore, and over and over they would sing out that they were dancing on the brink of the world.[30]

You wonder if they were speaking of this shoreline alone, or if they had something larger in mind. If Black Elk knew that anywhere is the center, they must have known that everywhere is the brink.

When Vizcaíno first sighted this bay he called it the loveliest port he had seen in all of New Spain. He named it for the Viceroy who had commissioned the voyage, and his report was so glowing that it kept the name "Monterey" alive in the imperial imagination for a hundred and sixty-five years. Portolá was sent north with the express purpose of finding this bay, and he passed right by it, didn't see it, or didn't know he had seen it. Judging by the diaries from that expedition, his party crossed those tablelands two miles below the meadow, some of them covered with mobile homes now, others still green with brussels sprouts right out to the sandstone precipice.

When later explorers identified this as the bay Vizcaíno described, they set up a presidio over there, on the sheltered side of the peninsula, and the first seat of government. When the Californios decided to secede from Mexico, in 1835, the revolt started there, in Monterey. By that time, of course, Yankees were trickling across the deserts and through the Sierras, or arriving a few at a time in the merchant ships beating around the Horn, men like Henry Cowell, who reached California in the heat of the Gold Rush and reached this particular hillside in 1865. He ran cattle here, as they still do, cut timber, quarried limestone. At one time he owned a wharf down there, where high-masted ships would take on Cowell Company hides and tallow and lumber. Volleyball champions now compete every summer on the beach that was named for this man.

His great ranch and various other holdings up and down the state eventually became the Cowell Foundation. When the university began shopping around for a new campus in the late 1950s, the Foundation made this tract available. The campus planners managed to preserve many of the old ranch buildings, as well as some of the redwood groves and these grassy slopes, and thus preserve the flavor and the view. Now the meadow I am sitting in borders a university playing field, a field so expansive, with a view so attractive that the space is often used for public events. This afternoon it is sprinkled with joggers and rope-skippers and a soccer team working out. The last time I sat here, nearly two years ago now, Tibetan temple chants filled the meadow, broadcast through great six-foot theater speakers positioned in the grass.

It seemed bizarre, in one sense, to be watching herefords graze, in full view of a bay named for a Spanish viceroy, with tennis balls arcing in the distance, while we listened to ritual temple music from Tibet. Bizarre, yet commonplace. The daily mix. It happened to be the fall of 1979, in the same month I made that first jaunt outward, down to

Hungry Valley with Gary Griggs, and the occasion here was an appearance by His Divine Holiness, the Dalai Lama, who is surely the most illustrious personage ever to visit this county.

Heads of state never stop here, whether in power or out, exiled or deposed. If they reach California at all, they pass through San Francisco, or Sacramento or L.A. The last head of state to make a local appearance was Teddy Roosevelt, who paraded through town in 1903. The Dalai Lama, of course, is in a class by himself, trained as both a political and a spiritual leader. Though he has been for over twenty years a leader without a country, there is still a worldwide spiritual community that looks to him, and this is what accounts for his arrival in Santa Cruz, where Asian studies and disciplines abound.

According to traditional belief, the Dalai Lama is an incarnation of a Buddhist deity. At the age of two he was identified by a team of priests who had gone out searching for the new leader, after the death of Tibet's previous Dalai Lama in 1933. The young lad's name was Tenzin Gyatso. He already spoke a court dialect unknown in his peasant village. In exchange for a rosary that had belonged to the deceased leader he named the three priests who had come looking for him. He identified various possessions that had belonged to his predecessors, and it was found that he bore eight physical markings which distinguish all Dalai Lamas, evidence that he was indeed a reincarnation of Bodhisattva Chenrezi. In 1939 he began his reign as the fourteenth Dalai Lama of Tibet and remained there until 1959, when the Communist Chinese takeover forced him to flee to Dharamsala in northern India, where he has lived since, presiding over the one hundred thousand exiles who followed him there. His forty-nine-day tour in the fall of 1979 was his first visit to the U.S., the first a Tibetan leader had ever made to this country.

In Santa Cruz four thousand people turned out. As we waited, as the slow guttural chanting settled the air, as Chinese dragon kites with green heads and purple tails appeared in the sky overhead, I began to wonder what he would have to tell us—a man from one of the world's most ancient communities, coming into one of the world's newest, from a culture that had been for centuries insulated, tradition-bound, and singular, entering this unrestrained and outrageously plural realm. I looked around at the crowd, packed tightly across the field, quiet for the most part, respectful, many with their eyes closed, some in the lotus, others chatting casually as if waiting for a bus. I saw Panama hats, Mexican hats, Guatemalan hats, and baseball hats. I saw plaid shirts and jeans and skimpy tank tops. I saw shirtless men in swimming trunks and sandals, and blond women dressed like Gypsies, and other women dressed for racquetball. A bearded man passed in front of me wearing a vest and a large unwieldy ceramic pendant, with trousers rolled to his knees, carrying an empty Bacardi pint. There were many students and TV cameramen with the black, control-tower headphones, and a young mother suckling her child, and elderly women in rayon dresses shifting in their portable canvas chairs, while a dozen reporters on metal chairs sat in the roped-off press section with notebook pages fluttering.

What would he have to tell such a gathering? Where would he begin?

He arrived at last, with his retinue of monks in their wine-colored robes and shaven heads, and he began by making us laugh. He didn't do this with a joke or a punchline, like a toastmaster warming up an audience. He did it by laughing spontaneously, by infecting us with his own sense for comedy. We weren't ready for that. With a kind of nervous expectancy we were ready for some more transcendent or "religious" moment. A good Buddhist will always pull the rug out from under you.

His hair was cropped close, his face smooth as polished wood. He too wore a wine-colored robe and tinted aviator's glasses. Behind him on the low stage hung an ocher screen with square flags mounted across the top. Beyond that was the sun. After a few formal sentences in his native tongue, passed on to us by a translator, he switched to a halting, high-pitched singsong English, thanked us for being there and for having the patience to sit with this afternoon sun shining straight over his shoulder. Saying that, he lifted one elbow high and sliced a hand and arm downward toward our eyes at precisely the sun's angle. His laugh was so sudden, he was so clearly amused by the sight of four thousand people sitting on the grass and squinting up, we could not help laughing with him.

For the next ten minutes he made connection in another way. He talked about the basic traits that link all people. The faces may differ, he said, the eyes, the skin, the politics, but underneath the skin all people are the same. We all want happiness and not suffering. All people have the right to be happy, and no matter what system you live under, the most important thing to remember is respect for human dignity. In the modern world our obsession with material progress via science and technology must be balanced by inner, moral progress, which is accomplished through compassion, a sense of brotherhood, and respect for the dignity of each being.

Each of these ideas was punctuated by applause, sometimes by outcries of support. And each idea actually gained some kind of added force when he had to stop and search for words, creating space and anticipation between the phrases, giving each word, once found, more weight. It was impressive, because it was so direct, so un-decorated. He made no effort to entertain. He did not tell stories or speak in parables. Nor was there a hard sell of any kind. He was not hustling for converts, there was no pitch for money or support. He did exactly what you hope a spiritual leader will do. He renewed our con-tact with basic truth.

Some written questions had been gathered beforehand. The transla-tor read them aloud. Most of the questions voiced some apparent con-tradiction or paradox. One intriguing difference between the Asian mind and the Western mind is the attitude toward contradiction. The Western mind is often troubled by it, whereas the Asian mind takes it for granted that opposites coexist. In each case the Dalai Lama resolved the matter, not by eliminating one of the ingredients but by showing how they might be balanced.

Q: What is the relationship between compassion and solitude?

A: We all have need for periods of solitude. But the very nature of compassion is service to others. In order to serve, you must remain in society.

Q: How can you practice nonattachment and be involved in the world of social need?

A: Compassion means mercy for everyone, but not with any specific attachments. Love with attachment is limited and cannot expand. Compassion is love that can reach even toward your enemy. You need your enemy. Without him you cannot learn tolerance or inner strength.

Q: Suppose I am faced with some outrageous evil. How can I practice compassion when I am filled with anger by some act that demands a stronger response? Isn't anger sometimes a more justifiable emotion?

A: Compassion is the deepest, most basic feeling. But other emotions might be required on the surface. When a child does something bad, the parent may grow angry, the parent may have to use force to help the child learn. But underneath the anger and the force there is the deeper sense of compassion.

Such questions continued for half an hour. Then the crowd fell silent. There was a brief, reflective moment when the period of ques-tioning seemed, by mutual consent, finished. Yet some expectancy still hung in the air, a waiting for the one last question. It finally came, almost as an afterthought, thrown out to fill this little void, to bring us all to an ending. It was a woman's voice.

"Will you ever return to your country?"

He looked at her, then away. His head dipped slightly, a move that both conveyed the seriousness of the question and shrugged it off. He had not seen his country for twenty years, and there was a chance he might never see it again.

"As a Buddhist," he replied, "I practice nonattachment. I am attached to no thing, no person, no place on the earth."

Here he stopped to grin, amused by his own adjustment to another contradiction.

"And yet, as a Tibetan, yes, I think about Tibet. I often think of my homeland and think of the day when we might return."

Coming from the divine incarnation of a Buddhist deity, this was a touchingly human confession. What a human pair of irreconcilable opposites. The depth of his loss gave the statement its full weight. In this brief sermon, His Divine Holiness the Dalai Lama of Tibet, twenty years in exile, taught the sanity and sanctity and, judging by his frequent grin and laughter, even the entertainment value of contradiction and paradox, the intertwining yins and yangs that govern all earthly matters including regional identity, patriotism, and the future.

If you take the long view, as Buddhists do, assuming that nothing lasts—if you look, for instance, at the history of California, with its long saga of exploitation, corporate greed, general eccentricity, and volatile rate of change—you are wise to take a vow of nonattachment.

Sitting on this hillside I take that vow, and I wonder how I would feel if I had been born to live my life in a simpler place, such as the Orkney Islands or Tasmania, where only one or two things are happening at any given time, where a person might have a fifty-fifty chance of grasping what is going on. That is the way with one's homeland. You do not choose it. You do not choose its character or its contradictions, whatever they may be. It is where you start from, where you come from. You are very lucky if you ever get to see it clear. And then, just when you think you've had a moment of clarity, *Bam!*, here comes another double whammy.

In the very moment I take that vow, I cannot help but be struck by the fact that this view, after all these years, is still intact. And how can I not be attached to it? You would have to be made of stone not to harbor some powerful feeling for whatever place on earth has left its imprint in your eyes and ears and nerve ends, especially on such a day as this, in the crisp sunny air of early autumn. Summer light is buttery here. Autumn brings a harder edge to the sheets of glare. The air begins to bite as the sun falls, the sky presses closer to each distant object, tightening all the curves and corners.

To the right is ocean, to the left the Salinas River delta, which has no profile, so that from here it seems to be a broad channel between the Gabilan Range and the Santa Lucias, which rise beyond Monterey. The peninsula looks detached. Below the peaks a fog bank is hovering, like low clouds around an island. This view, with its layers of coastal history, is layered yet again, silvered with glare, and it can still make the eyes glisten and the spirit sail, make you yearn to save whatever can be saved, and stir to life the dream that brought you here or brought your parents or grandparents here. At this altitude, if you squint a little and edit out the PG&E smokestacks at the Moss Landing power plant, down there along the inside curve, you can still see this bay as Vizcaíno might have seen it, or as it was seen by the Indians before him, who looked at the endless stands of pine and redwood and at the open sea ahead and told themselves they were dancing on the brink of the world.

ACKNOWLEDGMENTS

A number of people contributed to the making of this book. Most of them happen to be Californians, either by birth or by choice. The one notable exception is Ash Green, the book's editor at Knopf. Watching from afar, he made this journey possible and then provided wise and patient counsel all along the way.

Many thanks to those who shared their thoughts and their hospitality during my travels: John and Marlea Berutti, Len Fulton and Ellen Ferber, Chuck Hinsch and Eva Yee, Jack Hicks, David Kelley, Will Baker, Wright Morris, Olaf and Suzanna Palm, Carol Jean and Dane Olsen, Paul and Maureen Draper, Bill and Frankie Jo Rintoul, Eric Hanscom, Harry and Mary Willis, Peter and Karen Dahl, Ramon and Pamela Ross, George and Katie Diskant, Peter and Sally Dixon, Marilyn Ferguson, Noel and Judy Young.

For their assistance in my various researches I want to thank James Hart and Berkeley's Bancroft Library; Charles Atkins and the staff at the Main Branch of the Santa Cruz County Public Library; Jim Taylor of the Army Corps of Engineers; Rene White of the Regis-McKenna Agency; Ron Dunton; Mort Grosser; Paul Lee; Tom Sullivan and Ali Webb in the Office of the Mayor of Los Angeles; Terri Jacobs, Research Director at *San Francisco* magazine; the members of San Jose's Asian Law Alliance; and all those who took part in the Images of California series, sponsored by the Institute for Governmental Studies at the University of California, Berkeley, during 1979 and 1980.

Once again I thank the Montalvo Association of Saratoga, California, and Patricia Oakes, its Executive Director, for the blessed weeks of a Villa Montalvo residency. And for their time and good counsel during the early and late stages of the manuscript I am deeply grateful to Leo Laporte, Lynn Luria-Sukenick, Mort Yanow, Tom Rickman, Judith Minty and Victoria Myers.

A multitude of writers—novelists, journalists, poets, historians—have contributed to whatever understanding may be reflected in these pages, many more than I can list here or individually thank. I feel most indebted to the following works, which I note both to acknowledge my admiration and by way of recommending them to interested readers: Josiah Royce, *California: A Study in American Character* (Boston: Houghton Mifflin, 1886); Joan Didion, *Slouching Toward Bethlehem* (New York: Farrar, Straus, 1968); Curt Gentry, *The Last Days of the Late Great State of California* (New York: G. P. Putnam, 1968); Neil Morgan, *The California Syndrome* (New York: Prentice-Hall, 1969); David Lavender, *California: Land of New Beginnings* (New York: Harper and Row, 1972); Kevin Starr, *Americans and the California Dream, 1850–1915* (New York: Oxford University Press, 1973); William Everson, *Archetype West: The Pacific Coast as a Literary Region* (Berkeley: Oyez, 1976); William Kahrl (ed.), *The California Water Atlas* (Sacramento: The State of California, 1979); and various works by the late Carey McWilliams, particularly *California: The Great Exception* (New York: A. A. Wyn, 1949). In the days when very few were looking, he saw it all.

J.D.H.

Santa Cruz, California
April 1982

---

1. California's population, as reported in the 1980 Census, was 23,510,372. The population of the United States in 1850 was 23,191,876, according to the 1981 *World Almanac*.

2. Henry Miller, *The Air Conditioned Nightmare* (New York: New Directions, 1945).

3. Diary of William Swain, 15 May 1849, J. S. Holliday, ed., *The World Rushed In:The California Gold Rush Experience* (New York: Simon and Schuster, 1981).

4. Garcia Ordoñez de Montalvo, *Las Sergas de Esplandian* (Madrid: 1510), from the translation by Edward Everett Hale, *The Atlantic Monthly*, 1872. Reprinted as *The Queen of California* (San Francisco: The Colt Press, 1945).

5. Lew Welch, *Selected Poems* (Bolinas, Calif.: Grey Fox Press, 1976).

6. Montalvo, *Las Sergas de Esplandian.*

7. This recurring dream, which is typical of many I have heard in recent years, was told to me in 1976 by a woman, a native of Palo Alto, then about 25 and a graduate student in psychology at Berkeley.

8. Gary Griggs and Barbara L. Walsh, *The Hydrology of Hungry Valley, California.* Report for the State Dept. of Parks and Recreation, July 1979.

9. Robert Benson, *Great Winemakers of California* (Santa Barbara: Capra Press, 1977).

10. John Steinbeck, *The Grapes of Wrath* (New York: Viking Press, 1939).

11. *The Stanislaus River: A Fresh Perspective.* A pamphlet issued by The Friends of the River, Sacramento, Calif., July 1979.

12. Letter from Mark Dubois to Col. Donald O'Shei, District Engineer, Dept. of the Army, Sacramento District Corps of Engineers, dated May 17, 1979.

13. Letter from Mark Dubois to Col. Donald O'Shei, dated Sunday, May 20, 1979.

288   *Notes*

14. Luis Valdez, "El Teatro Campesino," *Aztlan: An Anthology of Mexican American Literature*, edited by Luis Valdez and Stan Steiner (New York: Alfred A. Knopf, 1972).

15. As this book was going to press, the cattle industry had slipped from its place as the state's number-one agricultural producer. Rising prices and changing eating habits had cut beef sales by 25–30 percent in less than three years (*California Business*, March 1982). I did not revise the passage because it was true at the time I visited Marlea's ranch, and could become true again. The industry was still bringing in around $2 billion a year, and most ranchers were holding on, hoping the trend would reverse. Meanwhile, it suggests a useful rule of thumb. When the subject is California, where the rate of change is so accelerated, this is the most you expect from any claim or figure: it was true at the time.

16. *Wall Street Journal*, August 21, 1980.

17. Herbert Thurston, S.J., and Donald Attwater, eds., *Butler's Lives of the Saints*, Vol. III (New York: P. J. Kenedy, 1956).

18. Edmund Wilson, "The Boys in the Back Room" (San Francisco: The Colt Press, 1941), revised and included in the author's collected essays, *Classics and Commercials* (New York: Farrar, Straus, 1950).

19. Theodora Kroeber, *The Inland Whale: Nine Stories Retold from California Indian Legends* (Bloomington: Indiana University Press, 1959).

20. Robert Scheer, "Bradley Sees Today's Issues in His Past," *Los Angeles Times*, December 29, 1978.

21. Tom Bradley, "My Two Built-in Blessings," *Guideposts*, July 1977.

22. Marilyn Ferguson, *The Aquarian Conspiracy: Personal and Social Transformation in the 1980s* (Los Angeles: J. P. Tarcher, 1980).

23. Gary Zukav, *The Dancing Wu Li Masters: An Overview of the New Physics* (New York: William Morrow, 1979).

24. John Steinbeck, *Cannery Row* (New York: Viking Press, 1945).

25. John Steinbeck, "About Ed Ricketts," *The Log from the Sea of Cortez* (New York: Viking Press, 1951).

26. Robinson Jeffers, "Thurso's Landing," *The Selected Poetry of Robinson Jeffers* (New York: Random House, 1938).

27. Mike Hogan, "San Diego: The Cinderella City Comes of Age," *California Business*, February 1980.

28. Lew Welch, *Selected Poems* (Bolinas: Grey Fox Press, 1976).

29. John G. Neihardt, ed., *Black Elk Speaks* (New York: William Morrow, 1932).

30. A. L. Kroeber, *Handbook of the Indians of California* (Washington, D.C.: Smithsonian Institution, 1925).

A Note About the Author

James D. Houston was born in San Francisco and has spent most of his life on the Pacific Coast. He is the author of six novels, including GIG, LOVE LIFE, and CONTINENTAL DRIFT, which he completed with the aid of a writing grant from the National Endowment for the Arts. Among his other non-fiction works is FAREWELL TO MANZANAR, co-authored with his wife, Jeanne Wakatsuki Houston, the story of her family's experience during the World War Two internment of Japanese Americans. For the teleplay based upon the book they received the Humanitas Prize in 1976. In 1983 CALIFORNIANS received an American Book Award from The Before Columbus Foundation. He has also received a Wallace Stegner Fellowship, the Joseph Henry Jackson Award for Fiction, and two travel grants to Asia sponsored by the USIA Arts America Program. Educated at San Jose State University and Stanford, he occasionally offers writing workshops at the University of California, Santa Cruz, where he is a Visiting Professor in Literature.